Creative
Sustainable
Gardening

Creative

Sustainable

Gardening

Diana Anthony

Centre for
Alternative
Technology

To my daughter Sarah
and the people of the twenty-first century,
with love and hope.

Acknowledgements

My sincere thanks to Dr Nicholas Martin and Peter Workman of Crop and Food Research, Auckland, New Zealand for their assistance in helping me compile lists of common insect pests and their biological control agents.

My grateful thanks to my editors Tracey Borgfeldt and Jeanette Cook for their patience and invaluable assistance in helping me produce this book.

My most sincere thanks to my non-gardening husband, Brian Anthony, for the long hours and slow painstaking work he undertook on my behalf, typing lists of plants with both English and Latin plant names onto computer spread sheets; and for his support, patience and encouragement during the writing of this book.

Text Copyright © Diana Anthony 2000
Copyright © David Bateman Ltd 2000

First published in Great Britain in 2000 by CAT Publications, The Centre for Alternative Technology, Machynlleth, Powys, SY20 9AZ.

10 9 8 7 6 5 4 3 2 1

A CIP record for this book is available from the British Library.

ISBN: 1-8980-4923-8 (paperback)

Edited by Jeanette Cook
Design by Errol McLeary
Typeset by Jazz Graphics, Thames Coast, New Zealand
Printed and bound in Hong Kong by Colorcraft Ltd

CONTENTS

FIELDS OF CHANGE

It is a source of regret to me that due to the rapid advance of modern technology, some of the information contained in this book must be quickly outdated. Modern technology in fields such as science, chemical production, medicine, genetic engineering and cloning are advancing almost daily. How these advances will affect us and our world is a matter for the future.

Those of us entering the new millennium practising the codes, ethics and philosophies expressed in *Creative Sustainable Gardening* do so with a different dream. Our keywords of the late twentieth century have been organics, sustainability, permaculture, etc. In a world where chemical-based agriculture and horticulture are having a profoundly degrading impact on human health and the environment, our vision is to institute safer and better horticultural practices in the twenty-first century.

The challenges are not just about growing healthy, chemical-free food for our families – they are about looking at our lives as a whole to find ways to tread more lightly upon our beleaguered earth.

Diana Anthony

CHAPTER ONE
UNDERSTANDING THE DILEMMAS

I believe that gardens offer us something beyond the material world. They provide a spiritual component allowing us to participate in the wonder and mystery of creation.

Gordon Ford, *The Natural Australian Garden*

Our need to create gardens, to fashion from nature places of order and retreat, has evolved from ancient Asia, Rome, Greece and Egypt. Whether established to provide food, to provide a peaceful retreat for meditation or simply to satisfy a desire to nurture plant life, the garden is an arena that has given human beings a source of deep spiritual fulfilment and pleasure for many thousands of years.

Gardens have never been as important as they are in our lives today. In our stressful, crowded and competitive world they have become therapeutic, providing sustenance for the spirit. Many of the world's peoples must live in overcrowded landscapes eroded by industrial and urban sprawl, and the garden is the only personal green space to which they have access. It offers peace and a place

to be in touch with nature, the seasons and elements, as well as a theatre for recreational and leisure pursuits.

Gardening is rated as one of the world's most popular leisure pursuits, but as we enter the new millennium the face of gardening is altering dramatically. Shifting climates, water shortage, difficult socio-economic circumstances, industrial and technological development and over-population are all changing the traditional culture of gardening as we knew it. These changes will unite us as global gardeners in the common aim of designing New Age natural gardens that will help sustain our earth.

What is sustainable gardening? The analysis at its most simple is that if family A creates a garden of plants suited to their specific environment, family B heals erosion and deforestation with plantings of trees, family C plants a drought-resistant garden and family D converts a patch of lawn to a vegetable garden, and if families A, B,C

Opposite: The garden is a place of peace – a haven in a stressful world. Gardens have provided human beings with spiritual fulfilment and pleasure for thousands of years.

9

and D resort to low-toxicity horticultural management, and if we then multiply these four families by their millions and tens of millions, their gardens of the new millennium will have a vital role to play in maintaining both the health of the world's population and of our planet.

As both gardeners and citizens of the twenty-first century we're facing challenges such as we've never faced before. We have to accept the consequences and ongoing implications of issues such as global warming, changing climates, chemical agriculture and horticulture, environmental pollution, deforestation, wholesale extinction of plant and animal species, genetic engineering of crops, the fact that the world's food seed-stocks are in the hands of a small number of highly competitive giant biotechnical companies, and that water is already listed as our most finite source – and this is before we've scarcely had time to imagine living with severely diminished supplies when world population doubles by 2050.

The movement called 'organic gardening' which has been evolving over the last decade is currently gaining world-wide momentum. It is a movement now defined as 'sustainable or natural gardening', the practice of horticulture without recourse to the dangerous chemicals and fertilisers

that pose a grave threat to both the safety and health of mankind and to life upon earth. It is about employing appropriate native and exotic plants in harmonious integration with the natural landscape. It is about alternatives.

You're probably thinking at this stage, *Doom and gloom again! I know all about the holes in the ozone layer and how we're poisoning ourselves with chemicals. I don't want to read any more of that stuff.* We all have varying levels of understanding about these topics. But if we bury our heads in the sand and choose not to face their frightening realities, we choose also to lose our self-empowerment – the power each of us has as an individual to help halt the advance of global warming and the earth's degradation, and to safeguard our family's health and well-being.

Chemical or organic gardening?

Garden pests and diseases are, always have been and ever will be. The gardener fights back according to his or her personal philosophy. There are few subjects more emotive among horticulturists than toxic chemicals versus alternative low toxicity management. The subject causes a great divide – some of us drench pest ridden or diseased plants with cocktails of poisonous chemicals; others

Above: 'Family D converts a patch of lawn to a vegetable garden.'
Right: Planted with natives and exotics, this coastal garden is in harmony with the landscape.

In late 1998, The Worldwide Fund for Nature (WWF) gave details of its Living Planet Index (LPI), which analysed the deterioration of the world's forest, freshwater and marine ecosystems between 1970 and 1998. The result shows that human beings have destroyed a staggering 30 per cent of the natural world since 1970 – which means that the earth has lost nearly a third of its natural wealth in just less than three decades.

Global consumption of natural resources has doubled over the last 25 years and continues to accelerate. We put immense pressure on the natural environment through the production and consumption of resources such as fossil fuels, grain, fish, wood and water and the emission of pollutants such as carbon dioxide.

In addition to the decline in global resources we must also consider the degrading impact of chemical agriculture and horticulture upon human health, on the environment and on those resources we have left. We've made mistakes that can't be undone. This book is about learning through experience and thus being able to form conclusions.

'I filled a backpack with toxic chemicals and dispensed death vengefully whenever I saw a few aphids.'

of us go for witches' cauldrons that boil and bubble, producing stinking but efficient organic decoctions.

When, as a novice gardener, I began to create my gardens, I would drench my plants with any prettily packaged poison helpful garden centre staff would sell me. Night after night as I read my 'How To' gardening books, lurid and highly graphic pictures would leap from the page, pictures of pests and diseases grotesque enough to strike terror into any amateur's heart. Their very names smacked of foul decay – rot, corky scab, wilt, blight, fungus, leaf curl, black spot, rust, botrytis, and mildews that had the bonus of manifesting themselves in several different forms.

As though this weren't enough, there followed lists of disgusting pests whose destructive capacities were apparently legendary. I used to go to bed envisioning whole armies of arthropod vampires invading my new gardens.

So I bought a backpack and enough toxic chemicals to annihilate plant life from several acres and dispensed death vengefully whenever I

saw a few aphids. One day a friend, seeing me striding around goggled, hooded, booted and suited, commanded that I stop and think what I was doing.

I vacillated uneasily between the use of diabolical chemicals and the dread of plant decimation by gruesome pests and diseases. I read everything I could find on organic gardening. There wasn't a great deal, but enough to make me understand the ecological consequences of the unthinking and irresponsible manner in which I had dispensed death from the air – killing everything, insects good and bad, and severely disrupting nature's balance. I began to question the effects and consequences of my actions not just upon the garden, but upon the environment as a whole. I embarked upon a steep learning course of common sense, trial and error.

For the first two years – while I struggled with alternative sprays, composting, mulching, soil conditioning, and companion planting – everything in the garden looked terrible; my plants were chewed, full of holes, pock-marked and

'To harm one is to harm all' – a monarch butterfly settles on jonquils, and a dove incubates its eggs in a rose bush.

razored. At the beginning of year three I thought I couldn't handle it any more, was totally losing control. Then, quite suddenly, I realised that the garden was a myriad of insect life, full of birds and their song and the plants were growing lustily and looking healthy.

I almost held my breath over the next season waiting for the healthy abundance to fall victim to an onslaught of hideous disease and pest infestation. It didn't happen, and I realised that, at last, I'd got soil conditions and the natural balance between the pest and beneficial predator insect population right. The equation? Healthy soil, healthy plants, healthy people.

Ecologically sound

The science of ecology is the study of the relationship and interaction between people, animals and plants and their environment. To harm one is to harm all. It is important to recognise ourselves as part of that whole. If we can recognise the natural balance and harmony in both the garden and our environment and do the best we can not to upset it, but to work with it and for it, we are

making an invaluable contribution to the future well-being of our world – the world of our children and of their children to come.

Creative Sustainable Gardening is not a dry and learned tome but a book that considers how, as individuals, we can make a difference. Hand in hand with sound practical advice on choosing and instituting sustainable gardening techniques and low toxicity management, we'll learn how to create water efficient gardens, and we'll explore creative landscaping with native plants and hardy exotics, with trees and shrubs, with edible gardens and with heirloom seeds.

We'll study planning, designing and planting sustainable gardens for specific environmental conditions and locations; for example, drought tolerant gardens, small-space and low-maintenance gardens, those in coastal areas and those suffering from changing or extreme climatic conditions. We'll explore creative landscaping in relation to the limitations imposed by these specifics and study the exciting styles of the millennium garden and those of the future. The 'doom and gloom' bits will be balanced by lots of positive practical action and creativity.

We'll review with optimism what each of us in our capacity as gardeners, horticulturists and lifestyle block owners can do to institute safer and better horticultural practices and to help heal, and in some cases halt, the environmental abuse of the twentieth century.

Towards the end of his life Albert Schweitzer said, 'Man has lost the capacity to foresee and to forestall. He will end by destroying the earth.' In our hearts we may suspect that ultimately this might be true. It is also true that we cannot undo what is done. But we can't, we won't, give up that easily. We should instead go forward with practical action and optimism because we owe our grandchildren's children the right to endure. We can choose, each and every one of us, from this moment to limit, and in some cases halt, the terrible tide of poisoning and degradation of the earth they will inherit.

If you wish to become a creative sustainable gardener, to do your bit to save the world, the best place to start is in your own backyard. Think global – act local!

As gardeners of the new millennium we can create beautiful displays that are also ecologically sustainable.

Gardeners' global glossary

Stunned by global gobbledegook? Before you attempt to negotiate your way through the following chapters, here is an ABC of words and phrases to help you understand the language of some of the planet's most crucial issues:

Alternative energy: the harnessing of wind, water and solar power in place of fossil fuels (coal, natural gas and petroleum) to create energy for human activities.

Atmosphere: the whole mass of gases surrounding the earth. The earth's atmosphere reaches 640 km (397 miles) above the surface, but 80 per cent of its air is concentrated in the troposphere (lowest layer of earth's atmosphere) which extends 11 km (7 miles) upwards. Although nitrogen and oxygen make up 99 per cent of the earth's atmosphere, other atmospheric gases are vital for the survival of life on earth.

Biodiversity/biological diversity/balanced ecosystem: the essential existence of a wide variety of plants and animal species in their natural environment.

Biological control: bug eat bug! The control of destructive organisms, especially insects, by non-chemical means, such as introducing a natural predator of the pest.

Biosphere: part of the earth's surface and atmosphere inhabited by living things.

Carbon dioxide: colourless, odourless incombustible gas that forms when carbon atoms combine with oxygen atoms; for example, during the process of burning or decay. Carbon dioxide is a small but vital part of the atmosphere, and a key ingredient in photosynthesis, the process in which green plants make the food upon which all animals depend. Its heat trapping characteristic helps make life on earth possible.

Carcinogen: a substance causing unnatural cell division thereby producing cancer. The adjective is *carcinogenic.*

Chemical fertilisers: artificial fertilisers that give short-term increased crop yield but destroy the natural soil organisms essential to its life, health, and structure.

Chlorofluorocarbons (CFCs): Gases used as coolants in refrigerators and air conditioners, as propellants in aerosol cans, as foaming agents for insulation and food packaging, and as industrial cleaning agents. They are long-lasting compounds that absorb infra-red energy more effectively than carbon dioxide. In the upper atmosphere, chlorine from CFCs destroys the ozone layer, which protects life on earth from the sun's harmful ultraviolet radiation.

Clone: a group of cells or organisms of the same genetic kind that have been reproduced artificially and asexually from a single plant or animal.

Cloning: the use of those extracted cells or organisms by scientists to produce identical replicas of the original species.

Ecology/ecosystem: science of the relationship and interaction between people, plants, animals and their environment.

Fossil fuels: fuels containing carbons that are believed to have formed from living materials, trees for example, millions of years ago. Coal, natural gas, and petroleum are fossil fuels.

Genetic modification/engineering of crops: genetic modification is the process of artificially transferring genes specific to one type of organism to another, thereby altering their natural genetic structure.

Global warming: an increase in the overall temperature worldwide, believed to be caused by the greenhouse effect, resulting in catastrophic changes to the world's climate.

Greenhouse effect: the gradual rise in temperature in the earth's atmosphere due to heat being absorbed by the sun and being trapped by gases such as carbon dioxide in the air around earth.

Integrated Pest Management (IPM): horticultural management programme in which cultivation practices such as companion planting, biological control of insectiferous pests, and non-toxic or low-toxicity plant derivative sprays are integrated for benign pest, weed and disease control.

Maximum Residual Limits (MRLs): the maximum allowable residues of herbicides and pesticides in plants and crops that will enter the food chain of humans and animals. The MRL is the amount of residue considered 'safe' for consumption. However, MRLs differ widely from country to country.

Mutant/mutagen: chemical agents capable of altering the structure of genes and chromosomes, the carriers of genetic material entering the food chain of both humans and animals.

Nitrogen: in gaseous form, nitrogen takes up four-fifths of the earth's atmosphere. Nitrogen is also an element in such substances as proteins, fertilisers, and ammonia.

Nitrous oxide: a gas emitted from nitrogen-based fertilisers. Nitrous oxide is another human-produced gas that traps heat in the earth's atmosphere.

Ozone: a form of oxygen present in the earth's atmosphere in small amounts. A layer of ozone between 22 and 30 km (13½ and 18½ miles) above sea level makes life possible by shielding the earth's surface from most ultraviolet rays. Ozone can be man-produced and is used to purify water and as a bleaching agent. As an air pollutant ozone damages materials and living tissues, and causes severe headaches and sore eyes.

Sustainable horticulture: care of the earth and care of the people with minimal recourse to chemicals. Employment of natural methods to feed and condition the soil, to grow food, and maintain the health, energy and fertility of the world's natural diversity of plants, animals and people.

Synergy/Synergystic effect: chemical enhancement of the effects of one substance by the presence of another.

Systemic broad spectrum herbicides and pesticides: toxic chemicals that are absorbed into plant tissue in order to kill chewing and sap-sucking insects. Their killing power is indiscriminate; they kill both beneficial and undesirable insects thus creating an unnatural balance.

Ultraviolet: invisible radiation from the sun, which has shorter wave lengths than visible violet light. Ultraviolet light includes tanning rays, but also includes the more powerful wave lengths that cause sunburn and skin cancer. Most of these damaging rays are blocked from reaching the earth's surface by a layer of ozone gas in the stratosphere.

Recommended reading
Global warming – understanding the forecast, Andrew Revkin, Abbeville Press, NY

CHAPTER TWO

SUSTAINABLE VERSUS CHEMICAL HORTICULTURE

The soil is a living organism and remains healthy and productive if it is used and fertilised biologically. 'Bios' is Greek for life; biology is the science of life and biological means according to the laws of life.

We know that all life on earth is dependent upon the soil. The soil is a living element filled with millions of minute creatures and plants all beavering away on our behalf to produce the nutrients necessary to sustain plant growth. Yet from the nozzles of backpacks, from agricultural machinery and from the air we spray poisons all over it!

We use systemic pesticides containing toxic elements that are absorbed into plant tissue to make them poisonous to sucking and chewing insects. Often the toxins are so strong the insects are killed by mere contact with the deadly vapours emanating from the plant's flowers and foliage. Systemic poisons enter the human body by both

Above: All life upon earth is dependent on the soil; yet we spray poisons all over it.

skin contact and inhalation, and also by ingestion of food from crops that have been sprayed with them.

Many insect pests become immune to pesticides, and this creates a need for ever stronger and more harmful preparations. When a species of insectiferous pest is entirely destroyed the beneficial insects that are their natural predators starve, and this creates further imbalance.

During the fifties and sixties when chemicals such as DDT, malathion, and parathion were dumped wholesale across the face of the earth, beneficial predatory insects such as ladybirds, which devour aphids and other pests, were almost made extinct in some localities. Horticultural scientists say that in these areas their comeback in significant numbers has been slow.

Modern versions of organophosphate chemicals such as these are equally powerful and dangerous. Honey bees and other beneficial insects become wildly agitated on contact with them, perform frantic cleansing movements, and are dead within 30 minutes. As pollinators, bees are vital to

Can we be sure the produce on our supermarket shelves contains no carcinogenic chemicals?

all horticulture and agriculture, particularly to the fruit industry, but every season, all over the world, vast numbers are eliminated with chemicals such as carbaryl.

What's in our food?

Most developed countries impose maximum residual limits (MRLs) on food crops. The MRL is the maximum level of chemical residue considered to be 'safe' for human consumption. However, some countries allow far higher MRLs than other countries.

Chemically raised crops – such as tomatoes, cabbages, cucumbers, broccoli, celery, bananas and many other fruit and vegetables – may be sprayed with up to six different pesticides and fungicides during growth. In many countries inadequate government regulations state only that a withholding period must be observed between the final spray application and harvest. How well is this monitored? Who really knows that the luscious arrays of fruit and vegetables in our supermarket were not sprayed with carcinogenic chemicals two days before they reached the shelves?

We're simply not aware of the clandestine cocktail of chemicals that lurk unseen in the bags and packets we put into our supermarket trolleys. The acutely toxic chemicals marketed as Diquat

and Paraquat (usually used as herbicides) are also used to kill off the tops of onions and potatoes before harvest, and incidences of human poisoning from high residual remains in these particular vegetables is rapidly increasing. Potatoes are also high in residues of the pesticide Propham, which is used after harvest to stop them sprouting in their supermarket bags. This chemical is suspected of being a mutagen (having the ability to change chromosome and gene structure) and is implicated in birth defects.

The organophosphate pesticides fenitrothian, pirimiphos-methyl and others are found as high-impact residues in a wide range of cereal-based products, especially wholemeal bread, bran flakes, white bread rolls, wheatgerm, muesli and savoury cracker biscuits. Both chemicals are believed to be mutagens implicated in birth defects and to have synergystic effects (where the presence of one chemical enhances the effect of another) when used with other organophosphates.

The outlook is even more alarming when we discover that in addition to unacceptably high levels of chemical residues, 'healthy' grain breads and cereals are also treated with various fungicidal agents that are proven carcinogens to prolong their shelf lives. These include calcium propionate, a mould inhibitor. The use of this dangerous preservative allows manufacturers to pack the bread into polythene bags while it is still hot. Current medical research shows that the preservative builds up in the body over a period of time – particularly in young children – and causes health problems such as stomach aches, headaches, irritability and lethargy.

High levels of organophosphate fungicide residues are also found in jam, white wine, lettuce, tomatoes, apples and pears.

A monitoring survey of domestic fruit and vegetable pesticide residues, which was carried out recently in several countries by the British Ministry of Agriculture and Fisheries and Department of Health, has yielded some frightening statistics:

- 17 different pesticides in celery
- 17 different pesticides in cucumber
- 20 different pesticides in broccoli and other brassicas. These findings included hazardous levels of Captafol – a carcinogenic fungicide banned in some countries

By growing crops using sustainable methods, we can eliminate cocktails of chemical residues from our meals.

- unacceptably high residues of several chemicals in flour, in peaches, oranges, strawberries, boysenberries, bananas, apples and other fruit, and in many vegetables.

By choosing to grow as much as possible of our own food by sustainable methods, we can do a great deal to help eliminate cocktails of chemical residues from our meals. If you've neither the time nor space to grow fruit and vegetables, refuse to be beaten – hunt down certified organic or bio-dynamic produce growers and support them.

Chemicals in bran, wholemeal and wheatgerm flour products are not so easy to eliminate from our diet because few domestic growers can cultivate grain crops. We cannot bypass the chemical contamination by baking our own bread because the grain crop is sprayed throughout growth, which means that the flour is also contaminated.

Chemical versus sustainable

A sustainable system of horticulture will increase organic matter in soils, rotate and diversify crops, integrate trees with crops and animals and con-

serve biodiversity. The objective is to create long-term ecological health and stability rather than a quick return profit regardless of the cost to human health, the environment and the needs of future generations. A quick chemical fix undermines the long-term sustainability of the entire system.

Sustainable horticulture

Sustainable horticulture eschews the use of chemical pesticides, herbicides and fertilisers. It is simply a way of working with nature rather than against it, of recycling natural materials to maintain soil fertility and of encouraging natural and benign methods of pest, weed and disease control. The sustainable gardener is aware that there is a fine balance in the natural world that allows all the species to co-exist without any one gaining dominance.

By growing a wide variety of plants, we will attract and build up a miniature eco-system of pests and predators so that, provided the balance isn't upset by killing them with chemicals, no species will be allowed to build up to an unacceptable level. In the course of their lives the soil's teeming micro-organisms will release those nutrients required for healthy plant growth from its reservoir of organic matter. The plants, able to draw on the nutrients as and when they need them, will be stronger and healthier, and thus able to resist attacks by pests and diseases.

If we walk into the bush or into an ancient forest, we know we have entered a self-sustaining ecosystem that has nurtured and fed itself for centuries without any help from man. Sustainable gardening recognises the fact that the complex workings of nature have been successful in sustaining life over hundreds of millions of years, so the basic principles closely follow those found in the natural world.

In addition to creating a healthier environment, we can be certain that the fruit and vegetables produced in our gardens are safe, flavoursome and residue-free. An environment where sustainable gardening predominates also provides a habitat for the correct balance of good and bad insects.

Looking to the future

Looking at the shape of things to come, we are deeply aware of the rapidly escalating global bias towards conservational gardening. We have recog-

Disease resistant plants, such as this 'Abraham Darby' rose ..y, are essentials of sustainable management.

..ntials of the sustainable garden

.. summary below defines the elements of ..inable gardening:

- Avoidance of monoculture by planting a diversity of plant material and employing crop rotation.
- Selection of disease resistant plant varieties and those suited to the garden's natural environment.
- Maintenance of soil to a high degree of fertility with organic matter and fertilisers.
- Disease, weed and pest control using benign properties or plant derivative pesticides and herbicides. Use of chemicals only where alternative methods are not viable and then only with the greatest discretion.
- Companion planting to repel pests and to attract beneficial predatory insects.
- Constant vigilance for early signs of pests and disease, and instant action.
- Employment of less water-hungry plants and alternative lawns.
- Low maintenance in design and planting.
- The cultivation of edible gardens.
- Plantings of trees and shrubs.

nised the need for natural gardening methods to minimise the use of chemicals; for water conservation and the planting of drought-resistant gardens; for easy-care gardens – low on labour and high on performance with year-round appeal; for small-space gardens and for self sufficiency on the edible scene.

Although a change to sustainable agriculture systems and a reduction in global warming would greatly enhance world health, in the struggle to increase tomorrow's food supplies it would be unrealistic to expect – despite the aids of agricultural machinery, manufactured fertilisers and plant genetics – that we could dispense entirely with chemicals. What we can and must do is:

- understand their structure and their impact on human health and the environment
- seek to reduce their worldwide abuse and misuse
- replace them with more benign preparations wherever possible
- use them with the greatest discretion only when no other methods are viable.

The world of systemic pesticides and herbicides is a nightmare world where the indiscriminate scythe of toxic chemicals kills both good and bad insects, and where fish, birds and small animals eat the poisoned insects or plants and themselves die. It is a world where animals raised for human consumption graze upon poisoned grass and foliage, where the bee may carry poisonous nectar back to the hive before it dies. It is a world where every link in the ecological chain is poisoned until it reaches and is ingested by man. We're eating these chemicals and they're being stored in our livers and fat as carcinogens.

In her book, *Silent Spring* (1963), biological scientist Rachel Carson wrote: 'What sets chemical pesticides apart is their enormous biological potency. They have immense power not merely to poison but to enter into the most vital processes of the body and change them in sinister and often deadly ways.' Writing with great prescience in 1963, she predicted the future effects of chemical horticulture on the earth and its nations; the environmental issues she foresaw at that time are those which today threaten man's very survival. The book's title conveys imagery of vast tracts of the earth's face so poisoned by systemic pesticides and herbicides from the 1940s to the present day that huge proportions of bird and animal life have vanished, leaving the earth devoid of their natural music, dead and sterile.

It is a senseless paradox that we must go to our doctor to get a prescription for a perfectly harmless medicine, yet we can go into the supermarket and there next to the household cleansers and the jam are bottles of poisons deadly enough to annihilate many forms of life from several acres and which pose a grave health threat to people and animals.

Because there is not a huge skull and crossbones suspended above the shelves, we don't treat the bottle with the respect we'd normally reserve for a diabolical poison, but lob it unthinkingly into the basket with the groceries! Or into the trolley at the garden centre together with the chemical fertilisers with which we plan to 'feed and condition' the soil. Under such cheerful domestic circumstances we are choosing what in hindsight have become, and will continue to become, the weapons of our own destruction.

The chemicals

During an international conference in Nairobi in 1999, The Worldwide Fund for Nature (WWF) branded the pesticide DDT as harmful to all forms of life and called for a worldwide ban by 2007. It is still used in many developing countries as an inexpensive and 'effective' insecticide control for mosquitoes, flies and lice, but its cost in terms of the human equation is ill health and environmental degradation. There are now affordable alternatives to DDT available that can serve the same purpose but without the human cost – for example, chemicals consisting of synthetic pyrethroids and plant derivative repellents.

Together with the United Nations, WWF is trying to negotiate the reduction or elimination of emissions of 12 persistent organic pollutants (POPs), including DDT.

Modern horticultural chemicals are countless, and for this reason it is possible to list only the most 'popular' of those most commonly used in USA, UK, Australasia, Europe and developed countries. The following pages describe pesticides and herbicides used to control weeds and insects in horticultural, agricultural and domestic situations, their effect upon human and animal health, and their impact upon the environment.

The bee may carry poisonous nectar to the hive before it dies.

It is imperative to remember that any one insecticide or herbicide containing one or several toxic chemical agents can be sold under limitless trade names according to country. The manufacturers of toxic chemicals choose to cloak the sinister potency of their products by giving them 'comfortable' innocuous-sounding names such as 'Save-It', 'Shield', 'Blast', 'Bravo', 'Protect', 'Weed-a-Way', 'Guard-All', 'Zero', 'Roundup' etc. The names of the chemicals listed below will probably be unfamiliar to many gardeners, and you may be justified in saying 'never heard of them'. But they are the main agents in many of the bottles of chemicals bearing names you do know: the ones you take down off the supermarket or garden centre shelves for spraying your roses, vegetables or weeds. Read the labels and you'll find these names occurring again and again, no matter where you live.

Many sprays for 'protecting' roses, ornamentals and vegetables contain not one but sometimes

Horticultural chemicals are toxic to birds, fish and many aquatic organisms.

people and then go on (in minute print) to instruct the user to wear 'full protective clothing' during use – goggles, masks, rubber gloves, impermeable spraysuits and sometimes even breathing equipment. The chemicals are most often applied as crystals or as water soluble sprays and many contain chorines that give off dioxins.

Probable and possible carcinogens

The following probable and possible carcinogenic pesticides and herbicides list is based on the United States Environmental Protection Agency list, and many are in use under different trade names in most developed countries. All are highly toxic, may be banned in some countries, but not in others.

All are damaging to desirable vegetation and in the case of crops carry withholding periods (i.e. time between spraying and 'safe' harvesting) of between 3 and 30 days.

two or three of the acutely toxic agents discussed below; for example:

- The fungicide chlorothalonil is teamed with varying amounts of captan, maldison and carbaryl.
- A popular dust for vegetables contains rotenone, carbaryl and maldison and carries warnings only that it is deadly to fish.
- Many fruit tree sprays contain lethal cocktails of captan, carbaryl, dicofol, and maldison.
- Path weedkillers comprise mixes of probable human carginogens and mutagens simazine and amitrole. Lawn weedkillers contain dicamba, and acutely toxic soil-insect killers carry the chemical diazenon.

Organochlorines

Many widely used herbicides and pesticides are organochlorines, which are classed as persistent toxic pollutants. Organochlorines are chemicals formed when chlorine bonds with carbon. Most do not occur naturally, so most living things cannot detoxify themselves and become poisoned. The organochlorines can cause cancer and infertility, impair development, disrupt the immune system and damage organs.

Chemical companies claim that their products are rigorously tested for adverse effects upon

Probable human carcinogens	Possible human carcinogens	
acetachlor	acephate	norflurazon
alachlor	asulam	oryzalin
amitrole	atrazine	oxyflurofen
captafol	benomyl	parathion
captan	chlorothalonil*	pendimethalin
clofentizine	cyanazine	permethrin
daminozide	cypermethrin	phosmet
ethylene dibromide	cyperconazole	procloraz
	dichlobenil	propazine
etridiazole	dicofol	propiconazole
folpet	diclofop-methyl	simazine
haloxyfop-methyl	dichlorvas	terbutryn
	dimethoate	tetramethrin
maneb/mancozeb	hexazinone	triademefon
	linuron	triademenol
procymidone	metalochlor	triallate
propargite	methidathion	tribenuron
propoxur		triforine*

*Chlorothalonil and triforine are active agents of many systemic fungicides recommended for use on crops and ornamentals.

Now let's take the same selection of 'popular' and widely used pesticides and herbicides and look at their function, their effect upon human and animal life and their impact upon the environment.

Herbicide agents

The most dangerous include metalochlor; dichlorvas; methoxychlor; alachor; atrazine; 2,4-D; 2,4,5-T; dicamba; cyanazine; and simazine.

Metalochlor

Broad spectrum herbicide.

Health effects: possible carcinogen. Exposure symptoms include skin and eye irritation, cramps, nausea, anaemia, convulsions, sweating, shock and collapse.

Environmental impact: water soluble, contamination of water sources. Metalochlor is persistent in the soil according to type from between 6 and 100 days.

Alachlor

Broad spectrum herbicide.

Health effects: possible carcinogen. Chronic effects include eye degeneration and cataract formation, liver damage, and suspected tumour formation in animals and human tissue.

Environmental impact: soil biodegradable according to type within 2 to 20 months. Leaches into water, toxic to humans, fish and aquatic organisms.

2,4-D

Broad spectrum herbicide with strong benzine-like odour. Member of the acid herbicides that chemically stimulate plant growth hormones. This group of compounds also contain chlorine, which creates carbon dioxide formation.

Health effects: 2,4-D exposure occurs by skin contact and absorption, inhalation, or ingestion of contaminated food or water. Exposure symptoms include stupor, weakness, muscle spasms, dermatitis, convulsions and nerve damage. Suspected to be implicated in birth defects.

Environmental impact: moderately toxic to birds and animals, toxic to fish and aquatic invertebrates. Persists for about a month in soil. Volatile nature causes widespread spray drift damaging to all life forms.

2,4,5-T

Also a member of the acid herbicides that chemically stimulate plant growth. Used as both a broad spectrum herbicide, defoliant and brush-killer (e.g. gorse, woody plants).

Health effects: may cause chronic irritation to skin, eyes, nose and throat, psoriasis-like skin rashes, weakness, unnatural fatigue, muscle and joint pain, anxiety, headaches. Suspected to be implicated in birth defects.

Environmental impact: biodegradable within soil in approximately 14 days. Ingestion of 2,4,5-T by animals may lead to similar poisoning symptoms to those experienced by humans. Volatile nature causes spraydrift over wide areas. Dangerous to all forms of life.

The herbicides 2,4,5-T and 2,4-D were the components of the terrible Agent Orange which caused death and hideous suffering during the Vietnam war. By 1987, 2,4,5-T was believed to be responsible for causing birth defects. Public concern and pressure has resulted in the manufacturer withdrawing the chemical from the market in a number of countries, but stockpiling is such that it will still be illegally in use for a number of years. Often applied on a grand scale by air, these highly volatile chemicals, and others like them, form vapour which causes widespread spraydrift damage to people, plants and animals. Damage to plants is manifested in unnatural mutation and contortion of flowers and foliage.

Medical scientists report a link between these chemicals and the high rate of malignant tumours found in both working and pet dogs where the owners have used them on domestic lawns and on pasture.

Glyphosate (H)

Marketed under a variety of names, including Roundup, Rodeo and Network this organophosphate herbicide is in use worldwide. Glyphosate is a non-selective broad spectrum herbicide used to control grasses, sedges, and aquatic weeds. In some countries glyphosate formulas are also used as an insecticide for fruit tree insects.

Health effects: glyphosates are thought to be responsible for the most common forms of human

The rose garden: an enchanted environment poisoned with chemical sprays?

poisoning from chemical herbicide. Exposure symptoms include unnatural fatigue, trembling, anxiety, recurring head pains, headaches and skin rashes.

Environmental impact: the manufacturers of glyphosate formulas claim them to be soil and water biodegradable and non-toxic to birds, fish and animals. Roundup is toxic to earthworms.

Escort/Ally

The active ingredient of Escort is metsulfuron-methyl which is a systemic herbicide. Widely used to control broad-leafed weeds and woody plants such as gorse and blackberry.

Health effects: Escort/Ally is relatively new on the market and health testing on laboratory animals has not yet been proved conclusive. Trade secrecy concerning the remaining 40 per cent of the ingredients means that accurate assessment of its health effects are not yet available. The main cause for concern regarding this chemical is that it is closely allied to the sulphonylurea herbicides which are proven causants of a number of health problems in animals – blood defects, damage to testes and reproductive failure, and chromosomal aberrations in both plants and animals at extremely low concentration levels.

Environmental impact: the sulphonylurea herbicides are reported to have a synergystic effect on organophosphate insecticides, increasing their potency. They are persistent in some soils, espe-

cially silty loams, and have high potential at low concentrations to contaminate groundwater and to be extremely toxic to non-target plants including aquatic plants. The UK Ministry of Agriculture and Fisheries has restricted the use of metsulfuron-methyl in preparations such as Escort/Ally for these reasons.

Cyanazine

Possible human carcinogen. Broad spectrum herbicides.

Health effects: toxic to humans, moderately toxic to birds, fish, and aquatic invertebrates.

Environmental effects: water soluble so contaminates water sources. Biodegradable according to type of soil over 12-25 days.

Atrazine and simazine

Belonging to a class of herbicides called triazins, these herbicides are commonly used worldwide. Developed in the 1950s for broad spectrum control of broadleaf weeds and troublesome grasses, they are chlorinated persistent herbicides with the ability to leach through soil into ground water and to form dioxins.

Health effects: atrazine is implicated in breast, uterine and ovarian cancer, dermatitis, irritation of eyes, nose and throat. High level or prolonged exposure: tremors, organ weight changes, liver and heart damage.

Environmental impact: low toxicity to mammals,

birds and fish, toxic to aquatic organisms. Non-biodegradable and persistent in soil from 3 to 13 months.

Simazine
Broad spectrum herbicide.
Health effects: possible human carcinogen. Very toxic if inhaled, moderately toxic when ingested. Simazine may cause mild to acute dermatitis, male infertility, irritation of the eyes and mucous membranes. Acute exposure leads to convulsions, paralysis, cyanosis, slowed respiration, gastrointestinal pain, impaired renal function and diarrhoea.
Environmental impact: sheep and cattle drinking simazine-contaminated water suffer from identical poisoning effects suffered by human beings. Proven to cause mutations in barley and maize crops.

Diquat/Paraquat
Acutely toxic herbicide generally marketed as a formula called Regone, commonly used to kill off the tops of crops such as onions and potatoes before harvesting. The herbicide Propham is also used to stop potatoes sprouting after harvesting. Onion and shallot bulbs are often soaked in fungicidal mixtures for preservative purposes before planting.
Health effects: poisoning through inadequate monitoring of MRLs, resulting in hazardous amounts of residue in crops. Symptoms may include unnatural fatigue, skin rashes, acute sensitivity to solvents and other chemicals, decreased white blood cell count, unusual nerve sensations, loss of nerve sensation (e.g. tips of toes).

Amitrole
Widely used herbicide regarded as a probable human carcinogen.

Triclopyr/Grazon
Widely used as a herbicide for gorse.
Environmental impact: contamination of soil and crops.

Pesticides
Pesticides/fungicides which are especially dangerous include carbaryl, malathion, DDT, captan, dichlorvas, methoxychlor and chlorothalonil. All

are available under various trade names in any supermarket or garden centre.
Environmental impact: all chemical pesticides result in indiscriminate killing of both beneficial and pestiferous insects, toxic pollution of soil and vegetation, food crops and water sources. Many are probable human carcinogens and mutagens.

Carbaryl
Poisoning with this insecticide often occurs during summer, since it is a commonly used agent for destroying mites, thrips and biting insects.
Health effects: symptoms include unnatural fatigue, nausea, muscle pains, connective tissue and joint tenderness, and a headache starting from tense shoulder muscles causing pain in the back of the neck with referred pain in the frontal area above the eyes. Believed to be implicated in birth defects and infertility.

Benomyl
The active ingredient of the fungicide Benlate, Benomyl is also implicated in birth defects and, like carbaryl, is emerging as a link in increasing human fertility problems.

Captan
Regarded as a probable human carcinogen, Captan is widely used by both commercial growers and home gardeners, and is commonly found as residues in fruit and vegetables after use as a fungicide.
Health effects: present testing on animals indicates malignant tumours, in a number of organs, mutations, fetal death and birth defects.

Endosulfan
At present being assessed as a human carcinogen linked with breast cancer. Widely used on playing fields, golf courses and bowling greens to kill earthworms, and as a pesticide on vegetable crops. An organochlorine which emits dioxins.

Our role
What are we going to do about the use and abuse of chemical sprays? We, the average gardeners, farmers and horticulturists, who hitherto went about our small plots dealing death in modest little doses – but little doses that nevertheless contributed to a global whole.

If we eschew the use of chemicals wherever possible and move instead to sustainable methods of horticulture and agriculture, we take a giant step nearer to a future in which we can hope for improved sources of safe, clean, unadulterated food, water and air – was once our natural birthright.

Indiscriminate poison from the skies

The need for ever increasing food production over the twentieth century has been at the expense of a massive input of chemicals. This frequently poses an environmental issue for rural gardeners since they are often applied by large scale aerial spraying. The chemicals involved are often extremely volatile, changing quickly from a liquid to a vapour so that drift pollutes the land, vegetation, waterways and human homes for miles around.

If you are a victim of aerial spraying, report the incident by ringing your city or borough council – many will have an environmental hotline, or something similar. Give as much relevant information as you can. You can also immediately submit the following details to the nearest plant diagnostic laboratory:

- Name of crops/plants affected.
- Stage of growth.
- Evaluation of extent of damage, i.e. percentage of plants affected/dying/dead.
- Clearly labelled plant, soil and water samples.
- Copies of written report sent to appropriate local bodies, and subsequent results.

Uncontaminated food, pure water and clean air were once our birthright.

Victims of aerial spraying should take plant, soil and water samples.

CHAPTER THREE
SOIL MANAGEMENT

The real gardener is not a man who cultivates flowers; he is a man who cultivates the soil...if he came into the Garden of Eden he would sniff excitedly and say 'Good Lord, what humus!'

Karel Capek, *The Gardener's Year*, 1929

Before we study the essentials of Integrated Pest Management (chapter 4) we must first pay homage to the key player in our earthy drama – the soil, which is the cradle of all sustainable management.

With a mind totally uncluttered by any knowledge of the habits and requirements of plants, I came to gardening as a plant serial killer. Some nine years of vegetative demise revealed a Great Truth: the gardener gives his all not to his plants, but to the soil in which they are planted; the gardener dedicates to the soil continual rites of conditioning, enriching, feeding, moisturising and mulching.

Above: Sustainable soil management requires continual enriching and conditioning.

Body and soil

Soil is the beginning point. Technology cannot create soil any more than it can create life. Soil is made biologically by plants and animals. Deep rooted plants find fractures in the subsoil, mine them for mineral elements and fracture them a bit more for the next generation. They cycle these minerals into the topsoil, where the other elements needed by plants and animals to make the chemical compounds we call soil are available.

We know that all life on earth is dependent upon the soil – a living element filled with millions of minute organisms working together to produce the nutrients essential to plant growth. A healthy soil, its structure, drainage and nutritional values enhanced by generous proportions of organic

A healthy soil and healthy plants ensure healthy people.

matter, is the key to sustainable gardening and to all successful growing.

Bare essentials – the nutrients

All plants need oxygen, carbon and hydrogen, which they get from the air, sunlight and water. Equally important for healthy growth is the presence of essential natural chemical elements in the soil. These include the main nutrients nitrogen (N), Phosphorus (P) and potassium (K). Minor amounts of other nutrients – magnesium, calcium and iron – are also required, together with others in minute amounts called trace elements. All these groups are present in average soils.

Nitrogen

An essential plant food, this is a component of chlorophyll – the pigment that gives green plants their colour – and a vital part of the structure of plant protein. Nitrogen is the element in the soil responsible for plant growth. Deficiency occurs through leaching in open soils; plant foliage becomes yellow and stunted. Too much nitrogen causes the rapid growth of an abundance of dark green 'soft' foliage subject to attack by insects and frost. Too much nitrogen can also cause luxuriant foliage growth at the expense of flowers.

To treat a nitrogen deficiency use a high nitrogen fertiliser such as dried blood.

Brutal toil

Whether your soil is brutish clay, fertile but thirsty volcanic deposits, impoverished earth or poor sandy soil through which water poured day and night disappears without trace, it has to be conditioned. This means prising it apart with a crow bar if needs be to insert lashings of organic materials for enrichment and to improve its basic structure and moisture retention. Only then, regardless of weather extremes, will it receive your spade willingly and nurture the plants folded into its surface.

Buckling of the knees with every spadeful indicates wet and heavy soils. In addition to providing nutritional materials, you'll need to dig every planting hole much bigger (oh joy!) to facilitate ramming in those prohibitively heavy, coarse materials such as sand, pumice, scoria, gravel, or pipes to improve drainage. A less body crippling and gratifyingly efficient method to encourage good drainage is to build simple raised beds with untreated timbers and fill them with conditioned soil. The reward is that your plants may consent to live.

When you have, with all diligence, broken your back and thus improved both the fertility and structure of your soil, the next immutable law is to mulch before the first hot summer weather dries the beds into Gobi desert faultlines. These dried out beds are a particularly cruel form of planticide, one which leaves tender treasures gasping piteously and with their roots exposed, fit only for dried flower arrangements.

Phosphorus

The next most important element after nitrogen, phosphorus is needed in smaller quantities – about one tenth of the amount. Phosphorus or phosphate is mainly responsible for good root growth. A deficiency causes a blue-green tinge on older leaves and stunting due to an under developed root system.

To treat a phosphorus deficiency apply a dressing of bone meal fertiliser.

Potassium

Also known as potash, this is required in the same quantities as nitrogen. It affects the size and quality of flowers and fruit, and is essential for the synthesis of protein and carbohydrates. Potassium deficiency results in stunted plants with brownish-yellow foliage, small, inferior flowers and fruit.

Magnesium

An element needed in much larger quantities than generally appreciated, magnesium should be present in about the same quantities as phosphorus. Magnesium is also a constituent of chlorophyll, thus a deficiency causes yellowing between the veins of the leaves. Magnesium deficiency is sometimes caused by plants not being able to take up magnesium in the soil, usually because there is too much potassium present. This can also happen if the soil structure is poor due to the presence of insufficient organic matter.

To treat magnesium deficiency apply a dressing of seaweed meal, liquid seaweed or liquid animal manure.

Calcium

Another element required in relatively large amounts, calcium neutralises certain acids formed in plants and helps in the manufacture of protein. Deficiency is rare in soils conditioned with organic fertilisers. Some plants develop an inability to distribute calcium throughout their systems, though it is not fully understood why. This results in such symptoms as black heart in celery and Brussels sprouts, blossom end rot in tomatoes when the tip of the fruit blackens and rots, and tip burn on lettuce.

There is no specific cure for calcium deficiency. The only treatment is by correct cultiva-

Colourful juicy capsicums grown using organic nutrients.

tion methods, incorporating plenty of manure or compost to build up balanced nutrient levels in the soil.

Sulphur

Often classed as a trace element, sulphur is in fact needed in fairly large quantities. It is involved in the formation of chlorophyll and plant proteins.

Sulphur deficiency causes stunting and yellowing of the plant. The problem should be rare in soils conditioned with organic compost.

To treat sulphur deficiency apply a very light dusting of calcium sulphate (gypsum) over the surface of the soil.

Gypsum

Gypsum is a naturally occurring, non-toxic mineral that, on dissolving, releases equal proportions of calcium and sulphate and thus acts as a slow release fertiliser when applied to soil. It also works to break up clay by causing flocculation – the sticking together of clay particles into crumbs, thus improving aeration and manageability and root penetration. In compost bins it helps to increase the utilisation of nitrogen, while aerating the mass. Used with magnesium limestone, gypsum is more active. Use 240 g per 2 square metres (8 oz per 2 square yards) of a 9:1 mix of gypsum and magnesium limestone, and hoe into

Soil is made biologically through the actions of plants and animals.

the top 50 mm (2 in) of soil on a still day between autumn and spring.

Earthy characters – the soil types

There are roughly six basic soil types varying from pure clay through various grades of sandy loam to pure sand.

Clay

This soil type swallows gumboots whole and is quagmire or bake out according to season! When wet, clay soils stick to your boots, drain slowly and are heavy to work. When dry they set hard, shrink and crack.

Clay soils are comprised of very small mineral particles, packed so closely together that the movement of air and water is very slow. Water is held very tightly around the particles; this makes it difficult for the plant to obtain moisture, and thus growth is slow. The drainage and structure of clay soils is improved by the addition of generous amounts of organic materials.

Silts

Silt soils have larger particles than those of clay and although they clump together so that drainage is slow, they lack the qualities of clay. Fertilisers and lime are easily lost, so silty soils tend to be acidic.

Loams

Top of every gardener's wish list! Loams contain a mix of different-sized particles that cling together to form loose 'crumbs', thus providing a fine tilth. Loam also contains good supplies of organic matter. Plant foods are held by this material and by the clay particles, and drainage and aeration are helped by the coarser sand particles.

Sandy soils

These vary from the pure sand of seaside gardens to sandy loams and the acid sands of heathlands. They're composed of silica grains, which are chemically inactive and contain no nutrients. Because drainage is rapid, moisture and soluble plant foods such as potash and nitrates quickly leach away causing dryness and acidity, especially in vegetable gardens. Sandy soils are improved by the addition of lime, organic matter, liquid fertilisers, and the installation of an automatic irrigation system.

Chalk and limestone soils

Well drained and alkaline, these soils sometimes prevent iron and manganese being absorbed by plants such as camellias and azaleas. Potash deficiency is also likely, and organic matter is rapidly decomposed.

A wide range of calcium tolerant plants may be grown, and species that require shallow drainage do well.

The topsoil is usually shallow and solid chalk may lie on the surface. If broken, this allows roots to penetrate to find reserves of water. It's well worth importing loads of good quality topsoil to build up the depth of these soils and then to maintain and build them with the no-dig methods outlined later in this chapter.

Peat soils

These comprise decomposed organic matter with little mineral content. Peat is formed in high rainfall areas and creates extremely acidity with bog-like conditions that discourage plant life.

Soil testing – acid or alkaline

Before deciding on a soil feeding regime, you'll need to determine the pH of your soil – in other words, whether it is acid or alkaline – because this will determine your cultivation techniques and what sort of plants you choose to grow. Acidity or alkalinity is determined by the amount of lime in the soil.

There is no mystique about determining the pH of your soil. A simple soil test, which you can do yourself, will tell you what your soil needs to bring it to optimum standard and save you the time, labour and expense of adding elements that are already present in satisfactory amounts.

The pH of a soil affects how nutrients are released to your plants. If soil pH is too high or too low some elements may not be available. In strongly acid soils (pH 4–5) all the important elements – nitrogen, phosphorous, potassium, calcium, magnesium and sulphur – are in short supply. On soils of slight to medium alkalinity (pH 7.5–8.5), phosphorous again becomes available and so do the other five trace elements: iron, manganese, boron, copper and zinc. All plant nutrients are available between pH 6–7, with maximum availability at pH 6.5 – soil which is very slightly acid.

The basic test result gives you the soil's pH level – the measure of acidity. On the pH scale, 7 is neutral; below 7 the soil is acidic or sour, above 7 the soil is alkaline or sweet.

Most plants thrive in a pH between 5.5 and 7 (slightly acidic) and most average soils range between pH 4 and 8. If your soil result exceeds 10, you're living in a limestone quarry; below 3 and you're living in a peat bog! Clay soil is generally rich in nutrients but it is often quite acidic and needs compost and lime to raise the pH level.

Most garden centres stock basic soil testing kits comprising a syringe, pH testing fluid and filters, test tube, and a pH colour chart to determine the results. The pH filter is put in the base of the syringe and a soil sample added. The syringe plunger is used to push the mixture through the filter and into a test tube. This is then held up against the pH colour chart. The mixture will match one of the colour bands thus telling you the pH of your soil, but it won't tell you what nutrients are available or lacking.

Troubleshooting

If you've done a soil test and adjusted your feeding and conditioning regime accordingly, and you're still having problems growing the plants of your heart's desire, you'll need to send a soil

Soil rich in natural minerals and nutrients grows bumper crops.

sample away for a professional analysis of nutrient levels (see the yellow pages of your telephone directory).

There will be a fee for this detailed evaluation, but you'll be told both your soil's pH level and the levels of calcium, phosphate, potassium, magnesium and sodium – all the essential nutrients for healthy plant growth. The report will suggest ways to correct imbalances and how to maintain optimum levels.

Out of the limelight: lowering soil pH

Few garden soils are naturally limy unless in a predominantly chalk or limestone region, so lowering pH is less of a problem than raising it. In most cases, the liberal dressings of manure and compost applied during sustainable gardening practices will lower the pH sufficiently.

Don't worry about whether you've got the pH level of your plot absolutely right; the situation isn't so critical that your plants will keel over and die if you haven't. They'll do just that much better if the level is adjusted as much as possible to suit their kind and your basic soil type. If you yearn for lashings of acid-loving plants such as rhododendrons, camellias, azaleas or pieris and your soil pH is above 7, alkaline and sweet, then you'll obviously have to adjust levels by incorporating lots of acid sphagnum peat and lime-free sharp sand.

In the limelight: raising soil pH

An acid soil may be made more alkaline by the addition of lime, but the correction is fairly slow to take effect. Resist the temptation to speed things up by adding larger quantities – it will scorch plant roots. It's wiser to effect the change by applying light dressings regularly.

Apply lime several weeks before planting or, ideally, dress the soil with manure in the autumn and add lime in the spring. The amount applied must depend on your soil type. Heavy clay soils need more lime than light sandy ones. As an approximate guide, to increase the pH of a sandy soil by one unit, apply 1 kg of lime to every 100 square metres (2 lb per 100 square yards). A sandy loam will need 2 kg (4 lb) for the same area, a medium loam about 3 kg (6 lb), and a heavy clay roughly 4 kg (8 lb).

Types of lime

Lime is available in several different forms. The more expensive varieties such as ground limestone or calcified seaweed last longer in the soil.

- Slaked lime (calcium oxide) is the most readily available. Sometime sold as 'garden lime' it is superior to builders' lime (hydrated lime) because it lasts longer in the soil.
- Hydrated lime (builders' lime), commonly sold for use with cement, is perfectly suitable for garden use, but must be replaced annually.
- Ground limestone, often called 'dolomite lime' is the best type to use. More expensive than slaked or hydrated lime, it will last in the soil for several years and also contains magnesium.
- Calcified seaweed is very useful since it contains magnesium and several other plant foods as well as lime. It lasts two to three years in the soil but it is expensive.

Soil sustenance – feeding and conditioning
Animal manures

Bulky and fibrous, animal manures are unparalleled for both feeding and improving the texture of the soil. Like good wines, they improve with age. Used immature they are unpleasant to handle and may burn your plants. Well rotted manures are dry and crumbly and benefit all the soil's beneficial organisms from worms to bacteria. When using any animal manure or commercially prepared organic fertiliser, it is essential to water well immediately after application. Not just a hit and miss splosh over the surface! A good deep soaking is required, preferably from sprinkler heads rather than hoses.

Cow manure

Perhaps the best of animal manures, as being doubly digested it is usually weed free, effective and safe. But heed a cautionary tale: for a long time I was puzzled why some of the foliage on my tomato or cucumber plants (sown with lashings of good home-made compost) became twisted and contorted, looking as though it had been spray damaged. I have since learned that the fault actually lay in my compost, which contained a high proportion of cow manure from cattle fed on bought-in winter hay. The straw it contained had been derived from cereal crops that had been sprayed with herbicides, and in addition to composting the manure, I'd used the hay sweepings as mulch. Even in minute amounts, the herbicide residues had caused the plants to distort making them weak and unprofitable.

Poultry manure

Poultry manure is a very strong fertiliser – a little goes a long way. Don't neglect to age it well because, rich in nitrogen in the form of ammonium carbonate, it is fierce and can burn crops badly. Chicken manure produces strong leafy growth in almost all plants and is especially beneficial for leafy crops such as salad greens, spinach, beet, cabbage etc. It is also excellent for plants such as roses and hibiscus, for lawns, hedges and bougainvillea, and for citrus, which are gross feeders. Poultry manure is best applied as a thin layer about 1 cm (½ in) thick away from the stems or trunks of plants. Also makes a rich liquid manure – use 1 part of concentrate to 3 parts of water.

Sheep manure

Classed as hot because it produces considerable heat during decomposition, sheep manure has the highest nitrogen value and is richer in nutrients Excellent under a mulch of grass around trees and plants or steeped in water as a liquid fertiliser.

These domestic laying hens will provide very strong fertiliser.

Horse manure

Classified as a hot, dry manure, this is especially valuable for heavy soils since it has a fibrous structure and rots down quickly. The heat produced during its rapid decomposition makes it a valuable compost activator, and also kills weed seeds and diseases.

Pig manure

It is said that plants grow faster on pig manure in an attempt to get away from the smell! There is no doubt it is malodorous, and classified as a cold manure it is slow to decompose, but it is rich in nutrients when mature.

Goat manure

An excellent general purpose manure because the goat is a browser, feeding on a diversity of leaves, shoots and shrubs, rather than on grass alone.

Pigeon manure

Difficult to obtain, which is regrettable since it is the richest manure of all; it has four times more potash and nitrogen than poultry manure. The phosphorus content is also doubled, making it an ideal compost activator.

Human waste

The more complex subject of human waste as a soil fertiliser is discussed in Chapter 9.

Elixirs of life – liquid fertilisers
Seaweed fertiliser

A good time to collect seaweed is after rough seas, when large and varied quantities have been washed up. Spread it out, give it a hose down to remove salt and allow it to dry thoroughly. Chop it roughly (I run the mower over it on a high setting) and toss approximately 2 kg (4½ lb) of seaweed into 2 litres (3½ pt) of hot water in a large drum or bin. Cover and allow to stand for an hour then add another 14 litres (3 gal) of cold water and soak for eight weeks, stirring twice weekly. Use concentrate at 1 part seaweed to 14 parts of water.

Liquid nettle

A more or less complete fertiliser. Use 10 litres (2 gal) of water to 1 kg (2 lb) of fresh nettles. Steep in a covered container, stirring every two days. Sieve after two weeks and use diluted 10 parts of water to one part of concentrate.

Comfrey fertiliser

Fill half a container with comfrey leaves, top with water, cover and leave for three to four weeks to mature, stirring weekly. Don't be put off by the smell – just watch your plants grow! Use one part of concentrate to five parts of water.

Home-made liquid manure

It's very easy to make your own nutritious liquid

Comfrey – a five-star plant

No self respecting garden should be without this versatile and valuable plant! Ancient physicians called comfrey (*Symphytum officinale*) 'knit bone' because of its remarkable healing properties. The herb was and still is used extensively for the healing of ulcers, sores and skin complaints. The Henry Doubleday Organic Research Foundation in Britain has pioneered research into the qualities of this most valuable herb. A native of Europe, it belongs to the borage family and because of its vigorous growth habit is now spread throughout much of the world.

Comfrey has a deep tap root and once established it can be difficult to eradicate. New plants grow readily from broken roots so it can be invasive in the vegetable patch or herb garden. Confine it to areas where you really want it, such as the orchard, under trees, as a ground cover or in a bed of its own. A thick border of comfrey is an excellent weed barrier – its thick roots will repel invasive grasses around edges or fence lines. The deep roots grow down into the subsoil, bringing to the surface valuable minerals and nutrients unavailable to plants with a shallower root system.

The plant grows to 50 cm (20 in) has thick, prolific, furry leaves of deep rich green and bears small bell-shaped flowers. Cultivars include 'Hidcote Pink' with pinkish-violet blooms, blue-flowered *Symphytum* 'Eminence' and the most attractive cream-flowered 'Goldsmith', a low growing compact plant to 20 cm (8 in) with foliage variegated green, gold and cream. Comfrey leaves contain as much nitrogen as farmyard manure, nearly as much phosphorus and twice as much potassium, and are rich in B, C, and E vitamins and carotene. The intensive healing properties of the herb are due to an active ingredient scientifically known as allantoin.

Because of its high protein content, comfrey is used to feed pigs, poultry and other animals.

The leaves may be spread around the base of plants to form a fertilising mulch, put straight into the compost heap or made into a liquid fertiliser. For a bumper, well-flavoured crop of potatoes with good storage life, place comfrey leaves in the trenches prior to planting. As a green manure, hoe or lightly turn the leaves into the soil or around plants. Quick decomposition will free nitrogen from the leaves, and the topsoil will be enriched with calcium and other minerals. Comfrey is an essential of sustainable horticulture – you can't afford to be without it!

manure. You'll require a large plastic drum, a hessian sack and some animal manure.

Sheep manure is excellent because it is particularly high in nutrients, but cow, pig, goat or horse manure are all satisfactory too. About half a sackful will give a year's supply. As with compost, it's wise to have one drum 'maturing' and one in use,

thus always having plant food readily available.

Fill the drum three-quarters full with water. Collect half a sackful of animal manure and tie top with a double loop of string. Place a stout stake across the top of the drum and loop the string over it so that the sack is suspended in the water. Leave for about a fortnight until the water is rich

Applying liquid fertilisers

If they are of a commercial variety such as fish emulsion or seaweed extract, dilute according to the manufacturer's instructions. The golden rule when applying liquid fertilisers is never to do so when the soil is very dry – you may scorch roots. And never be tempted to try to grow 'knock the neighbours' eyes out' plants by using stronger concentrations than recommended! This will almost certainly burn the plants and may result in their demise.

Water the beds deeply if you can, or if short of water wait until after it has rained. If you're feeding plants in containers, simply fill up to the rim of the pot. For plants growing in soil, water the fertiliser on generously in a fairly wide area around the base until the soil is saturated.

For plants such as tomatoes, which need constant feeding, a good idea is to bury a flower pot or a bottomless upturned plastic drink bottle near the roots and fill that. Using this method the fertiliser sinks direct to the roots and you know how much you're giving the plant each time.

The advantage of liquid feeding is that, since plants can only take up nutrients in liquid form, the nutrients are available immediately.

Home-made liquid fertiliser can be dispensed from a plastic barrel.

dark brown. Remove the sack and cover the drum. Remains of manure can be added to the compost heap or spread on beds. To use the liquid manure as a foliar fertiliser, dilute the liquid with equal parts of water.

Fish emulsion

Despite being somewhat malodorous, fish concentrate is a rich and valuable natural fertiliser, which may be applied as a foliar or root feed. Contains phosphorous, nitrogen, potash, sodium, zinc, iron, copper, and other vitamins and minerals.

In emulsion form it is easily assimilated by plants, and has the advantage of being both a fertiliser and an odiferous deterrent to insect pests and to larger undesirable animal pests such as opossums.

Dried blood and bone

Sometimes plants take out more from the soil than we can put back in the form of compost or manure. This is when manufactured organic fertilisers make useful boosters. Canines will come from miles around to deprive your plants of these pungent nitrogen boosts by rolling in or eating them, so sprinkle them in volumes indicated by the manufacturer and water them in quickly. Dried blood on its own is water soluble so may be sprayed on, but it is expensive. Blood and bone is basically a slow-release form of nitrogen and is a safe and gentle fertiliser. These products are best used in spring and summer.

Magic mulches

As you study the principles of sustainable gardening you'll develop a healthy respect for mulch – it's addictive and habit forming! Mulches suppress weeds, keep the soil warm in winter and cool in summer, conserve moisture, and support and

Mulch conserves moisture, inhibits weed growth and provides soil nutrients.

encourage the myriads of beneficial organisms required by a healthy soil. These organic materials break down to improve soil structure and drainage, and last but not least, add nutrients to the soil. In areas where the soil must be covered – as in beds of young shrubs, a mulch of fine bark is both beneficial and aesthetically pleasing. Pebbles and gravel also create attractive and harmonious mulches beneath heat-loving plants like succulents, or in gardens of oriental design.

The healthiest plants are those that have constant supplies of nutrients available so that they don't suffer setbacks in growth. The provision of a good feeding mulch that breaks down easily is an inexpensive and effective way of doing this. We tend to think that nutrients will not reach the roots of plants unless the mulch is dug in, but in nature food is taken down into the soil by rain and the activity of earthworms. To take advantage of this, many plants have their most active feeding roots just below the soil surface; the downside is that they're easily damaged by weeding, mowing, or periods of prolonged dryness. Thus a good layer of mulch both feeds and protects.

Naturally you will have removed perennial weeds such as docks, dandelions, plantains and invasive grasses before mulching! Nothing will prevent wind-borne seeds germinating in the top of a mulch, of course, but a gentle stir round with the hoe on a dry day will dispatch them with the minimum of effort.

Types of mulch
Leaf mould
Make a chicken wire enclosure and stack leaves in it. They rot slowly by fungal action, which can take over a year, but leaf mould is a treat worth waiting for. Invaluable on sandy soils where, although it can't replace the nutritional value of compost, it will provide humus to help retain nutrients from the compost and improve structure. Water the leaves in layers if they're dry when you stack them, and water in summer to prevent drying out.

Grass clippings
Grass clippings from a weed free lawn (untreated with chemicals) make an excellent feeding mulch, but they must be sprinkled lightly and if possible mixed with other organic materials such as leaves. Because clippings are high in nitrogen, decay organisms attack them ravenously, especially in humid weather, transforming a heap almost overnight to a steaming, smelly, slimy pulp. This is unpleasant to handle and may burn plants, so clippings are best sprinkled no more than 2 cm (1 in) deep straight onto the beds from the catcher. This will prevent heat building up, and the layers can be added to gradually in successive weeks to form a nutritious mulch.

Although lawn grass has a high nitrogen content it has little fibre, but if combined with a rich carbon source such as untreated sawdust, cereal straw or autumn leaves it will provide the fibre required to improve the soil structure, and also become more of a balanced food.

Lucerne pea straw

Other nutritious mulching materials include lucerne hay or pea straw. As lucerne grows, its deep roots bring up minerals, trace elements and other valuable nutrients. These are stored in the plant, then returned to the soil as the mulch decomposes. Cereal straw is ineffective on its own since it is mostly carbon, but mixed with grass clippings, animal manure or blood and bone it forms a nutritious mulch. In some countries, food processing firms have nutritious waste products to dispose of, such as rice or cereal hulls, peanut husks, spent hops or cocoa pods. Whichever mulch you choose it should be kept to a depth of approximately 10 cm (4 in) thick. This will settle down to about 5 cm (2 in), which is still effective both for moisture retention and weed suppression, but it will obviously need topping up as it decomposes.

Bark

A favourite mulch for shrubberies is bark, which is fine for mature plants. But if the shrubs are young and there are interplantings of perennials, soft feeding mulches of compost or mixed clippings are far more beneficial.

To make a richly nutritious mulch to go beneath a top-dressing of bark, first spread a layer of compost right through the bed. Cover with a thick layer of newspaper to prevent weed seeds germinating and top-dress with the bark.

Although fairly rot resistant, bark will gradually break down and require topping up every three years or so. As it breaks down it will eventually contribute a dressing of rich black humus to the soil.

What about black plastic?

In the 'dark ages' (1970–1990) gardeners were encouraged to use layers of heavy duty polythene beneath vegetative mulch to give total weed suppression. But the problems soon became evident – the soil, starved of oxygen and light became sour and caused root die back. The polythene's slippery surface caused the mulch to slide off revealing its ugly surface which, once exposed to the elements, rotted and shredded allowing weeds to germinate freely. As we've seen, sheets of plastic have their place when used as weed control by solarisation, but should be used only on a temporary basis.

Eating machines – chipper-mulchers

Electric or petrol powered chipping and shredding machines facilitate the recycling of shrub prunings, roots, stalks and larger pieces of vegetation into mulch. Heavier duty models will take flax, palm fronds, vines, cardboard, papers and hard prunings; some incorporate a hammermill, which will grind up materials such as bark, seaweed, shells, and bones. A shredding machine is an advantage if you have a large garden producing quantities of prunings – especially if you live in an urban area and have difficulty in disposing of them. Feeding the vegetation into the machine takes energy and time, but you're recycling waste into a luscious pile of instant mulch rather than using the car to take it to a landfill.

An alternative method if your garden is not big enough to justify the acquisition of a mulcher is to spread the prunings on the lawn and run the mower over them on a high setting. The resulting mix of grass clippings and prunings can be used as excellent instant mulch or composting material.

I am managing my gardens on the no-dig system, which we shall discuss shortly, so when light-pruning shrubs and perennials I use my secateurs to re-clip the foliage and stalks straight back onto the beds. When covered with a mulch of grass clippings from the next mow, they rot down quickly as nutrients and help build up the soil.

Compost – nature's supreme fertiliser

Are you one of those gardeners who suffer from the misconception that there is some kind of magic and mystique about making compost? Read on. Here's how to rot successfully.

Compost is simply well rotted organic matter and the process of making it is easy, but some gardeners encounter problems – it's too smelly, it won't decay properly or it takes too long to do so. There are ways around these difficulties, and the benefits of compost in a healthy, productive garden are unparalleled. It enriches the soil and improves its structure and drainage, and provides plants with the nutrients that promote strong

Compost check
How do I know if the compost heap is working?
Started off with the right ingredients, compost should start to heat up after three days. If not, check that it is not too wet, too dry or in need of more air.

When is the compost ready?
When it is a dark crumbly mass and it is no longer possible to tell what went in, except for the odd foreign body (trowel, secateurs…).

Why has my compost failed?
It may be too wet, too dry, or lacking in ventilation (aerate by tossing or turning). It may have lacked nitrogenous materials. If compost fails to heat up, add nitrogen in the form of urine, hen manure, blood and bone, or green leafy lucerne.

Why is my compost a pale sludgy mess?
Too many kitchen scraps and insufficient plant material. Add more vegetative material and mix well.

My compost is an evil smelling heap!
Oops! It has insufficient ventilation and has become anaerobic instead of aerobic – it needs more air, toss and turn it thoroughly, and if possible add twiggy prunings to improve aeration.

growth, abundant crops and flowers.

Good compost is filled with every organic material, minerals, and millions of beneficial micro-organisms, as well as trace elements; it is nature's supreme fertiliser and soil conditioner. Soils rich in organic matter are a breeding ground for some of the helpful bacteria and moulds that attack many of the fungi responsible for plant disease.

From henceforth let nothing that can be converted to rich black sweetly friable compost escape your attention: grass clippings, fallen leaves, all vegetative kitchen waste, human and animal hair, prunings, contents of the vacuum cleaner bag, weeds, coffee grounds, seaweed, untreated sawdust, any type of animal manure, shredded newspaper and card, old potting mix – and anything else you can think of! It's best not to include food scraps, which may attract vermin, and to use grass clippings in light layers mixed with other materials such as leaves or prunings. Thick layers of grass heat up rapidly and can decompose quickly to a malodorous slimy mess.

Carefree composting
You'll require a robust bin such as the black polythene composters stocked by garden centres. They're lidded but bottomless and have holes in their sides for ventilation. When the compost is mature, the shell of the bin is lifted leaving a neat cone-shaped pile.

Alternatively you can construct a simple container of wooden slats, bricks or netting, which allows air circulation but is enclosed enough to allow heat to build up within the materials. It's best to build two bins side by side, so that by the time the second bin is full, the compost in the first should be mature. A three bay system is ideal; one containing mature, ready to use compost, one in the maturing process, and one in the making.

When you've collected enough material to start the bin, pierce the soil beneath with a fork to allow excess water to drain away and encourage the earthworms to start work. Place well-mixed materials in layers about 30 cm (1 ft) thick, with a sprinkling of activator between layers. The activator can be a commercial product (ammonium sulphate), human urine or animal manure. When the bin is full, cover it with a piece of old carpet or punctured polythene and leave it to heat up. The heating process takes about a month and ensures weed seeds are destroyed. The compost should then be turned once, recovered, and the process repeated once more before it is mature.

Compost tumblers filled with shredded ingredients produce garden-ready compost in about three weeks.

A sense of humus
To feed beneficial soil organisms, and through them ultimately the plants, it is essential to continually build up the humus content of the soil.

Humus is the end product of the natural recycling process. It is the material found in a good ripe compost heap, but the same process will go on in the soil wherever appropriate raw materials are provided.

Humus is the very fabric of the universe. Since our planet evolved, the weather has caused rock to disintegrate, ground boulders into sand and allowed tiny fungus and lichens to form specks of vegetable mould. Giant forests have flourished for a millennium before dying, and in decaying have given back to the earth nourishment that will sustain future life. When insects, fish and man evolved, they were able to survive because of this sustenance. They in their turn enriched the soil with their excreta, and finally with their bodies.

Green manures and cover crops
An empty bed should never be an idle bed! The sowing of green manures as a cover crop prevents nutrient greedy weeds forming and will produce the soil's own fertilisers and soil conditioners. During colder months plant a green crop such as lupins, oats or quick growing mustard.

Crops such as buckwheat serve more than one purpose – often used as a green manure, it also attracts hover flies, which dine on greenflies and blackflies. Cover crops such as these take up nutrients still present in the soil so that they will be safely trapped over winter. They will also collect carbon from the air by making sugar in their leaves during photosynthesis, which will ensure there is plenty of energy present to ultimately convert all the growth into useful humus.

To achieve this conversion one needs to cut down the plants when the carbon/nitrogen ratio is most appropriate. This happens when the plants begin to flower. Earlier there is too high a proportion of nitrogen-rich young growth and later, too much carbonaceous tissue.

In the past the recommendation has been to dig the crop in, but horticultural scientists now believe that digging destroys the structure of the soil. They recommend cutting the crop down and leaving it to rot on the surface as a thick mulch. It doesn't matter if it hasn't rotted down entirely by the time you wish to plant new crops. Simply draw the mulch aside and then replace it around the young plants to feed and protect them.

An alternative is a winter mulch with a mix of paper, lawn clippings and autumn leaves. In poor soils or on land that is being prepared for vegetable growing, the amount of processing humus can be increased by covering the slashed green manure with this mix. It is unwise to spread mature compost in late autumn because prolonged heavy winter rains may leach the nutrients down below root zones before they can be used. It is better to apply the raw green mulch materials to the soil for decay organisms to work on and then boost their efforts with compost when the spring crops go in.

A quick fix
Nitrogen fixing green manures: Alfalfa (*Medicago sativa*), alsike clover (*Trifolium hybridum*), black medic-hop clover (*Medicago lupilina*), cowpea (*Vigna unguiculata*, which also has powerful roots for breaking up compacted soil), fava (broad) beans (*Vicia faba*), lupins (*Lupinus augustifolius*), red clover (*Trifolium pratense*), winter tare (*Vicia villosa*).

Non-nitrogen fixers: Annual ryegrass (*Lolium multiflorum*), buckwheat (*Fagopyrum esculentum*), comfrey (*Symphytum* spp), millet (*Millium effusum*), mustard (*Sinapsis alba*), phacelia (*Phacelia tanacetifolia*), rye (*Ecale cereale*).

Raised beds – an uplifting experience
Few of us naturally inherit open, well-drained earth; heavy, wet or clay soils are most gardener's lot and are a universal problem. They bring instant rot to seeds, and death by drowning to tender seedlings. We can do much to prevent

Raised beds are filled with enriched soil.

responding size. Drive in short 'stay' pegs at strategic intervals on either side of long planks to prevent bulging or cracking. Ensure the bottom of the beds are free from perennial weeds and grasses. Score the soil by stabbing it repeatedly with a garden fork or light crowbar to loosen impacted earth and to encourage basal drainage. Line the framework with a good layer of the Saturday classifieds – earthworms adore newsprint and will quickly wriggle up to begin their good work.

During drought months bed surfaces may be mulched with organic materials such as shredded bark, pea straw, well rotted manure, or shrub and grass clippings to conserve moisture and inhibit weed growth. A raised bed system is also invaluable where a garden must be created on a sloping site. In addition to providing easily maintained blocks of conditioned soil, stoutly built raised beds in tiers and terraces provide the garden with both a strong, erosion-free framework and create an attractive design feature.

Those gardeners of long ago had sussed out the fact that in addition to preventing waterlogging, raised beds were much easier to weed, feed and maintain.

No-dig gardening

For many years we've obediently tilled the soil as instructed by the horticultural cognoscenti. Autumn and spring we've given it 'a good digging over', or (courting lumbar collapse) dug whole beds over to 'one or two spade's depth'. Were we right to 'bury the soil'? Horticultural scientists studying soil structure now believe that it is damaged by heavy digging, and I for one am convinced they're right.

In nature, spent plant material and other organic waste is deposited on the earth's surface so that it is alive, teeming with organisms and bacteria all busily converting organic matter into plant food. This great army of microscopic creatures concerned with the recycling of organic material is intended to live on the soil surface, not interred at spade depth. Many of these organisms also inhibit or prevent the development of the parasitic fungi responsible for plant diseases. The soil surface is merely the table on which we lay the food.

In soils conditioned with a continuous supply of organic matter, earthworm armies are also pres-

waterlogging by conditioning the soil to make it freer draining or by building simple raised beds – a system used over many centuries.

Woodcuts in ancient gardening chronicles show gardeners cultivating herbs and vegetables (which almost all require light well-drained soils) in this manner. Their construction is not difficult and involves few tools other than hammer and nails or lengths of strong wire and pliers. No-join edging materials include railway sleepers (heavy enough to abut naturally), straw bales, breeze blocks, bricks or large stones. Round poles or half poles may be stacked to the desired height and nailed or wired together. Planks of timber should be untreated to avoid the leaching of undesirable chemicals into the soil, but must be durable enough to last. I've constructed excellent raised beds with inexpensive offcuts of untreated macrocarpa from a local mill.

Measure the length and width of the desired bed, and if you're using timbers, cut them to cor-

Constructing a raised bed is a relatively simple operation.

ent and their constant tunnelling supplies the aeration needed by plant roots. They pull decomposing material from the soil's surface to lower depths, at the same time bringing up soil from lower levels, fertilising both with their rich castings. The topsoil is alive with teeming activity unseen by the human eye!

Earthy treasures

If your soil is raw orange clay like mine, in order to break it you may need to incorporate sand, fine-grade scoria or pumice in addition to the nutritional elements. If all this smacks of too much hard labour, treat yourself to a trailer-full of good quality topsoil and add your own organic materials. The light, open structure of a mix such as this creates a no-dig situation and is easily conditioned with top-dressings of organic humus and fertilisers when necessary. Seeds will reward you by germinating therein, and your seedlings by consenting to live and growing lustily.

A straw and paper garden

The idea is to build a no-dig garden on top of existing ground using newspaper, lucerne hay, straw, compost and any good organic mulch. As with raised beds, it will be necessary to provide solid edging to confine materials. This type of garden doesn't require any digging to build or maintain, so lay down your spade and let nature do the work for you.

No-dig beds can be built to suit three basic earth environments – over lawn or existing garden, on top of hard, rocky or compacted ground, or over poor soil.

To build this garden over existing areas, select a sunny site and spread a 1 cm (½ in) layer of newspaper. Ensure the newspaper is well overlapped to prevent the lawn growing through. Capture some earthworms from your 'wormarium' (see end of this chapter) and bed them on top. Cover the newspaper with pads of lucerne hay, straw or vegetative mulch topped with a light dressing of organic fertiliser such as well rotted manure. Cover with a layer about 20 cm (8 in) deep of the same mulching materials slightly loosened and top off with compost to a depth of 10 cm (4 in).

If you're aiming to convert your rockery or compacted clay to a productive patch, lay down a foundation of roughly equal parts of old leaves, small prunings and twigs and shredded seaweed to a depth of 10 cm (4 in). Top this with newspaper and build up the layers as described above. Keep the mulch lightly watered, which will assist decomposition and encourage the worms to start work.

The no-dig beds should be ready for planting within six weeks. After a few months – say, once the leafy summer crops have finished – the layers of garden will have decomposed and melted down into each other. Top up the beds with another generous layer of compost or manure and sow seeds or plant seedlings for winter crops such as onions, spinach, brassicas, turnips and carrots. No digging is required.

Potatoes can be grown in this garden almost year round in temperate zones. Tuck the seedling tubers well into the mulch and as they sprout ensure they're covered with mix to prevent 'greening', which is toxic. During the colder months crops that are not harvested may be protected under a layer of hessian and collected at leisure.

As with the traditional bed, fertility in the no-dig garden is maintained by crop rotation in addition to the dressings of compost, organic mulches and fertilisers. Weeds that sow into the top layer are easily pulled since the surface of the no-dig garden is soft and friable at all times.

As you build up the rich layers in your no dig beds, it is very important not to allow them to become heavy and compacted, which can happen over a period of time. Regardless of soil type or quality, roots need to breathe – they need oxygen just as much as they need sunlight and rain. In between crops, fork the layers lightly, loosening and aerating them

If you yearn for lashings of acid-loving plants – such as rhododendrons, camellias, azaleas or pieris – and your soil pH is above 7 (alkaline and sweet), then you'll obviously have to adjust levels by incorporating lots of acid sphagnum peat and lime-free sharp sand.

The hotbed

The traditional hotbed is not only a useful aid for propagation (cuttings 'take' more successfully) but can also help produce an early crop of salad vegetables. This is the method the Emperor Tiberius used to grow his favourite cucumbers, and gardeners in grand Victorian gardens managed to produce pineapples in the same way. Traditionally it utilises heat generated by aerobic decay (as in a compost heap), though the same effect is generally produced today by special propagators or artificial under-soil heating.

To make a traditional hotbed, poultry or any other manure will do, but horse manure is best – great if you have access to local stables! Begin in midwinter by piling strawy horse manure (as fresh as possible and well wetted with urine)

under a plastic sheet for a week until heating begins. Using a cold frame as a container, dig out 30 cm (1 ft) of soil and fill the hole with manure, treading it firm, until level with the ground. Cover with 10 cm (4 in) of equal parts of soil and compost, and cover for a few days until the bed heats up.

Sow seeds such as lettuce, radish, turnip and cauliflower. Keep the frame closed until seeds germinate, then ventilate daily when safe from cold. Left-over manure can be piled around the frame for added warmth and insulation. After everything's been harvested, top up with manure and compost and plant another crop.

A can of worms – farming earthworms

In addition to being great fun, farming earthworms adds another dimension to sustainable soil management in the domestic horticultural situation. The humble earthworm evolved from marine worms long before there was even any soil on our planet. As the earth's seas retreated, the marine worms adapted themselves to life on land.

The Egyptians farmed worms in ancient times, using them extensively in their agricultural economy. The ravishing Cleopatra admired them so much that she had them declared sacred! And Charles Darwin, who lived from 1809 to 1882, worked for nearly 70 years to give us understanding of the unique creature's vital role in the health and well-being of our earth. In his book *Origin of the Species* he says: 'The common earthworm had efficiently fertilised and tilled the soil thousands of years before man ever put a digging implement into the earth.'

It has to be said that we gardeners have also known a thing or two about all this for many centuries. We've long harnessed worm power for recycling kitchen waste – breeding them in home compost heaps or enriched soils. Vermi-compost is a mixture of worm castings and compost material not yet consumed by the worms. It is an excellent garden compost, superior to ordinary composted material.

The value of vermicast

A number of countries now employ earthworms to gobble up whole rubbish tips and landfills, with the highly valuable end product of worm castings – vermicast – which are a first class fertiliser. Ver-

A typical home worm farm.

micast is the material that has passed through the worm's gut (i.e. worm manure). It is loaded with beneficial bacteria and nutrients in plant-useable form. A plant growth-promoting hormone has also been identified in plant growth experiments using vermicast. Scientists have proved that worm castings are richer in nitrogen, phosphorous, magnesium, potassium and calcium than an average well-cared-for topsoil.

Field trials show that 200 kg/ha (440 lbs/2½ acres) of vermicast gives the same plant growth response as compost at the rate of 40 tonnes/ha (40 tons/2½ acres), and that as a protein source in animal diets, worm protein has a biological value 30 or 40 times more than fish meal.

Raised public awareness of such facts have led to the manufacture by entrepreneurial commercial enterprises of small portable home-unit worm farms and bins, which can even be used by apartment dwellers. Earthworm breeding farms have become a lucrative commercial venture. The worms are sold as breeding stock to new worm farmers and gardeners, to local waste disposal bodies, as household organic waste disposal units, to aviarists for feeding birds and to fishermen for bait. They are also sold for composting human waste, and to farmers for processing and adding value to solid animal waste such as pig manure, which is hard to dispose of. Worm castings are sold as vermicast fertiliser, incorporated into pot-ting mixes and soil conditioners and processed into worm tea as liquid manure.

The domestic worm farm

Inexpensively priced home worm farm units and bins with full operating instructions are available from garden centres and horticultural magazines. Made of recycled black plastic, they usually consist of four trays and work on the simple principle that as the worms eat their way up through the food in the trays, they leave behind rich black vermicast and liquid fertiliser in the lower levels.

The bin should be sited in a cool but not cold, shady place away from direct sunlight. The bottom tray, referred to as level 1, is a collector tray, which has a solid base and tap. Liquid drains through the upper trays into the collector tray where, drawn off and diluted with water, it is used as a rich liquid fertiliser. It is important not to put worms, compost or scraps in the collector tray because they may block the tap outlet.

Home-made farms

You can make your own worm farm by building a series of simple interlocking wooden trays that rest one upon the other like the plastic trays described above. Be sure that the wood is untreated – treated wood contains chemicals that will kill earthworms and contaminate their liquid manure, resulting in severely damaged plants.

Alternatively you can house your worms in old drums sawn in half, or in polythene bins, but make sure aeration and drainage holes are added.

The owners of a mail order nursery near my home use large, simple wooden boxes on a rotation system to recycle all their office paper. Dampened and crumbled up, the paper is thrown in together with food scraps and the worms do the rest!

Adding the worms
Starter packs of 1000 composting worms are usually sold with the bins, together with an initial supply of bedding material. Composting worms

are called 'tigers' and 'reds' because of their reddish striped bodies and darker coloured species are referred to as 'blues'. They live, feed and breed happily at the top of the soil under natural leaf litter and organic waste.

The other sort of worms, true earthworms, are more specifically soil dwellers and enjoy humus and soil rather than kitchen waste as their basic diet. They appear much bigger than the composters, but this is usually because they are older.

One of the main objectives of your farm is to breed a ready supply of composting worms for domestic use – in composting toilets, to enhance the fertility of the surface mulch on your garden, and to recycle waste. But remember that composting worms require moist conditions all year round because they don't tunnel deep to find

Common queries about vermiculture

How much will my worms eat?
This depends on how many worms you have. Worms don't eat to live, they live to eat! And they can eat half their own body weight daily and double their population every few months.

If you start your farm with a thousand mature worms (mature worms have a distinct ring-shaped swelling around their body), they'll weigh approximately 450 gm (1 lb) and they will consume up to 225 gm (8 oz) of waste per day. After a few months when you've doubled your stock you can feed them more. Baby worms don't eat much and will take about three months to mature. You will soon be able to observe the rate at which your farm's wriggly residents are consuming food and adjust their banquets accordingly.

Are there any foods I shouldn't feed my worms?
Earthworm alert! It is best only to feed your worms on known food waste from your own household. Never feed them manures from unknown sources – for example, cattle, horses, sheep and goats that may have been treated with chemical vermicides to kill parasitic worms. The vermicides remain active in the manure for some time and can kill off all your worms in one day.

If you use manures, ensure that they are mature and very well rotted.

Will my worms compost garden refuse?
The domestic worm bin is designed for the breaking down of soft organic waste. Large, bulky or woody garden refuse is best composted by the conventional aerobic composting methods.

Will my farm breed too many worms?
You can never have too many worms! They will regulate their population to the confines of available space and the amount of food you give them. In the average domestic worm bin (about the size of a small dustbin) worm concentration should reach capacity – about 15,000 to 20,000 worms – after two to five years.

Will my farm be okay when I go on holiday?
A home worm farm can be left for at least a month. Just feed the worms a good quantity of food waste – about ⅓ of a trayful – and ensure the contents are moist and the farm is in the required cool shady position.

There is an excellent range of books and videos on earthworm farming available from libraries and bookstores.

A well-mulched garden with raised beds.

moisture like their earthworm cousins. So place them only in well mulched beds or moister areas of the garden. They will not do well in hot dry garden areas and soils.

Using castings and liquid fertiliser

Vermicast is a valuable fertiliser for any garden, improving the colour, quality and quantity of fruit, vegetables, flowers and ornamental shrubs. The pH of vermicast is neutral (7) and suitable for all types of plants including exotics such as orchids. Castings may be used as pure organic fertilisers or as additives to compost, seed raising and potting mix.

- **Seed raising mix**: Three parts of compost to one part castings
- **Potting mix**: Two parts aged compost to one part castings, and half a part of vermiculite.
- **Top dressing**: Spread a layer 12 mm (½ in) deep of worm castings around plants. Water it well in.
- **Liquid fertiliser**: Apply around base of plants and water well in. The fertiliser can be diluted up to 50 per cent with water and still contain nutrients.

Whether you live in an apartment, a high rise building or have only a tiny plot you can have fun providing the supreme organic fertiliser for your garden or indoor plants. So go to it. Harness worm power in your garden. Tuck up your worms in bed and tell them to 'go forth and multiply'!

The ultimate truth

We've learned that humus and the soil are inseparable elements, and our education as gardeners is almost complete. Our concrete clay should now disintegrate and crumble with a sigh, thin sandy soils breathe body and substance, and each eagerly receive the plant treasures committed to its care. To have created soil that is warm and malleable, that receives spade and trowel gladly, that is dark and crumbly in texture, is our great victory. It lies there beneath our boots – deep, soft and beautiful. We are compelled to bend down and pick up a fistful, crumble it through our fingers to test its body, weight, fragrance, colour and texture.

We accept, finally, that there is no excuse in our gardener's heart for soil that is compacted, wet, cold, greasy, thin and sterile. 'My soil is so poor' announces to the world that one is not a sustainable but a slovenly gardener.

We are all guilty of varying degrees of plant murder, until comprehension of the old adage hits us between our unseeing eyes – that the welfare of plant treasures is in direct correlation to the condition of the soil in which we place them. The Ultimate Great Truth is 'the answer lies in the toil'.

CHAPTER FOUR

BENIGN PEST, DISEASE AND WEED CONTROL

On every stem, on every leaf ... and at the root of everything that grows, is a professional expert in the shape of a grub, caterpillar, aphis, or other expert, whose business it is to devour that particular plant.

Oliver Wendell Holmes Jr

This is a very crowded planet – there are about 30 million species of insect pests. Despite chemical warfare they remain one up on man, for in destroying the bad we must also destroy the beneficial. This creates an imbalance where beneficial predatory insects starve because we have severely diminished their pestiferous food sources. In addition, many pests eventually become immune to the chemicals, and in order to control these pests we become trapped on a vicious treadmill that forces us to use ever more powerful systemic sprays for their destruction.

By employing benign pest, disease and weed control, we are able to control the feared pestilence and prevent it from causing horticultural decimation of biblical proportions, without

Above: Chemical annihilation of pollinators such as these monarch butterflies will result in low garden fertility.
Opposite: The sustainable garden allows a balance of beneficial insects and the creatures on which they feed.

entirely wiping out the creatures that provide the necessary sustenance for beneficial predators.

Integrated Pest Management

Integrated Pest Management (IPM) is not a single issue. It includes the following factors for controlling pests, diseases and sometimes weeds using elements already naturally present in the environment and ecological chain:

- Biological control of pests by naturally occurring enemies.
- Non-toxic or low toxicity plant derivative pesticides and herbicides.
- Biological, mechanical and non-chemical methods of weed control.
- Provision of host plants on which beneficial predatory insects may breed and feed.
- The employment of companion planting to both attract and repel specific insects.

If total annihilation of bad insects takes place, the beneficial predatory insects that have survived

Basic principles of IPM

The key to IPM in my large gardens at Valley Homestead has evolved through experience, and along the way I made numerous mistakes and tried many things that didn't work! Successful IPM has been maintained by a combination of the following principles:

1. The use of pesticides, fungicides and herbicides made from non-chemical/low toxicity substances – i.e. plant derivatives such as garlic, pyrethrum and neem oil concentrates.
2. Awareness that even organic pesticides (e.g. pyrethrins), if applied at incorrect strength or at the wrong time of day, can kill beneficial insects as well as pestiferous ones.
3. The growing of disease-resistant plant varieties and discarding of disease-prone species, so that the need for spraying is minimised.
4. The growing of plants that are well suited to the individual soil and climatic conditions, and avoiding those for which artificial conditions must be created.
5. Employment of companion planting methods, in conjunction with appropriate benign sprays, so as to attract beneficial insects and repel undesirable ones in specific areas.
6. Avoidance of monoculture, which attracts large numbers of specific insect pests in one area. This is done by setting plants in clumps or rows of different species that both attract and repel specific insects, ensuring a natural balance between the two.
7. Provision of plant hosts on which beneficial insects may breed or feed – i.e. encouraging natural predators in order to provide a biological 'bug eat bug' method of control.
8. Acceptance of a tolerable level of disease and pests, one which can be maintained by non-chemical methods, rather than demanding a pest and disease-free garden achieved by the use of non-specific chemicals.
9. Understanding that the welfare of our plants is in direct proportion to the health of the soil in which we place them.
10. The practise of crop rotation, which avoids a build up of plant-specific diseases in the soil and prevents the same nutrients being continuously taken up until crops fail.

The practice of IPM involves all these principles working together as a whole to promote a sustainable system of horticulture.

the spraying will starve. Beneficial insects not only include the natural enemies of garden pests. There are also the plant pollinators, such as bees, and their annihilation by chemical spraying leads to a poor pollination rate and low fertility throughout the garden. The aim is to maintain a happy balance by using the correct spray at correct strength, at the correct time, and only on those areas in which an unacceptable level of undesirable insect infestation or disease may be seen.

The sustainable gardener has a different perception of the old adage 'prevention is better than cure'; he or she uses benign sprays, and only when strictly necessary, and works towards a 'live and let live' philosophy. This means allowing a balance of good and bad insects to exist for mutual benefit, which is what nature intended before man destroyed that balance. There's room for us all!

As sustainable gardeners we've agreed that toxic pesticides and herbicides are harmful to the environment, to plant and animal life, and that they poison nature's food chains. In adopting the IPM philosophy, we eschew non-specific chemical treatments (which have indiscriminate killing power) and use natural methods of pest, disease and weed control. These methods either attempt to follow nature's own controls or are designed to eliminate or control only the unwanted pests or plants. The aim is to grow as wide a diversity of plants as possible to attract both beneficial predatory insects and the undesirable pests on which they feed.

Beneficial insects exert natural control by eating those that are pests. If the former are eliminated by non-specific pesticides, or by organic preparations used at incorrect strength, any pests which survive will flourish. Their natural predators destroyed, they breed unchecked and one becomes locked in an unrelenting cycle. It is your choice as a sustainable gardener to have an acceptable degree of diseases and pests and to strive for a natural balance rather than resorting to toxic chemicals.

Pest and disease identification

Much of the first part of this chapter is devoted to information on insect pests, and ways of attracting beneficial predatory insects into your garden and making them work for you. But first we need to identify the pests they can help us control, and to establish whether the problem is in fact a pest at all or whether it is caused by a disease (which will be dealt with later in this chapter). The trouble shooting charts that follow are designed to help you identify the most common problems.

Pest and disease identification

Symptoms on leaves

Problem	Detail	Probable cause
Wilting	General	Short of water; a root pest or disease; wilt disease
Holed	Generally ragged	Small pests (millipedes, flea beetles, woodlice), capsid bugs
	Elongated holes; usually with slime present	Slugs or snails
	Fairly large holes over entire leaf	Caterpillars
	Holes confined to edges	Beetles
	Semi-circular pieces taken from edges	Leaf-cutter beetles
Discoloured	Black	Sooty mould
	Predominantly red	Short of water
	More or less bleached	Nutrient deficiency, short of water or too much water
	Silvery (plums)	Silver leaf
	Irregular yellow patterns	Virus
	Irregular tunnels	Leaf miners
	Surface flecking	Leafhoppers
	Tomatoes – leaves, distorted and yellow	Virus
	Tomatoes – yellow veining on foliage	Magnesium/nutrient deficiency
	Brown (scorched) in spring	Frost
Spotted	Brownish, angular, with mould underneath	Downy mildew
	Brownish, irregular or rounded; no mould	Leaf spot
	Dark brown or black; not dusty	Scab
	Small, dusty, brown, black or brightly coloured	Rust
Mouldy	Black	Sooty mould
	Grey, fluffy	Grey mould
	White, velvety	Mildew
	Brown (tomatoes)	Leaf mould
	White, beneath leaves (potatoes)	Blight
Infested with insects	White, moth-like, tiny	Whiteflies
	Green, grey, black or any colour	Aphids
	White, woolly (greenhouse)	Mealy bugs
	Flat, encrusted, like limpets	Scale insects
	Large, six legs, worm-like	Caterpillars
Curling	Insects present also	See insects above
	Tightly rolled in spring (roses)	Sawflies
	Puckered, reddish (peaches and almonds)	Peach leaf curl
	Puckered, yellowish (pears)	Pear leaf blister mites
Cobwebs present	Plant wilting	Red spider mites

Symptoms on fruit

Problem	Detail	Probable cause
Pieces eaten away	Fruit close to ground	Slugs or mice
	Tree fruits	Birds or wasps
Distorted	With rounded bumps (apples)	Capsid bugs
	Black powder within (sweet corn)	Smut
	Ribbon-like scars (apples)	Sawflies
	Split (tomatoes)	Short of water
Discoloured	Uneven ripening (tomatoes)	Virus or nutrient deficiency
Mouldy	While on plant (tomatoes)	Grey mould or blight
	While on plant (tree fruits)	Brown rot
	In store	Fungal decay
Spotted	Tree fruits	Scab
	Tomato	Ghost spot
Maggoty	Tree fruits	Caterpillars (codling moth)
	Peas	Caterpillars (pea moth)
	Raspberries	Beetles
Dropping prematurely	Pears	Pear midge
	Apples (in early season)	June drop (normal; not a pest or disease)

Pest and disease identification

Symptoms on flowers

Problem	Detail	Probable cause
Dropping	General	Short of water
		End of flowering period
Tattered	Masses of tiny holes	Caterpillars
	Large pieces torn away	Birds
Removed entirely	Usually discarded nearby	Birds
Distorted	Usually only a few plants affected in a bed	Virus
Discoloured	Powdery white covering	Powdery mildew
Mouldy	Fluffy, grey mould	Botrytis grey mould

Symptoms on stems

Problem	Detail	Probable cause
Eaten through	On young plants	Slugs or snails
	On older plants	Mice or rabbits
	On young trees	Rabbits or deer
Infested with insects	Green, grey, black or any colour	Aphids
	White, woolly, on tree bark	Woolly aphids
	Flat, encrusted, like limpets	Scale insects
	Large, six legs, worm-like	Caterpillars
Rotten	At base of young plants	Stem and foot rot
	On trees and shrubs	Decay fungus
Blister on bark of trees	More or less spherical	Gall
	Target-like	Canker
Dying back	General	Short of water
Abnormal growth	Like birds' nests	Witches' broom
	Leafy plant	Mistletoe
	Buds swollen (blackcurrants)	Big bud

Symptoms on roots and bulbs

Problem	Detail	Probable cause
Decayed	General	Decay fungi
Parts eaten away	General	Small soil pests (millipedes, wireworms, leatherjackets)
	Corms and bulbs	Vine weevils
With irregular swellings	Brassicas and wallflowers	Clubroot
	Potatoes	Eelworms
	Peas and beans	Root nodules
Maggoty	General	Fly larvae
With warty spots	Root vegetables	Scab
Irregularly distorted	Root vegetables	Clubroot

Insect pests: lives of the great eaters

Greenfly, it's difficult to see, why God who made the rose made thee.

A.P. Herbert

Most insect pests can be put into one of four categories: chewers, suckers, raspers, and parasites. In gardening terms, a pest is defined as an animal that damages a plant or causes it to malfunction. Pests range in size from microscopic mites to itinerant cattle or goats. Sucking and chewing insects include beetles, caterpillars, aphids, whiteflies and many others generally referred to as sap-suckers. Chewers extend their repertoire by sometimes tunnelling into branches of wood and roots, and into flower and fruit buds. With the exception of the aphid, which achieves its prodigious population explosions by giving birth to hordes of living young, most insects reproduce by laying eggs and passing through an immature larval form. Both larvae and adult cause considerable damage to our plants and win by sheer superiority of numbers.

Airborne invaders

From the sky, from the horizon, airborne invaders zoom into your garden on inbuilt radar. One moment your plants are clean, healthy, vigorous; the next they're hosts to writhing masses of animate vitality or present a curiously defective appearance, their buds, flowers and foliage so chewed they resemble colanders or lace table-mats.

Smallest among airborne sucking and chewing machines are thrips, aphids and whiteflies – all equipped with hypodermic mouth parts with which, dracula-like, they siphon off the life-sustaining sap of their defenceless hosts. Once they've landed, massed colonies of aphids are usually fairly conspicuous, brazen beasts. Whiteflies are more sly, preferring to lurk on the underside of leaves, from which they erupt in angry clouds when disturbed. Thrips form scattered squadrons on leaves and flowers, sucking sap from the surface cells only, which gives foliage a mottled unattractive appearance. Though not airborne, minute enemy forces also include red spider mites.

Battalions of larger pests include beetles, sawflies, wasps, and other bugs – powerfully built, winged strike-forces. Having arrived at the menu destination of their choice, they set about destruction by devoted mandibular chewing, which ensures a much more dramatic plant demise than the slow death effected by sap suckers.

Next come butterflies and moths with radar honed in on fruit trees, vegetables such as brassicas and many ornamentals. Their mission is not to chomp and chew, but to effect plant destruction by depositing huge numbers of eggs from which voracious offspring emerge with all speed. Every female white butterfly is capable of producing several hundred eggs, and cabbages are reduced to shreds in minutes by the new born caterpillars.

Simply spineless

Invertebrate pests include woodlice, millipedes, slugs and snails (molluscs) and microscopic eelworms. Woodlice and millipedes are valuable recyclers, generally living on damp rotting wood, paper and decaying vegetative matter; they usually only attack vegetation for moisture when conditions are very dry. So co-exist and let live unless they're really a problem.

Small, legless, land-based invaders include nematodes and eelworms, which cause havoc by limited, wriggling, eel-like movements. They comprise a troglodytic army of galactic proportions. Other legless creepers and crawlers conducting campaigns on the soil surface include slugs and snails; using the propulsion of a large muscular foot they, like their fellow molluscs, adopt the role of a guerrilla bandit force – lying low by day and striking as soon as darkness falls. They effect plant destruction with a fearsome multi-toothed tongue – the radula – devouring almost any vegetation in their path, and leaving a graffiti slime to record their passing.

Aphids en masse, a gardener's nightmare!

Marshalling the troops

Sometimes the solution to a problem is found by approaching it from a different angle. Instead of asking yourself 'Why have I so many pests?' ask instead 'Why have I so few predators?'

For every insect you consider a pest there are a number of other insects that will find it the most delectable of foods. Together with provision of the correct host plants on which beneficial predatory insects may breed and feed, the second line of defence is to foster a strong, stable population of birds, frogs, lizards and hedgehogs. One of the main IPM methods used to encourage this balance is companion planting (see chapter 5).

Ladybirds for example, are a most precious garden resident. One ladybird is reputed to eat at least 100 aphids a day and also relish scale insects, mealy bugs, leaf hoppers, whitefly, mites, the potato beetle and the bean beetle.

Benign control for insect pests
Aphids

These are small prolific, sap-sucking green/white/pink flies, which give birth to living young. They are controlled by naturally occurring insect enemies (see biological control, page 53) or plant derivative pesticides such as pyrethrum.

Ants

Ants are valuable predators and recyclers, so try not to destroy them unless necessary. They've been accused of carrying sap suckers from plant to plant (to 'milk' their sweet secretions) but this is questionable. However, ant nests can kill plants above them so if they must be eradicated, mix 1 part borax or derris to 4 parts icing sugar and sprinkle around the nest as bait. To destroy ants in nest, spray nest with 1 part kerosene, 1 part liquid detergent and 1 part vegetable oil. Spray surface ants with pyrethrum. Apply tree-banding grease around the trunks of shrubs and ornamentals.

Caterpillars

Some looper caterpillars are particularly voracious – they can double their weight (and strip a plant) in just two days! They hide on the underside of leaves, and some will burrow into tomatoes. Caterpillars may be picked off by hand, and you can then use derris dust or *Bacillus thuringiensis* spray to despatch stragglers.

Codling moth

The orchardist's nightmare, codling moths are about 20 mm (1 in) from wing to wing, greyish-brown with a circular, slightly shiny, dark area near each wing tip. They lay their eggs in or near fruit – usually apples. The caterpillars feed for three to five weeks on the fruit before they travel down the trunk of the tree looking for a place to pupate. Trap the caterpillars by fixing a corrugated cardboard or cloth band soaked in liquid derris, grease or old sump oil to the trunk of the tree. Inspect weekly and get rid of the pupae. For the moths, try one of the following:

Pheromone hormone traps: These commercially available traps are baited with the scent of the female codling moth's sex hormones. They will, of course, catch only the extremely frustrated male moths, who think they are being lured to a sexually receptive female. The female dies unfertilised so the traps are very helpful in reducing codling moth populations in the immediate area.

Lure pots: These will trap not only codling moths, but also a number of other fruit tree pests. Fill a glass jar with 1 part port to 7 parts water, or 1 part molasses to 10 parts water. Top up with a little oil to deter mosquitoes and to stop moths escaping.

Earwigs

Most species of earwigs are 'goodies' which recycle dead and decaying matter and eat smaller insects. The European earwig does have the behavioural problem, however, of crawling into flowers and stone fruit for a snack. They love to hide, so if they're troublesome, crumple up loose balls of newspaper and leave them out overnight; uplift and dump them, full of their earwig residents, into a bowl of water next morning. Use the protein-enriched paper as mulch!

Flea beetle

This is a small beetle that chews many tiny holes in flowers and foliage and destroys seedlings of brassicas, radishes, turnips and wallflowers. They're controllable with derris dust (Retenone), a tropical plant extract pesticide that kills many pests including caterpillars.

Green/bronze beetles

Famous chewers include green vegetable beetles and bronze beetles. The larvae of the latter complete their life cycle underground where they snack on the roots of plants. The green vegetable beetles are commonly called 'stink bugs', and in fact these green eating machines are bugs, though they closely resemble beetles in form. In their immature stage, sap-sucking green vegetable bugs are not green, but black with white spots. The best method of control is to keep up a watch early in the season; if you can destroy the first generation

Adult codling moth.

to hatch on your plants in early spring, their successors will be considerably less in number throughout the remainder of the season.

Green beetles colonise in great numbers on edible and ornamental plants, and they bring out my sadistic worst when they persecute my tomato crops. The foul odour they give off when squashed is a warning to their mates that predators are at work. The others 'play possum' – they drop off the infested plant and play dead – whereupon you can flatten a number of your first victim's friends. They may also be lured to a similarly unpleasant end with companion plantings of cleome (spider flower). The bugs congregate in large numbers on this plant, and may then be shaken off and destroyed.

Stink beetles can be given a dose of their own medicine – literally. Hand-pick and hurl beetles into a jar of soapy water; then put the awful mixture in a kitchen blender. (It's probably a good idea to get your partner's approval first!) The evil-smelling green goo must stand, then be strained and diluted and sprayed on plants infested with the departed's relations. Macabre it may be, but the smell of death of their own kind dispatches them with all speed!

Biological control involves the use of a tiny wasp parasite (*Trissolcus basalis*), introduced from Egypt, which lays its eggs inside those of the green vegetable bug and kills the developing embryos.

Mealy bugs

If your plants start sprouting puffy cotton wool-like protuberances on the undersides of leaves, the powder-coated mealybug is in residence. Like woolly aphids they protect themselves with a waterproof overcoat, so it's death by suffocating oil for them. Otherwise the biological predator *Cryptolaemus montrouzieri* will dine on them for you (see information on biological control, later this chapter).

Mites, red spider mite

Mite presence is indicated by a silvery flecking on the leaves, together with small webbings on the undersides – particularly prevalent on roses. On larger cultivars, mite presence is usually indicated by rough brown patches originating from bud axils, which spread onto the foliage.

Above: Green vegetable bug feeding on tomatoes.

Below: *Cryptolaemus montrouzieri* feeding on mealy bug.

One of the great biological control success stories is the employment of the natural predator *Phytoseiulus permilis* to help growers combat spider mites. This very small and hungry predator in an orange overcoat eats everything from other pestiferous mites to small caterpillars twice its size!

Slug and snail traps will not harm humans, birds, or pets.

Scale insects

Scale insects are intriguing little creatures. They are immobile because they shed their legs with their skin! They excrete a waterproof 'roof' over their heads and are thus controlled only with vegetable or mineral oil, which suffocates them.

Slugs and snails

Crunch these rapacious raspers underfoot by torch light, or hand pick them and drop them into salty water – you can use traps made from jars or tins partially filled with beer and pushed into the soil.

Alternatively, effective traps can be made from large-sized lidded yoghurt cartons. Cut holes one quarter of the way up the sides, large enough for the snails to crawl in. Put small quantities of home-made bait into the base – 1 part bran, 1 part derris dust and 2 parts grated raw potato, moistened with molasses. The snails will eat it, froth up and die, yet the bait is non-toxic to humans, birds and pets. Cut a small round hole in the lid and base of the carton and secure into the ground by pushing through a small short stick. The bait may also be sprinkled safely around all plants. Renew on a regular basis and after rain.

In addition to toxic pellets (metaldehyde) there are commercially produced benign products available containing coarse gritty sand and shell, which work on the principle that gastropods dislike creeping over anything sharp and gritty. I've found these to be a deterrent, but not as efficient as home-made bait and traps. There is also a new spray-on copper-based product available, which is said to be an effective deterrent because molluscs dislike the smell of copper. Directions instruct spraying it around, rather than on plants, but in testing the product I found it difficult not to contaminate seedlings and have reservations about the build up of copper in the soil. The spray would also be an expensive option in a large garden.

Biological control of slugs and snails involves the release into the soil of nematodes with an almost impossible to pronounce name – *Phasmarhabditis hermaphroditica*. These carry bacteria designed to deal to snails and specific other soil dwelling pests.

Thrips

Silvering of leaves on such shrubs as rhododendrons, pyracanthas, fuchsias and many other plants is usually due to thrips, whose black droppings will be found on the underside of the leaves. The silvering is the result of the insect rasping away the leaf surface which doesn't recover even if the thrips are killed. With evergreen plants the unsightly silver leaves will remain indefinitely until they are shed. Look carefully for the start of new attacks on the new green foliage arising beyond the originally damaged ones – remove and destroy infested leaves by soaking in water as part of a manure tea or sludge.

Thrips on shrubs are efficiently controlled with the plant-derived pesticide pyrethrum, or by biological control with the predatory mite *Amblyseius cucumeris*, which also preys on onion and flower thrips.

Whitefly

An insect about 2 mm ($^1/_{12}$ in) in length and a relative of the aphid. Whitefly is found under the leaves of many plants and vegetables, especially in warmer areas and is a troublesome glasshouse pest. The adults are minute white-winged insects, which fly up in infuriated clouds if disturbed. They lay eggs on the undersides of mature leaves; these hatch first into green, flat wingless nymphs, which eventually develop into the winged form. Only the mature stage is susceptible to common

insecticides, which necessitates frequent spraying to catch each batch of insects as they become adult. But as a result of frequent spraying, this pest has built up an immunity to common pesticides.

There are however, some non-chemical methods of control. One is to smear a piece of yellow plastic (whiteflies like the colour yellow) with a petroleum-based gel such as vaseline or gearbox oil. Attracted to the colour the insect gets stuck in the gel.

Biological control involves the parasitic wasp *Encarsia formosa*, which is about half the size of the whitefly and lays its eggs in the whitefly nymph. When the egg hatches it kills the nymph. These parasitic wasps, developed as a major biocontrol, come on a card which you attach to an infested plant with a twist tie.

Above: Whitefly nymphs parasitised by the predatory wasp *Encarsia formosa. Above left:* Greenhouse whitefly adults emerging from puparia.

Biological pest control

The use of natural parasites and predators already present in the environment to control pests is nothing new, but it's a much under-used and under-valued practice pushed aside by widespread chemical usage. It began in China in the thirteenth century, where farmers caught and released ants into their citrus and litchi fruit trees to guard them from pest attack.

Today biological control is being used with increasing success in modern agriculture and horticulture. In recent years, for example, a predatory Australian ladybird species, *Crytolaemus montrouzieri*, was introduced into California to control decimation of citrus orchards by pests. The

Benign treatments for common pests

Pest	Host	Treatment
Aphids	Many plants	Hose off
Ants	Some plants	Borax or derris dust, icing sugar bait
Beetles (bronze and green)	Vegetables/ornamentals	Cleome – host plant
Caterpillar	Brassicas	*Bacillus thuringiensis* spray
Codling moth	Apples, other fruit	Pheromone traps/grease bands
Flea beetle	Vegetables, ornamentals	Derris dust
Greenfly (aphid)	Vegetables/ornamentals/greenhouse	Sticky yellow traps/bowls of yellow water
Nematode worms	Squash family, potato	Plant marigolds
Scale	Roses	Vegetable/mineral oil
Slugs, snails	Many plants	Traps, bran bait, dispatch by hand or foot!
Thrips	Camellias, azaleas, rhodos, other shrubs	Pyrethrum
Woolly aphid	Many plants	Vegetable/mineral oil

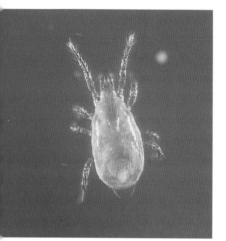

Biological control insects in action. Clockwise from top left: White butterfly parasitised by *Cotesia rubecula*; *Aphidoletes aphidimyza* feeding on *Aphis gossypii*; *Phytoseiulus persimilis* attacking two mites; *Amblyseius cucumeris*; adult *Encarsia formosa*; and *E. formosa* parasitising whitefly scale.

small beetle is now exported worldwide for this purpose.

The use of parasites and predators is also proving invaluable in both domestic and commercial greenhouses and shadehouses, where the warm enclosed environment and free meals are much to their liking. Horticultural marketing and packaging boards are making these specifically bred predatory insects readily available for home gardeners to purchase. If you're interested, contact your local vegetable growers' association or biodynamics association, or look through the advertisement pages of any gardening or horticultural magazine for breeding stockists. But bear in mind that a number of these predators, such as the ichneumonid wasps, should already be resident in your garden if you've made it predator hospitable.

In home and commercial greenhouses the introduced predator or parasite may eliminate the pest so rapidly that the predator might be in danger of starving. As with all pest control, observation and monitoring of plants is necessary in case new supplies need purchasing.

The term biological control describes the control of exotic pests by their naturally occurring enemies, enemies that are often introduced from the pest's home of origin. The dramatic control of prickly pear in Australia by the introduced caterpillar *Cactoblastis* is just one example. The manner in which the various methods work differ. The biological control agents for caterpillars, *Bacillus thuringiensis* (Bt), and the bacteria-bearing soil nematodes both depend on the bacteria attacking and degrading the target pest, thus bringing about its demise. The gall midges and parasitic wasps work by laying their eggs into the pest. These then hatch and the resulting larvae eat the pest – an unpleasant but effective end! The ladybird beetles, both in larval and adult form, feed directly on mealy bugs.

Bt carries bacteria in a liquid suspension and is sprayed directly onto the plants and pests. The bacteria-bearing nematodes do not themselves kill pests – more devious, they introduce bacteria by penetrating their victims' bodies, thus, like the wasps, causing a somewhat ghoulish demise. They are supplied packed in moist clay, and each culture sachet contains literally millions of live nematodes, each carrying a bacterium specific to insects. They should be introduced to moist but not wet soils – they will wash away in waterlogged earth.

Bacteria carrying nematodes help reduce the use of the particularly dangerous chemicals that are poured into the earth to kill soil dwelling pests.

Commercially available control organisms

Insectiferous pests are controlled by natural enemies that do not harm beneficial insects. Biological control predators are often used in conjunction with a benign and appropriate spray programme that avoids killing the predators or parasites. The following chart shows biological control insects and other agents that are commercially available for domestic gardens, and the conditions under which they should work best.

How to use biological control insects

Most biological control insects are delivered by courier post. When yours arrive, carefully check the directions for application and for how long and under what conditions the organisms remain viable after you receive them. Never place them directly in hot sunlight or in the refrigerator. Try to release them onto crops immediately.

Thrip controlling *Amblysieus*, may be distributed in two ways: either shaken through the crop, or tied to crop stems in sachets with clipped corners, which allow the mites to escape.

Red spider mite control, *Phytoseilus*, come packed on bean leaves in tissue-paper-lined plastic punnets. They contain approximately 1000 adult female predators, plus juveniles and eggs. For a greenhouse crop you'll need about 4000 predators per 1000 m² (¼ acre), and for outdoor crops, 4000 predators per hectare (2½ acres). (More concentrated numbers of predators are required for the greenhouse because in this warm humid climate pests breed all year round and at much higher rates, and are not subject to the natural control provided outside.) Place the predator-bearing

Biological control insects

Pest	Biological control organism	Where to use/temperature
Aphids	*Aphidoletes aphidimyza* (predatory gall midge)	Greenhouse/min air temp 10°C (50°F).
Aphids	*Aphidius ervi* (aphid parasite)	Greenhouse/ min air temp 18°C (65°F)
Green vegetable bug	*Trissolcus basalis* wasp	Outdoors
Caterpillars	*Bacillus thuringiensis* (bacterium spray)	Greenhouse or outdoors
Mealy bug	*Cryptoleamus montrouzieri* (ladybird beetle)	Greenhouse/min air temp 20°C (68°F)
	Leptomastix dactyloptii (parasitic wasp)	Greenhouse or outdoors
	L. abnormis (parasitic wasp)	
Two-spotted spider mites	*Phytoseiulus persimilis* (also preys on other pestiferous mites)	Greenhouse – outdoors in summer/min air temp 16°C (61°F)
European red mite	*Typhlodromus pyri*	Outdoors
European and two-spotted mite	*T. occidentalis* (predatory mites bred to control pestiferous mites in deciduous fruit)	
Scale insects	*Metaphycus helvolus*	Greenhouse/min air temp 22°C (72°F)
Slugs	*Phasmarhabditis hermaphroditica* (nematode-carrying bacteria)	Outdoors/min soil temp 5°C (41°F)
Soil pests (some)	*Steinernema carpocapsae* (bacteria-carrying soil nematode)	Outdoors/min soil temp 14°C (57°F)
Thrips	*Amblyseius cucumeris*	Greenhouse/outdoors
Vine weevil larvae	*Heterorhabditis megadis* (bacteria-carrying soil nematode)	Outdoors/min soil temp 12°C (54°F)
Vine weevil larvae	*Steinernema carpocapsae* (bacteria-carrying nematode)	Greenhouse/ min air temp 14°C (57°F)
Whiteflies	*Encarsia formosa* (parasitic wasp)	Greenhouse/min air temp 18°C (65°F)

The recommended minimum temperatures vary slightly between marketing companies but, within defined limits, all predators work better at the upper level of the temperature range, which is the one given here. However, many predators will breed and feed at slightly lower temperatures. They often overwinter in weeds and clovers, or as welcome residents in greenhouses during the colder months. Certain pollen-producing plants encourage high populations of predatory mites. For example, Rhodes grass (*Chloris gayana*) is used as an inter-row plant in Queensland citrus orchards, and *Phacelia tanacetifolia* is planted with many food crops in a number of countries.

bean leaves under and around the crops or staple them to stems.

Predatory insects such as the Australian *Cryptolaemus* ladybird beetle also usually come in punnets. After opening the lid, dislodge them by lightly tapping the container onto plant foliage. Cryptolaemus beetle release rates for orchards are 800 to 2000 beetles (20 to 50 punnets) per hectare. For shade/greenhouses the release rate is one to two beetles per square metre (1¼ yd²). This may sound like a lot of beetles, but remember that after your initial expenditure, provided they are given plenty of pests to eat and reasonable weather conditions, your biological control insects will get down to some pretty serious feeding and breeding activities!

All biological control agents will come with full instructions from their breeders. Their distribution and use in Europe, UK, USA and Australasia is subject to strict rules and regulations, about which you'll be left in no doubt!

The biological predators listed above are those that are most commonly used throughout Australasia, England, Europe and USA, but many more exist, some specific to their country of origin. In the USA, for example, sweet potato whitefly and scales are decimated by the small black beetle, *Delphastus pusillus*, thrips by the fearsome sucking bug, *Orius insidious*, and the soil-dwelling predatory mite *Hypoasis miles* dines on thrip pupae and gnat larvae, which are also soil dwellers.

Australia and parts of America, troubled greatly by housefly and blowfly, employ specific parasites for their control. Insects such as praying mantises are common to a number of countries and are also employed as biological agents to control a wide variety of insectiferous pests.

The good guys: beneficial predators
Ants
Ants feed on many insects including caterpillars, various larvae, fruit fly, codling moth and other maggots in the soil. The predatory ant *Myrmecia varians* eats large quantities of psyllids and other small insects.

Assassin bugs (Australia)
Assassin bugs eat beetles, grasshoppers and caterpillars. They are about 18 mm (¾ in) long, brown to reddish-black; some have flattened mantis-like bodies.

Beetles
Soldier beetles eat codling moth and other larvae, sap sucking insects, locusts, grasshopper and fly eggs. They are up to 18 mm (¾ in) long, with a small semi-triangular head and long body. They range in colour from yellow through to dull orange to blue-black and lay their eggs on the ground.

The tiger beetle, *Calosoma schayeri*, shreds army worms and cutworms and a range of large insects, including codling moth. Many beetles are miscast as baddies of the insect world, but, with the exception of the well known sap-sucking beetles, the majority of the species are pest eaters.

Centipedes
Centipedes eat caterpillars, slugs and other pests. Don't confuse them with plant-eating millipedes – centipedes have only one leg per segment, millipedes have many.

Damsel flies (Australia)
Both adults and nymphs consume large quantities of aphids and other sap-suckers. Damsel flies are similar to dragonflies but more delicate, smaller eyed and slower moving. They hold their wings erect when resting (dragonflies' wings are held horizontal).

Dragonflies
For your gardener's book of records – dragonflies are among the fastest insects on the wing, capable of flying 14 m (15 yd) per second. They're excellent mosquito predators but will also take bees and even Christmas beetles. They've also been known to snatch young cabbage white butterflies from the air!

Frogs and beneficial toad species
Through chemical agriculture and horticulture, water pollution and destruction of habitat, these gentle, harmless creatures are threatened with global extinction. They dine on insects, slugs and snails. We must do our utmost to give them safe haven on our land by incorporating a water garden of any shape or size surrounded by sheltering, shady shrubs.

Hoverflies (*Synphus ribesii*)

Hoverflies are the best predators of all for aphids. It is estimated that hoverfly larvae can eat one aphid in a minute, 50 a day and up to 900 in their lifetime!

They also eat a wide range of scale insects, mites, the larvae of pear and cherry slugs and young caterpillars. There are a number of species; some are like small stout bees, others like thin-waisted wasps. They are most easily recognised by their distinctive hovering motion and appear in abundance throughout spring and summer. Hoverflies can also withstand cold better than other aphid predators and remain active at lower temperatures.

Attractor plants for hoverflies include buckwheat flowers, *Phacelia tanacetifilia, Limnanthes douglassi* (poached egg plant), cucurbit flowers, flowering brassicas (cut off the tops before the seeds set, so new flower heads form), flowering sages, dill and parsnips.

Ichneumons (*Netelia productus*)

These parasites are often referred to as flies or wasps. They lay eggs in the bodies of many pests and eat caterpillars, including those of the codling moth and cabbage white butterfly. They will also eat sawfly larvae and pear or cherry slug. Around 30–40 mm (1¼–1¾ in) long, they're orange-yellow in colour and have long wasp-like legs, narrow waists and are often banded.

Lacewings (*Micromus tasmaniae*)

Second only to the hoverfly in the pest control stakes, both adult lacewings and their larvae eat a wide range of garden pests, including aphids, scale, mealy bugs, mites, whitefly, thrips, pear and cherry slug and a wide range of sap-sucking insects, and butterfly and moth eggs. They favour much the same host plants as hoverflies.

Ladybirds

Both adult and larvae eat scale, aphids, whitefly, mealy bugs, woolly aphids and other sap suckers. One ladybird larva may eat a hundred aphids and several thousand aphid larvae. Ladybirds are being bred and introduced in USA, UK, Australia and New Zealand for biological control. Ladybirds don't just come in the familiar red-with-black-spots species – they vary in colour from

Adult hoverfly.

Spotted ladybird feeding on an aphid.

orange and red to blue or green. Ladybirds can be harmed by oils, Bordeaux mixture, derris dust and pyrethrum sprays.

Lizards

These small reptiles eat slugs, snails, flies and other insects, depending on species.

Praying mantises

Active both by day and night in the interest of pest control, diligent adult mantises eat caterpillars, bugs, beetles, moths and other insects, and young mantises eat aphids and leaf hoppers. There are many species of the insect, of which the most common are the green and brown varieties distinguished by their 'praying' position of lifted forelegs.

Healthy gardens don't happen by accident. Companion planting and encouraging beneficial insects can work wonders.

Breeding mantises is a fascinating project for children. Mantises lay their eggs in frothy masses on tree trunks or fences. To protect the eggs from being parasitised by wasps, keep them in an open container indoors. They will hatch in about five months, but separate them immediately or they'll turn cannibal! Although basically carnivorous they will feed on raw apple, potato, shreds of meat, fruit and dead or live insects. Release into a safe sheltered garden area when large enough.

Robber or assassin flies (Australia)
These voracious predators eat almost anything they can catch and will also sting humans. They are long, thin, hairy flies with thick legs and wing spans ranging from 25–75 mm (1–3 in). The cylindrical larvae live in soil or old timber.

Scorpion flies (Australia)
The males prey on flies, bees, caterpillars and beetle larvae. They pupate in the soil surface. They vary in appearance but all have long spindly legs and long transparent wings with opaque veins.

Spiders
Spiders live almost entirely on insects, not just web-caught flies and mosquitoes. They will also eat caterpillars including codling moth larvae, flying termites, butterflies, whiteflies and many others.

Stilt flies
These are aphid-eating, small, thin, tapering flies up to 15 mm (½ in) in length and greenish-brown in colour. They thrive in moist leafy places.

Wasps
Many species of wasp either prey on or parasitise pests and their eggs. They eat a wide range of caterpillars, including those of the cabbage white butterfly and codling moth, and pear and cherry slugs. Some also eat scale insects. Chalcid wasps, which are minute and metallic blue, black or brown, parasitise beetles and mealy bugs as well as a range of insect eggs, scale and caterpillars. Paper wasps eat caterpillars, spiders, pear and cherry slugs and aphids, but they disgrace themselves by devouring monarch butterfly caterpillars.

How to attract beneficial predators
Provide water
In areas where mosquitos are not a problem, you can create a small pond surrounded by plants or a bird bath with leafy shrubs around it. Predators such as dragonflies, damsel flies, frogs and certain beneficial toads breed near water; others such as ichneumon wasps and birds need to drink.

Don't dig

Many predator eggs and nymphs live in the soil, so the less the ground is dug the more predators will survive.

Provide year-round flowers

Lists of attractor and host plants for beneficial predatory insects follow in chapter 5. Try to ensure there are at least some flowers in bloom throughout the cooler seasons on which beneficial insects may breed and feed. Many dine not just on nectar but on the insect pests trying to colonise the same plants. If you live in an area where winters are long and intense and it's very difficult to have flowers in bloom, spray evergreen and other plants with a yeast and sugar solution, or one made of a commercial yeast spread such as Vegemite or Marmite. This attracts lacewings, hoverflies and other sugar lovers.

Provide nesting boxes and food for birds

In America, tobacco plantations provide nesting boxes for predatory pollistes wasps and for birds. Feed insect-eating birds during winter and ensure they have access to thawed water. Many birds die because regular water sources become frozen for prolonged periods.

General aids to pest management
Hygiene

The prompt removal of old edible crop residues – fallen fruit from the base of trees, tomato plants, etc – is beneficial This prevents a build up of 'grazing' fruit fly and other pests. Employ a few chickens to do this work – they do a mean job! A neat and tidy garden is more likely to remain healthy than one cluttered with rubbish, debris and the remains of old plants, all highly hospitable to pests and diseases looking for a good home. But don't go to the other extreme and clear away natural vegetation that is not floral or edible. This would achieve the same result as deforestation – removing the natural habitat of countless beneficial insects, animals and organisms.

Mechanical methods

Wash aphids, blackfly, whitefly off plants with strong hose, dust off with a small paintbrush or soft toothbrush dipped in oil. Hand pick larger pests – slugs, snails, beetles, caterpillars – squash (or if squeamish!) – drop into a bucket of water.

Traps

These include cardboard traps around tree trunks, pheromone lures to catch codling moths and cut worms, yellow-painted and greased boards to attract and immobilise aphids, whiteflies and greenflies, aphid traps made from ice cream containers of water with yellow colouring and detergents, and slug and snail traps.

Barriers

These include grease bands to deter ants and crawling insects, nets and cover cloth to keep away destructive birds, and cover cloth to seal in brassicas so that cabbage white butterflies can't lay their eggs on the foliage.

Repellents

Details of masking, repellent and companion plants are given in chapter 5.

Organic sprays

No matter how good the growing system is, factors such as unseasonable weather conditions and

This pollen-rich daisy attracts the predatory hoverfly, a beneficial insect.

the influx of pests (as a result of lack of predators or a general pest/predator imbalance from pesticides used nearby) may all cause sudden problems. The methods described in the next section should be used as temporary measures while the problems are identified and remedied. Organic sprays break down quickly and are least harmful to humans and the environment, but use them only as a last resort. Remember too, that some 'natural' plant derivative substances like pyrethrum and derris dust are not entirely safe – they're harmful to some beneficial insects and toxic to fish. Any spraying, organic or not, may kill predators and even sprays that are 'target specific' – designed to destroy one type of pest – remove predators' food sources and cause them to die or depart from your garden.

Always remember that the best way to control pests is to have a healthy soil, and provide specific flowering plants on which predatory insects may breed and feed.

Let us spray: low-toxicity pest control

It is argued that natural control methods used by organic gardeners are not always as effective as more orthodox treatments. It is true that most environmentally friendly plant-derivative sprays are non-systemic; that is, they do not, as with toxic chemicals, enter the system of the plant and afford continued protection.

The following sprays will repel, and in some cases kill pests, but remember that, with the exception of neem, which enters the plant's system, they are all contact sprays and need to be applied regularly (especially after rain) to be effective. They involve a little more work, but they will not harm your family or the environment and will allow a diversity of insect life to thrive in your garden thus maintaining a natural balance.

Plant-derived insecticides

Plant-derived insecticides fall into two categories, pesticides and anti-feedants. Put simply, this means the pesticides kill the pest, while the anti-feedant repels and acts as a prevention to pest infestation.

It is true that a certain level of pests and disease will remain, because organic preparations kill or deter only when they come in contact with the bodies of the insects they are designed to deal

Woolly aphids on underside of plant foliage.

with. Thus they need to be used more frequently and it is essential that all parts of the plants, including the undersides of the leaves, are thoroughly covered. It is possible to minimise even the use of benign sprays by inspecting one's vegetables regularly. Brassicas, for example, are prey to infestations of caterpillars at certain times of the year. Turn a few leaves as often as you can and rub out the pests and their colonies of egg clusters. Keen eyes are an essential factor in benign pest and disease management.

It's neither difficult nor expensive to make one's own pesticides, but remember even plant-derivative sprays can be harmful if used too frequently or at the incorrect strength. Most are harmless to people but it's best to take every precaution when making them. When boiling or steeping plants don't use everyday cooking utensils, and keep away from food preparation areas. Wear a mask, don't inhale fumes and ventilate the room. Wear gloves and long sleeved shirts when preparing and spraying. Label all home-made sprays clearly and store in a cool, dark, safe place. Don't consume sprayed crops within 24 hours, or longer if spray is more toxic.

It is beyond the scope of this book to give recipes for all the plants that can be made into sprays, but those given below are widely used and have proved effective. See the quick reference charts throughout this chapter for others.

The shelf life of plant-derivative sprays is limited and they are most effective used fresh. Incorporate a little well dissolved pure soap into spray as a sticking agent.

Once you have identified a pest, you can use a spray that controls it without doing damage to the helpful insects and the creatures that eat them. By experimenting with plant combinations and with making repellent sprays, then closely observing the results, you can discover what combinations suit you and your garden best. The strength of the spray will vary according to which pest you need to deter, trap or kill, but never be tempted to make it too strong – you may kill the predators of the pests you're trying to deter and burn the very plants you are trying to protect!

The following plants can be used to make pesticide sprays or dusts of varying strengths. When masking and repelling plants won't work it may be necessary to use 'killer plants' to kill pests until their numbers are reduced.

Killer plants: Basils, chilli peppers (wear gloves and do not touch face or eyes while chopping fruit), derris root, elder, eucalyptus, feverfew, garlic, hellebore, lantana (a noxious weed in some countries), larkspur, marigolds, melaleuca, mustards, onions, parsnips, pyrethrum (toxic to fish, don't spray near water; toxic to bees and other beneficial insects, use after sundown), quassia, rhubarb (leaves toxic to humans), tomato, turnips, white cedar and wormwood.

Garlic and pyrethrum concentrate: Widely available from most nurseries and garden centres. The garlic acts as a pest repellent and the pyrethrum flower extract as a broad spectrum insecticide. Spray after sundown when beneficial insects have stopped working the flowers.

It is possible to make your own garlic and pyrethrum sprays if you wish, but I've found a 200 ml (7 fl oz) commercially prepared bottle of this combined concentrate lasts for several years for spot spraying in a large garden.

Garlic spray: Chop six large cloves of garlic, place in a blender with 6 tablespoons of medicinal paraffin oil and pulverise. Leave pulp to stand for 48 hours. Grate 1 tablespoon of oil-based soap into a container and add 570 ml (1 pt) hot water, stirring until soap has melted. Stir into garlic pulp. When cool, strain into jars and store in the refrigerator. Use 2 tablespoons garlic mixture to 1 litre (2 pt) of water.

Pyrethrum spray: The silver leafed pyrethrum daisy (*Chrysanthemum/ Tanacetum cinerariifolium*) contains substances called pyrethrins, which act directly on the nervous systems of insects such as aphids, mites and caterpillars and some beneficial insects. To make this spray, take 1 tablespoon of well crushed flowers and mix with sufficient spirit alcohol to wet the flowers and release the pyrethrin extracts. (Flowers may be harvested, dried and stored for use at other times of the year). Place crushed mixture into 2 litres (4 pt) of hot water and add a squirt of natural soap (not detergent) to aid stickability. Allow to stand, strain into air-tight jars when cool.

Marigold spray: This repels most sap-suckers and will kill aphids. Cover marigold flowers with boiling water. Leave to stand overnight. Strain and spray.

Nettle tea: Effective against powdery mildew. Spray undiluted from tea drum.

Rhubarb sprays: Rhubarb leaves are poisonous. The toxin that kills insects is oxalic acid, so take great care with its preparation, use and storage. Boil 1 kg (2 lb) of leaves in 2 litres (4 pt) of water for 30 minutes but do not use an aluminium saucepan. When cool, remove the leaves, strain the fluid and mix with enough pure soap to make it frothy.

Tansy spray: Although it is a plant-derivative spray, tansy has some toxicity and has the disadvantage of needing to be washed off edible plants before use. Avoid inhalation. Tansy spray will not kill predators. It is an anti-feedant – it repels insects and inhibits their feeding. It breaks down quite quickly and needs to be reapplied every two or three days. To make tansy spray, pour 1 litre (2 pt) of boiling water over 2 firmly packed cupfuls of roughly chopped leaves. Cool, strain and use within a few days.

Wormwood (*Artemisia absinthe*) or **Southernwood** (*Artemisia abrotanum*) **infusion:** Wormwood is a bitter aromatic herb containing volatile oils made up of various organic acids and glucoside absinthe. The spray repels and kills fleas and other pests such as flies, moths and mosquitoes. It is effective against aphids and when applied over and around the base of young plants is an excellent slug and snail repellent. But like all organic infusions it needs to be applied regularly to be effective. Wormwood tea is an excellent insecticide for sap-suckers such as bean, tomato and onion fly and whitefly.

Cover chopped leaves and flowers with boiling water and leave for three hours. Strain and dilute 1 part spray with 4 parts water. Since this mix does not need straining (unless to be used as a spray) I keep a bucket filled with steeping leaves and pour it out, leaves and all, wherever gastropods have become a nuisance.

Other pest control agents
The following preparations are also generally acceptable to sustainable growers:

Derris dust (Retenone): A plant-derived pesticide from the roots of the South American *Derris elliptica* plant or from tropical plants such as babaco, crushed to a powder. Although of low toxicity to human beings, birds and animals, it is toxic to fish, other aquatic organisms and tortoises. Derris dust kills a number of pests.

Diatomaceous earth: This is made from finely ground skeletons of marine organisms. Use against soft-bodied pests such as aphids, thrips, mites, snails and termites, or hard-shelled pests such as bugs. The fine dust should penetrate their carapaces and gradually wear them away. Spray fortnightly. Mix 200 g (½ lb) diatomaceous earth with 1 litre (35 fl oz) soapy water.

Dipel (*Bacillus thuringiensis*): A bacterial form of biological control – germ warfare – that plays havoc with digestive systems of caterpillars. It must be consumed to be effective. Dipel was a silkworm disease in Japan and a disease of wax moth larvae. The spores are killed by sunlight and must be reapplied weekly. Spray under the leaves as well as on top. This soil bacterium *Bacillus thuringiensis* produces a toxin known as 'Bt', which is regarded as a safe insecticide. It is harmless to people, spiders and beneficial insects but kills caterpillars, beetles and other pests – includ-

Plant-derivative sprays

Plant name	Latin name	Controls
Basil	*Ocimum basilicum*	Aphids, asparagus beetles, fruit flies; general pesticide
Catnip	*Nepeta cataria*	Colorado beetles; attracts beneficial parasitic wasps; general repellent
Chamomile	*Chamomile nobile*	Anti fungal spray and aphid repellent
Chestnut	*Castanea sativa*	Beet moths
Chilli	*Capsicum* spp	Repels and kills insects and animal pests
Chive	*Allium schoenoprasum*	Apple scab; mildew on cucumbers, gooseberries, summer squash and pumpkins; general repellent
Citronella	*Cymbopogon* spp	General insect and animal repellent
Citrus fruit	*Citrus*	Fall armyworms and bollworms
Coriander	*Coriandrum sativum*	Aphids, spider mites; repels insects on fruit trees
Derris root	*Derris elliptica*	White cabbage butterfly, caterpillars, chewing insects
Elderberry	*Sambucus*	Aphids, carrot flies, cucumber beetles, peach tree borers, root maggots
Eucalyptus	*Eucalyptus*	General insecticide and repellent
Feverfew	*Tanacetum parthenium*	General pesticide; kills and deters wide range of insects
Garlic	*Allium sativum*	Kills and deters a whole range of pests including aphids, caterpillars, codling moths, Japanese beetles, root maggots, rusts, snails
Horseradish	*Armoracia rusticana*	Fungicide for fruit trees and other plants
Horsetail	*Equisetum*	Slugs and snails
Hyssop	*Hyssopus officinalis*	Repels white cabbage butterflies; fungicidal spray
Ivy	*Hedera helix*	Corn wireworms
Johnson grass	*Sorghum halepense*	Willamette mites on vines
Mint	*Mentha*	Colorado beetles and ants; repellent and masking plant
Neem	*Azadirachta indica*	Systemic botanic pesticide; kills wide range of insect pests but harmless to beneficial insects
Parsley	*Petroselinum crispum*	Asparagus beetles
Pelargonium	*Pelargonium*	Cabbage moths, corn earworms and Japanese beetles
Pepper	*Capsicum*	General insect repellent, also kills insect pests
Quassia	*Quassia amara*	General pesticide and repellent; kills and repels insect pests
Rhubarb	*Rheum rhubarbarum*	General insecticide and blackspot treatment; kills wide range of pests
Sage	*Salvia officinalis*	Cabbage worms; kills aphids, deters carrot fly; masking plant
Southernwood	*Artemisia abrotanum*	Cabbage worms, aphids, whitefly, slugs, snails, cabbage butterfly
Thyme	*Thymus vulgaris*	Cabbage worms, onion worms; masking plant
Tomato	*Lycopersicon lycopersicum*	Asparagus beetles
Wormwood	*Artemesia absinthe*	Fleas, aphids, whitefly, slugs, snails, cabbage butterfly

ing the Colorado beetle, which decimates potato crops in America. The infected caterpillars are not toxic to birds or other predators.

Eucalyptus oil spray: Like other oils, eucalyptus oil kills scale, aphids, etc, and will repel many pests.

Neemseed oil insecticide: Oil from the neem tree (*Azadirachta indica*) is the only botanical systemic pesticide yet available, and is highly efficient for controlling a large variety of plant feeding pests including whitefly, scale, mealybug, thrips and nematodes. Neem preparations are environmentally benign and may be used in horticulture, agriculture, on flowers and turf. Azadirachtin, the main ingredient of neemseed oil, has proven harmless to beneficial insects and predators. It has been used for centuries in India as a food preservative and to prevent insects eating stored grain. A systemic, it repels and deters leaf-eating and plant-sucking insects by suppressing their appetite and affecting bowel activity. Applied at the early stages of insect growth, it can influence the development of eggs, larvae and pupae. At the larvae and nymph stage, neemseed oil disrupts the metamorphosis process.

If you do not wish to purchase commercially prepared neem, an effective insecticide may be made with a cake of neem soap from a Trade Aid shop. You will need (a strong arm) a grater, a 5 litre (1 gal) bucket, a whisk and a sieve, and storage jars or bottles. Grate a quarter of a cake of neem soap into the bucket, pour on about a litre (2 pt) of boiling water to make a liquid, stir thoroughly to dissolve lumps, then add remaining water. Strain the liquid into bottles or jars.

Quassia: A general insecticide and bird repellent for fruit. Use quassia for aphids, mites, caterpillars, sawfly larvae and pear slug. Quassia is harmless to almost all predators and bees. It contains a lactone with a very bitter taste, hence its value as a bird repellent – but it washes off so must be renewed after rain. Quassia chips may be bought from organic suppliers. Simmer 30 g (about 1 oz) quassia chips in 1 litre (35 fl oz) of water for one hour. Add more water as it evaporates. The liquid should be yellow. Strain, mix in enough soft soap to form a lather (about 30 g) and dilute with 5

Ingredients for benign pesticides.

parts water for aphids or 3 parts for sawfly larvae, pear and cherry slug, or mites like red spider mite. To make a quassia infusion steep 30 g quassia chips in 570 ml (1 pt) cold water for two hours, strain and use.

Sulphur: Some sulphur preparations contain additional unacceptable pesticides. Study labels.

Vegetable/mineral oils: Vegetable oils kill pests or their eggs with a light film of suffocating oil. Use in a mixture of soft soap. Boil and stir vigorously until dissolved. Dilute with 20 times the amount of water. This spray separates quickly so don't store it once it has been mixed with water.

Organic protection for trees and fruit
As we have already discussed, trees, particularly fruiting varieties, can be protected against flightless insects with sticky bands and collars, pheromone traps and lure jars, which trap the larvae as they crawl up the trunk from the ground. Codling moth traps can be used from spring through summer for codling moth in apples and pears.

Pests and diseases on trees can also be controlled by frequent applications of the organic sprays already discussed, but at a slightly stronger concentration.

Fruit tree spray programme

Fruit	Spray	Pest/disease
Late summer– early autumn		
Apples	garlic and pyrethrum	codling moth
Pears	garlic and pyrethrum	pear slug
Citrus	garlic and pyrethrum	aphid, mealy bug
Autumn–winter (during leaf fall)		
All stone and pip fruit	cutonic copper with vegetable/mineral oil	leaf curl and blast
Berry fruit		fungus diseases
		insects and eggs
Spring (at bud swell and burst)		
Apples	garlic and pyrethrum, just before bud burst	insect pests
Stone fruit	garlic and pyrethrum, just before bud burst	insect pests
	cutonic copper, just before bid burst	fungal diseases
Citrus	garlic and pyrethrum, just before bud burst	

The copper and mineral oil preparations mentioned in the spray programme above are particularly good for prevention and treatment of brown rot and leaf curl on peach, plum and nectarine trees. Garlic and pyrethrum double up as pesticide and repellent, but as pyrethrum is toxic to bees, it should be used after sundown.

For lush, healthy citrus, 20 g (1 oz) of Epsom salts can be added to 10 litres (2 gal) of water with the copper and garlic.

Use Burgundy and Bordeaux mixtures for canker and fungal infections as necessary. Bordeaux paste is also useful for collar rot and pruning wound.

Commercially prepared non-chemical preparations

Preparations containing the following benign agents are sold under many names in different countries. Label reading is all! Ask for assistance in choosing a benign pesticide or herbicide, but check that the lotions and potions recommended contain no additional ingredients to those listed below.

Copper: Copper hydroxide preparations are usually presented in the form of a wettable powder that controls fungus and bacterial diseases such as blight, downy mildew, black spot, leaf curl and shothole on fruit, vegetables and ornamentals.

Mineral spraying oil, vegetable oil, all-purpose oil and others: These non-toxic mineral or vegetable oils control scale, mites and mealybug on a wide range of ornamentals, fruit and vegetables.

They are compatible with copper hydroxide fungicide preparations and are generally used together as an organic insecticide and fungicide. The combination is popular as a general 'clean up' spray before and after pruning and during winter. The oils are for use in both winter and early summer.

Fatty acids (potassium salts and soaps, vegetable based oils): Available for the control of aphid, greenfly, mealy bugs, mites, thrips and whitefly on roses, vegetables and ornamentals, these pesticides are manufactured from biodegradable fatty acids, vegetable oils (coconut) and potassium salts in the form of a soluble concentrate. The same ingredients combined at more concentrated strength are employed as benign herbicides and work by destroying cells in the tissues of undesirable plants. The use of fatty acids at different strengths for both protection from pests and destruction of plant material heavily underlines how vital it is to use *exactly* the strength recommended by the manufacturer if it is only the insect's pests you wish to attack, rather than destroy your precious plants.

Neemseed oil: This preparation, a valuable aid in controlling garden plant pests, is also available commercially for use on fruit trees.

Pyrethrum: Low toxicity plant derivative pesticide derived from the silver-leafed pyrethrum daisy, *Chrysanthemum cinerariifolium*. The plant contains substances called pyrethrins, which act directly on the nervous systems of insects. It is safe for humans and animals but toxic to fish, bees

A multi-purpose mixture

When it has been necessary to spray I have had success with a multi-purpose solution, which is a 'three-in-one' repellent, insecticide and fungicide: It contains garlic, as an insect deterrent; pyrethrum, as an organic insecticide; and copper hydroxide, as a preventative and protection against fungal and bacterial diseases.

These three preparations are all compatible and combine to offer protection to edibles, roses and ornamentals against insectiferous pests, as well as fungal and bacterial diseases. (The dilution rates for commercial preparations are clearly stated on the packets, and those for the home-made sprays have already been given in this chapter.)

If, like me, you are a rosophile, you will have to accept that where there are roses, there are black spot and downy mildews. Even when the plants are drenched with toxic chemicals, these disfiguring diseases remain to some extent.

Newspaper offices and printers are good sources for recycled tin banding. They will often let you purchase the thin aluminium sheets used as inking pads for a modest price. These make excellent bands, but don't hammer them into the tree with big nails. Tack, staple or wire them on lightly.

Rings of old tyres and bottomless drums will also protect young trees against goats and cattle but again, remember to take them off as the trees' trunks grow – both these items are virtually impossible to cut through!

Peckish possums

Gardeners in New Zealand are locked in mortal combat with the possum, an herbivorous pest that operates well above ground level (and is not the same family as the carnivorous US opossum).

Faced with the devastating results of possom damage, even the most placid of us will shudder with rage, horror and disbelief. This furry creature turns gentle gardeners into vengeful hunters armed with guns, flashlights, bait, traps and cages. It makes serial killers of us all and drags us from

and other beneficial insects. Use after sundown. The extract is sometimes sold as a 'domestically safe' pesticide for indoor use for fly/flea control as a refillable pyrethrum 'bug bomb', in which the propellant is simply water. It has to be charged occasionally with an easily worked pump on the bottom and refills are available. Cover pet goldfish.

Animal pests

In addition to insect pests, from time immemorial gardeners have also suffered the depredations of animal pests. Following are a few you may encounter in your domestic garden, and what to do about them.

Rabbits, hares, goats and possums

To prevent rabbits, hares and goats ring-barking young shrubs or trees wrap aluminium foil, tarpaper or tin around the trunks at the base. Tin banding will also keep away possums, but remember to replace them as trees and shrubs grow. Bands cutting into their flesh and choking off their life blood will kill them faster than any pest!

A tree banded against animal pests.

The possum, an herbivorous Australasian marsupial that has reached epidemic proportions in New Zealand.

our beds uttering foul oaths or incantations that smack of witchcraft. Night after night, the dogs' hysterical barking warns that the enemy is in the garden, leaping about full of *joie de vivre*, holding feasts of Bacchanalian proportions amongst the rose bushes (oh, no!), and tender trees and shrubs.

Possum controls for the home gardener that do not involve poison include trapping in cages and shooting, and the use of humane traps that kill instantly. Humane traps usually contain a highly efficient guillotine system that causes instant death. The bait is put on the tip of a steel spike, and the trap is sprung by means of a pull cord. When the peckish possum puts its head into the small hole at the front of the box, a powerful spring-loaded bar drops, breaking its neck instantaneously.

Possums are curious creatures and are easily trapped in cages, but the downside of this method is that for nocturnal creatures the system is not so humane. I've seen terrified, starving possums left all day in cages in hot sunlight, so if you use cages be out at first light to shoot the animals so they do not suffer unnecessarily. The animal has a very distinctive, blood-curdling, growling laugh and is easily located and shot at night with the help of a strong flashlight.

Disposal of carcasses can be a problem, but if you dig a small trench near one tree or shrub at a time to bury your possums, (not too near the roots) you'll be providing it with rich bonus nutrients.

In most parts of Australia, possums are a protected species and may not be killed by members of the public. It is necessary to contact your local pest control officer for help with their disposal or removal.

Cats and dogs

One way to repel unwanted cats and canines is to drive them away by 'sound'. The 'sound' method comprises an electronic device that emits incredibly high pitched tones inaudible to humans, which are harmless but annoying to animals. The device consists of a small plastic box attached to a peg which is left in place in the soil. Power is supplied either by batteries or a lead from a small transformer.

Another method is to capitalise on their advanced sense of smell. A number of preparations containing odours offensive to cats and dogs are readily available worldwide. The latest of these is an ointment called Skunk Shot 2, a laboratory produced replica of the evil-smelling oil skunks emit when threatened. This is effective for one month, its performance is unaffected by rain and the smell is undetectable to humans except at very close range.

Birds – a love/hate relationship

Birds are beautiful, their song a privilege, but some are number one enemy in the edible garden. Blackbirds, thrushes and sparrows are supreme predators, reducing troublesome pest numbers, but they reverse the good they do by devouring fruit and seedlings, and the amount of damage they do in the beds with their powerful beaks and feet is awesome. They'll dig up a row of seedlings in seconds, scooting carefully worked-up soil and mulch all over pathways. The amount of time and labour entailed daily in trying to replant dehydrated seedlings, and in sweeping up the mess and replacing it, negates the objectives of the low maintenance garden.

My edible gardens have a distinct mummified appearance early in the season, swathed, bandaged and pegged in acres of cover cloth to protect plants, mulch and soil. Cloches covered with chicken wire or netting, or cages of netting if you're trying to grow soft fruits, are also effective.

Benign weed control

Lord, give me the courage and tenacity of a weed.

'Gardener's Prayer', Karel Capek, 1929

Ever since human beings began domestic gardening some 4000 years ago, we've been arguing over which plants are weeds. There are a few, like oxalis and ground elder, that even the most *laissez-faire* of horticulturists will agree are weeds. But weeds can be valuable; many are host plants on which beneficial insects may breed and feed; others such as blackberry, bracken (high in potash), nettles, dock and broom break up or enrich the soil with their roots. The dock has a deep tap root, which brings up nutrients from deep in the soil where shallow rooted plants can't reach. When dock leaves are used as mulch the nutrients are returned.

Some weeds like purslane (*Portulaca oleracea*), lamb's quarters (*Chenopodium album*), garlic mustard (*Alliaria petiolata*), common nasturtiums, shepherd's purse (*Capsella bursa-pastoris*), and dandelions (*Taraxacum officinale*) are highly nutritious as human foods.

Nettles (*Urtica dioica*) encourage earthworms and butterflies, are nitrogen fixing and a traditional plant tonic. Nettle tea discourages fungal diseases and helps increase frost resistance. The plant is, however, horribly invasive if not strictly confined, spreading by both rhizomes and seed. Remove heads as soon as they form, and confine the plants to an area where you can control them by harvesting frequently for mulch (leaves only) and liquid manure.

Weeds adore bare and freshly dug soil. Having lain dormant in the earth, when exposed to sunlight, oxygen and moisture they leap into luxuriant life. They are nature's ground cover, preventing large scale erosion of the earth's surface by colonising bare topsoil, which might otherwise wash away in rain or blow away in wind, leaving infertile subsoil.

The bottom line is that a weed is a plant in the wrong place. If you don't want it there, it's a weed.

The predominance of a particular weed tells you a good deal about your soil conditions. Buttercups, quack grass (*Agropyon repens*), plantains, dock and ground ivy indicate heavy poorly drained soil; thistles, knotweed, and white clover colonise compacted ground; the presence of common yarrow, thistles, and plantains indicate infertile soil but *Amaranthus* spp, lamb's quarters and chick weeds thrive in fertile earth; red sorrel, plantains, oxeye daisy and many mosses thrive in acid soil and shepherd's purse, chicory and mugwort (*Artemesia vulgaris*) in alkaline.

Attacking the uncleared section

Being faced with a large area infested with weeds is daunting in the extreme, and an understandable mistake we all make is to invest brutal toil in attempting to clear the whole patch at once. It's wiser to gain control slowly but completely – a small area at a time. Mow, slash or strim-weed the whole area to take off all seed heads. Rake heads into heaps and cover heavily with thick polythene to heat kill them, or gather and drop into barrels of water for liquid and rotted sludge manure. Don't compost them.

Having levelled the site and removed all seed heads, take a manageable section at a time and clear of weeds by hand pulling, spraying with benign herbicide, or by solarisation (see below).

Then apply a sealing layer of nutritious vegetative mulch and plant straight into it (punch holes if you're using thick layers of newspaper or weedmat). Plant or develop this 'clean' area for its designated purpose, before tackling another section. As they mature, desirable plants will choke out weeds by depriving them of air and light, and in an area that is a manageable size, you'll have far better chance of controlling others that germinate.

In the meantime, until you're ready to develop the uncleared sections, keep all weeds in these sections topped so that they cannot reseed.

Non-toxic herbicides

These are sold under various 'environmentally friendly' trade names such as 'Nature's Way' but, as yet, they are regrettably few in number. Most are comprised of biodegradable, potassium salts and soaps in the form of a soluble concentrate. They are basically the same as those used in benign pesticides but at much higher strength. They work by destroying the cellular structure of the plant tissues.

Non-chemical methods of weeding
Sun scorch – solarisation
If you've a large area to clear, harness the sun's power with some sheets of plastic. Together they can destroy many of the weed seeds, stolons, rhizomes, tubers and bulbs near the soil's surface. Solarisation is not a quick method, but as a bonus you'll also destroy some disease causing pathogens and soil dwelling pests. Remove the truly gigantic weeds by hand, then cover the area with thick, clear plastic and leave the soil covered for at least a month. The heat will encourage germination of all surface weed seeds, whereupon they'll quickly fry! Don't dig the area before planting – this will only encourage millions of buried weed seeds to germinate. Build up no-dig beds as detailed in chapter 3.

Smother crops
Certain crops can help inhibit weed growth not only by covering the soil, but because they produce toxins in their roots and leaves that make the soil inhospitable for other plants – the mechanism, called allelopathy, is discussed in chapter 5.

Allelopathic species include annual ryegrass (*Lolium multiflorum*), oats (*Avena sativa*), winter wheat (*Triticum aestivum*) and winter rye (*Secale cereale*). These four make good smother crops, and when you work them into the soil, their decomposing residues inhibit annual weeds. Other smother crops include buckwheat (*Fagopyrum esculentum* – available in health food shops) and white clover (*Trifolium repens*). Many home gardeners won't have room to grow these crops, but may use instead traditional green manure crops such as lupins, mustard greens and sunflowers to inhibit weeds on temporarily uncultivated soil. (If you use sunflowers, don't buy expensive pre-packeted seed – buy a kilo of cheap bird seed and do the job for quarter the price!)

Weedmat
This is lightweight, water-permeable fabric usually made of spun or pressed plastic which pre-

vents plant growth. For new plantings a hole is made into the weedmat. The fabric is particularly useful for laying in areas such as pathways and under trees and shrubs where, hidden by a top layer of mulch, it offers long-term weed suppression. The same effect can be achieved by sheets of plastic, but it will eventually rot and if in place over a long period it excludes oxygen from the soil and kills essential nutrients; this may render the area difficult to plant in future years.

Dense planting
Plant crops and flowers as densely as possible; bare ground invites weeds. As long as you've conditioned your soil well, it will be able to support the plants and their intermingling foliage will conserve moisture and prevent light reaching weed seeds. With mildew-prone plants, dense planting can, however, have the downside of encouraging fungal diseases. With vegetables such as brassicas, and with shrubs such as roses, ensure there is adequate air circulation and sunlight between plants.

Beautiful barriers
Plant a weed barrier that is both aesthetically pleasing and practical. Cannas, agapanthus, comfrey, daylilies, marigolds, and herbal hedges (lavender, santolina, etc) quickly clump up to form dense floral barriers, which will fulfil the dual purpose of attracting beneficial predatory and pollinating insects. Agapanthus self-sows freely and can become invasive in subtropical areas; control by decapitation – remove and destroy globular seed heads when your weed barrier is dense enough.

Edging strips
To prevent grasses from creeping into beds, invest in solid edging strips of wood, concrete, bricks or pavers so that edges are easily mowed. Another way to control their spread is to create a barrier. Remove the soil in a strip 5 cm (2 in) wide and deep between the grass and the paving to make it harder for the grass to spread outward. As new runners attempt to creep they are easily nipped in the prime with clippers or strimmer. The floral barrier plantings above will also prevent grasses

Sunflowers are a traditional smother, green manure and food crop.

running under fence lines and other areas where you don't want them.

Mulch magic

Many perennial weeds can be controlled with applications of deep mulch. Those that do germinate will be loosely rooted and easily removed. Refer to chapter 3 for details of organic materials that may be used as weed inhibiting ground covers.

Lawn lore

If you wish to have turfed areas, the best way to prevent lawn weeds is to give the turf the same feeding, watering and TLC extended to other plant treasures.

A curious paradox is that we shower flowering plants with food and drink, but fling in grass seeds and expect the lawn to remain healthy and luxurious without any care from us at all. Grass is a plant like any other and needs just as much feeding and watering. A thin, patchy lawn is the perfect bed for weed seeds and what you'll end up with is a 'CDW' ('cut down weeds') lawn. We all suffer from the mow-low syndrome at times, but a scalped lawn exposes grass roots to dehydrating sun and wind causing them to dehydrate and die back – and that's when the weeds move in. We wouldn't dream of treating our flowers like this!

Try never to procrastinate so long with mowing that broad-headed weed seed heads form

– if you're going on holiday, bribe a friend to mow or a pay a contractor. Prevention is truly better than cure as far as lawn weeds are concerned.

Biological control

When applied to weed control, the term biological control is rather wishful thinking. It conjures up visions of a mysterious silent army of insects or micro-organisms that silently wipe out huge weed populations. Dream on. . . The reality is that although certain fungi, beetles and mites are used on agricultural and horticultural land for the control of weeds such as gorse, ragwort and thistles, their use is not (as yet) really applicable to the common annual and perennial weeds which colonise domestic gardens.

Eating machines

But all is not lost, although control of weeds in domestic gardens by micro-organisms may still be a dream, a form of biological control in rural gardens can include the larger weed-eating machines such as pigs, goats and sheep, and in urban plots, those such as chickens and rabbits in moveable cages or arks.

Gourmet goats

Goat grazing is also effective for blackberry and gorse clearance. If the plants are woody and ancient, slash them down for the goats to reach in one area at a time. Match the area to be cleared to goat power: if there's not enough food the animals will starve; if given too much they will only browse, and the weedy shrubs will regrow and gain control again quickly. Goats will also eat weeds such as ragwort, dock, rushes and broom if little else is available. As the animals are moved to another area, sow the cleared space immediately – the grass or crop should do well in soil enriched with years of dropped blackberry leaves now mixed with goat droppings. Pigs, horses and sheep will also eat young plants or regrowth on old ones.

Mechanical control

First, a word of warning: never use a rotary tiller in an area infested with weeds such as invasive grasses or wandering jew, which grow from runners, rhizomes or stolons. These machines chop the weeds into little bits, each piece capable of producing an infant plant. Similarly, when mowing or cutting them down with a weed strimmer, take care to rake and clear up every piece or you'll end up with a worse problem than you started with!

Do not compost these materials, instead, recycle them into vegetative manure as described below.

If you're breaking in or clearing land for horticultural development, it will be necessary initially to bring out your heavy artillery – brush cutters, chain saws, weed eaters, strimmers, tractors, diggers and bulldozers for large woody shrub weeds and scrub. Battery operated weed strimmers now available facilitate greater range of mobility.

Control of gorse and ragwort
If biological control is impractical in your domestic situation, blackberry and gorse usually require mechanical clearance. The plants need uprooting by bulldozer, front-end loader or tractor and pushing into heaps for burning. This is quick and effective but it is imperative that grass or crops are sown immediately. Burning off alone may work as long as the flame guns are hot and powerful enough. Regrowth must be treated immediately.

There is no easy organic technique for getting rid of these troublesome woody-stemmed weeds other than by gaining control, and then keeping control as part of one's overall ongoing management plan. Have faith! You will win in the end, and without recourse to toxic chemicals that may injure both your family and your land.

Recycling weeds
Most weeds make excellent compost, but don't include those bearing mature seedheads. Even the heat of a well managed heap may not destroy hardy specimens, and they'll germinate to colonise the garden again. Not only that, but they'll emerge as super-weeds in all that lovely nutritious mulch! It's best to throw weeds into a bin of water – many are rich in nitrogen and potassium and will make excellent liquid manure 'teas'. The seeds will rot in water, so they're safer recycled in this way. With weeds that grow from runners, rhizomes or stolons, drop them into a large polythene bag, add just enough water to cover them and leave them to rot down into a somewhat odiferous but nutritious black sludge. This may then be used safely as a vegetative manure.

Attacking hardened offenders
Bindii or Onehunga weed
These lawn low-downs are small plants covered in tiny prickles, very painful when walked on barefoot. They show up light green as juveniles. Apply a pinch of sulphate of ammonia to each, or two-day-old undiluted urine.

Bracken
Bracken will not stand frequent mowing, slashing or bruising, but this must be done as soon as new fronds emerge and continued until no new growth appears. Bending and bruising the fronds means the plant exhausts itself trying to repair repeated damage. Confine scratching hens in the area and they will effectively clear bracken.

If you've a large area to clear, an old bed frame, a wooden pallet or something similar dragged over the plants during the growing season will damage them badly and help you gain control. Bracken is high in potash and makes good mulch and compost.

Couch, kikuyu and other invasive grasses
The best way is to build and plant a new no-dig bed over the existing area as detailed in chapter 3. If you wish to clear the area for a purpose other than planting, cover it in early spring with newspaper, plastic sheeting or heavy mulch to a depth of at least 20 cm (8 in), leaving the cover on for at least a season. During very dry hot weather a sprinkling of sulphate of ammonia will also kill these villains, as will three-day-old urine. Old urine is highly ammoniac and ammonia kills grass (as all turf-proud dog owners will attest). Boiling water will also kill small areas, and a smother crop such as a thick planting of marigolds will choke out couch – their leaves and roots produce an allelopathic substance that inhibits its growth.

Dandelions, dock and other weeds with deep tap roots
Try to get the plants young and deal to them with the 'vampire method' – stab into their hearts with a knitting needle, then rub salt into the wounds (squirt a little salt into the holes). You can also use

boiling water, but this does brown off the surrounding area. Another alternative is to spot-weed with heat weeders, which will be discussed shortly.

Oxalis, onion weed and nut grass
The traditional penance gardeners who harbour these troublesome weeds must pay is time consuming, tedious and labour-intensive hand weeding. The good news is that I've discovered that repeated searing of mature top-growth with a gas weed-wand (discussed shortly) exhausts the bulblets and they give up fairly quickly. Sear regrowth until no more appears.

If you would prefer to dig up the wicked little bulbs, dig to a fork depth and carefully shake out the soil so that the roots are not broken from the bulblets. You may prefer to shake the soil into a coarse sieve, but whether shaking or sieving, it will be necessary to repeat these processes a number of times to ensure the removal of every bulb. Try to avoid using the soil from an infested area in another area, or in the compost; it is unbelievably easy to transfer just one tiny bulb elsewhere and start a whole new colony.

Paspalum and plantain
Decapitating with a sharp mattock will remove these weeds. Roots left in the soil will not regenerate.

Thistles
Behead or grub them up with a sharp grubber. If you've a large area to clear, mow or slash them. Raked and collected, they make a high silica compost or green liquid manure. Thistles are a sign of over grazing and colonise quickly on thin or bald-spotted pasture. Stop grazing until a good grass cover grows again, or resow. Once the grass is doing well thistles will soon die out.

Cooking and steaming
In many countries, local councils are still spraying tank mixes of chemical cocktails in parks, reserves, games fields, around schools and hospitals and along residential verges. More enlightened bodies have instituted the use of scalding water, steam, gas or flame machines as alternatives that are environmentally friendly and harmless to human health. In Australia, New Zealand, USA

Scorching and steaming are environmentally friendly solutions for weed control.

and UK, the use of pressurised hot water and gas powered systems for vegetation control in public areas is increasing.

Fighting with fire
Don't despair, in addition to benign herbicides there is another weapon in the horticulturist's armoury. The company Primus Gas, among others, have produced the ultimate in tools for painless and environmentally friendly weed destruction – no bending, no stretching, no digging and best of all, no toxic herbicides. Smug with virtue you may survey immaculately weeded edges, brick pathways and drive without back and knees groaning and creaking from grovelling in the soil. Your finger nails need not be ragged and rimmed with dirt, nor need you be fit for nothing else after a weeding session but to collapse in a terminally exhausted heap.

You needn't win the lottery and take into your employ an army of under gardeners. The gas powered Primus Gardener allows one to stroll nonchalantly around, malevolently directing a spiteful tongue of flame over vegetation of dubious parentage. The blast of heat passed over the weed causes the cell structure to collapse, leading to dehydration and instant death.

Benign weed control with the Primus Gas Gardener.

The weeder is a lightweight hand-held metal rod with a curved handle which fits snugly into the palm of the hand. Economical to run, the handle end is fitted for the insertion of a refillable or disposable gas canister for use in domestic gardens, or for linking by hose to a large 2 kg (4½ lb) gas bottle for use over larger areas such as orchards, life-style blocks and public reserves. The best models are ignited by an electronic piezo ignition switch on its steel shaft, which fuels a tongue of flame that is easily adjustable according to how monstrous or puny the weeds are. The idea is not to actually burn them, tempting and satisfying though this is; but to allow the blast of searing heat from the flame to pass over causing cellular collapse and root exhaustion. They are easy to use, and of great benefit to older gardeners and those with bad backs for whom bending and stretching is difficult.

The Primus gardener is unsuitable for large perennial weeds. Smaller broad leafed perennials – e.g. daisies and docks – may need several weekly treatments, but annual weeds die with one application. When the weeds have collapsed they do not need uplifting, and an additional bonus not effected by hand weeding is that the weeder eliminates the next generation of weeds by incinerating seeds that have fallen around the parent plant.

Invaluable for zapping weeds on terraces, gravel and paved paths, the tool's adjustable directional flame allows it to be used in flower beds and on broad-leafed lawn weeds. Since no herbicides are involved, the weeder eliminates the danger of spray drift – which would damage precious plants – and it may be used to within 50 mm (2 in) of valuable plants.

Hot and steamy

Recently on the market are hand-held steam weeders. Although they negate the need for chemicals, as yet they are a little cumbersome and have the disadvantage of requiring both electricity (and long flexes), hose and water supplies. For these reasons, unlike the gas powered gardener, which gives one complete freedom of mobility, the area a steam weeder can cover is dictated by power and water supplies. The steam weeder heats the water to close to boiling point so as to produce a constant flow of hot steam.

Both the gas powered weeder and the steam weeder have the advantage of being suitable for use in wet and windy weather.

Commercial herbicides

These are marketed under a wide range of individual trade names that vary between countries, but their active ingredients are fatty acids. Read the labels carefully and check that no other undesirable agents have been added. All are non-systemic – which means they kill by contact rather than by absorption into the plant system. Regular applications and full plant coverage is essential.

Toxic herbicides: biting the bullet

'Aha,' you say, 'but what about when there is no alternative to gaining control but with toxic chemicals?'

Purists will be justified in considering it nothing less than heresy for a book dedicated to low toxicity management to advocate the use of chemicals to gain initial control. There are however a few specific times when idealism has to be balanced with realism; such as when the piece of land one wants to develop is hopelessly invaded by noxious weeds, suckering grasses or mature gorse that cannot initially be destroyed by alternative or biological control methods. And not everyone has access to farm machinery!

An example of this occurred on our land where a particularly invasive suckering bamboo had taken over large areas. Its stranglehold was so extensive even machinery could not have pulled it out, and we'd no vehicular access in that area anyway, so in order to destroy its wicked root system and make the land productive we had to chain-saw the mature canes to the ground and spray Amitrol into the cavities. As regrowth occurred the new leaves were painted with the chemical, thus confining the preparation solely to the unwanted vegetation. In situations such as these it is necessary to use chemicals, but only with the utmost discretion and because there is no alternative practice for reclaiming the area.

Nevertheless in using this chemical we have to accept that we destroyed millions of living micro-organisms in the soil and, to some degree, polluted the atmosphere.

A vast eternal labour

Weeding is said to be the gardener's vast eternal labour. The bottom line is 'after the brutal toil of gaining control, keep control'. Weeds are a bit like eating disorders: once you've conquered the problem and are in control, never let it be in control of you again. Identify your most severe problem and allot a section of time daily in your management programme to controlling and eradicating your specific weed problem.

Plague and pestilence: dealing to disease

Pests and weeds have no scruples; they appear in the most lovingly tended gardens. But like people and animals, plants may also fall ill. Sometimes there's little we can do about this, but taking good care of the plants we grow is the key to success. A small number of well fed, well watered healthy vegetable plants will often give a greater yield than a whole patch of identical plants left to fend for themselves. Just as in the home, poor diet, neglect and unhygienic practices encourage disease and pest infestation.

A disease is an affliction of a plant caused by an organism other than an animal. In practice this means infection with a virus, a bacterium or a fungus, all of which feed on the organic materials contained in other living things. Some fungi such as botrytis or grey mould ('plants in fur coats') live on both dead and living materials.

Disease resistance

Some plants have a greater natural resistance to pests and diseases than others. Many of the older varieties of both vegetables and flowering plants have come down to us by virtue of their being tougher and able to survive. Modern plant breeders can only make use of resistance that occurs naturally in wild plants. Where these are significantly different from the cultivated forms, it may be impossible to breed the resistance into the cultivated plants without losing other essential desirable features in the process; but breeders strive constantly to hybridise plants with high health, prolific flowering and long-lasting blooms, and to give us sturdy vegetable cultivars with high yields. In effect, we have at our disposal both hardy heirloom plants and the best disease resistant, prolific cropping, modern hybrids – the best of both worlds! Study plant catalogues carefully when ordering and note which varieties offer resistance to diseases such as mildews and virus.

Viruses: complex and mysterious

Viruses are invisible to the human eye, they are complex and can exist only within the living cells

Mottled foliage usually indicates a viral disease.

of another organism. Their presence is usually betrayed by mottling or irregular colouring within a plant's foliage. Virus contamination present in a plant's tissues is likely to be passed onto its offspring.

The crops most seriously affected are those propagated vegetatively; that is, by cuttings, corms, bulbs and tubers rather than by seed. This is one group of diseases for which purchasing healthy and certified virus-free stock is essential, but it is very difficult to refuse cuttings of choice plants from friend's gardens or to bypass the 'bargains' on plant stalls. However, harden your heart when purchasing long-term plants such as fruit trees and specimen trees and purchase only certified virus-free stock.

Apple scab.

Disease identification and control

Disease	Appearance	Control
Apple scab	Dark green/brown spots on foliage. Fruits cracked and disfigured with fallen leaves.	Rake up and remove. Prune corky patches, scabby twigs.
Bacterial canker	Serious disease of cherries, plums and other stone fruit. Gum oozes from bark – affected branches die.	Cut out diseased branches. Spray with copper in autumn, Burgundy or Bordeaux mixture at other times.
Black spot	Major rose problem – black spots with yellow edges on leaves. Premature leaf fall defoliates bush.	Rake and destroy all fallen leaves. Ensure bushes have adequate air circulation. Spray with Burgundy/ Bordeaux/ Copper hydroxide mix.
Brown rot	Common fruit disease. Fruit turns brown and rings of yellowish mould appear.	Use preventative sprays of copper. Destroy all affected fruit. Store only sound fruit and inspect at regular intervals
Botrytis (grey mould)	Grey fluffy mould appears on stems, leaves, flowers and fruit. Worst outdoors in wet season and poorly ventilated greenhouses	Avoid basic causes, poor drainage, over-watering and inadequate ventilation. Remove and destroy infected fruit and leaves. Control with sulphur, or bicarbonate of soda in solution as spray.
Bulb, corm and tuber rot	Browning and decay of underground storage organs	Dry thoroughly before storing. Discard soft or rotten bulbs.
Canker	Serious disease of apples and pears which can be fatal	Cut off damaged twigs. Cut out canker from stems and branches. Seal cuts and spray tree with Burgundy mix.
Club root	Swollen and distorted roots – affects stocks, wallflowers and cabbage family	Ensure land is well drained and adequately limed. Destroy diseased plants and do not grow cabbage family plants on site for several years.
Damping off	Serious disease of seedlings particularly in trays. Base of affected plant becomes blackened and withered – stem collapses	Do not use soil as potting medium. Use sterilised seed mix and do not overwater. Remove affected plants.
Die-back	Common disease of roses, fruit trees, shrubs. Die-back spreads slowly downwards from branch tip.	Cut out all dead wood. Try to improve drainage, light and air circulation.
Downy mildew	Grey mildew particularly troublesome in vegetable plot. Leaf surface turns yellow and greyish mould appears.	Ensure soil is well drained. Practise crop rotation of vegetables. Pick off and destroy infected leaves as soon as disease appears. Improve air circulation to crop.
Leaf spot	Blotches, spots or rings on foliage, especially on celery and blackcurrant. Leaves may fall prematurely.	Feed with a fertiliser containing potash. Pick off diseased leaves, avoid overcrowding.
Peach leaf curl	Large reddish blisters appear on foliage of peaches, cherries, apricots etc. Use copper sprays.	Pick off and destroy leaves at first sight. Use copper sprays.
Potato/tomato blight	Spreading brown patches appear on leaves and infected potato tubers rot in store. Attacks prevalent in hot humid weather.	Remove infected stems a fortnight before lifting potatoes. Inspect stored crops. Spray crops with copper hydroxide as preventative.
Potato scab	Scurfy patches occur on tuber surface. Disease is only skin deep – eating quality unaffected. Prevalent on light soils.	Use compost but not lime before planting. Resistant strains are available.
Powdery mildew	Garden menace! White powdery deposit on leaves, stems, buds and fruit on roses. Worst in hot dry weather	Mulch in hot dry weather. Spray with baking powder, cooking oil and soft soap.
Root rot and food crop rots (e.g. brown rot)	Affects all plants, particularly vegetables. Leaves wilt and turn yellow, roots and stem bases blacken and rot.	Avoid cold and wet conditions. Improve soil drainage, lift and destroy infected plants. Rotate crops.
Rust	Raised pustules, brown, orange or black appear on leaves. Attacks numerous plants, is a serious disease on roses.	Use a fertiliser containing potash. Remove and destroy infected foliage. Use Bordeaux spray but roses may require chemical treatment.
Stem rot	Brown patch develops at stem base but roots are not affected. Serious disease on tomatoes.	Disinfect greenhouse between crops. Cut out diseased area if slight. Remove and destroy plant if badly affected.
Virus	All sorts of distortions, discoloration and growth problems are produced depending on plant	No cure. Destroy affected plant if you're sure it's a viral infection. Keep sap sucking pests under control.
White rot	Leaves of onions and leeks turn yellow and wilt. Fluffy white mould appears at base of bulbs. Worst in hot, dry weather.	Rotate crops. Destroy diseased plants.
Wilt	Leaves wilt even in moist soil and tissue inside stems is often stained brown.	No cure. Do not grow susceptible plants in area again.

Fearsome fungus

Fungal diseases are legion, particularly trouble-some and are indiscriminate about their choice of plant hosts – they grow their creeping grey beards on all sorts. The majority of fungi get their nourishment from dead material, but some eat living organisms. They cause many gruesome diseases: damping off of seedlings, wheat rust, smuts, wilts, mildews, club root, potato blight, botrytis, root rots, storage rots, scab, canker, silver leaf, peach leaf curl, honey fungus, coral spot and Dutch elm disease. As a general rule, the best way to avoid fungal take-over is to ensure that the soil is well drained, the crops have adequate air and light, and that they're not overcrowded. Regrettably, the gardener has little control over the hot humid weather conditions or prolonged periods of damp that fungi adore.

Mildews thrive on damp foliage so avoid overhead watering which also spreads fungal spores – for this reason many flowers and most vegetables are best watered at root level.

Disease identification and control

Consult the chart opposite for identification and management of common diseases.

Low or non-toxic fungicides

Bordeaux mixture

A standard organic fungicide containing copper sulphate and calcium hydroxide (hydrated lime). Effective against a wide range of parasitic fungi

and bacteria. Pathogens do not seem to develop resistance to it as they do to many fungicides. Always use the mix within an hour, when it will stick well and withstand light rain. After an hour it will start to separate.

Bordeaux is used as a spray at bud swell for deciduous plants, after blossoming for evergreens and at half strength on grapes and vegetables throughout the season for downy mildew. Bordeaux paste is useful for collar rot and pruning wounds.

Burgundy mixture

Used for the same diseases as Bordeaux mixture. Dissolve 22 g (¾ oz) copper sulphate in 1 litre (35 fl oz) of hot water and leave to cool overnight. Dissolve 30 g (1 oz) washing soda (sodium bicarbonate) in 1 litre of cold water, and mix the two solutions together. Do all the mixing in plastic buckets and use immediately.

Chamomile tea

A mild fungicide. Cover a handful of flowers in boiling water, or use a tea bag, and spray when cool. Chamomile tea is useful for damping off (trickle round seedlings), or for spraying on fruit every few days to ward off brown rot.

Chive tea

Used in the same way as chamomile tea, but is also a general insect repellent, so avoid using it where you know you have high proportions of beneficial insects. It is effective against apple scab if sprayed in late winter before bud swell.

Condy's crystals

An effective old fashioned remedy for powdery mildew. Dissolve 7 g (⅓ oz) potassium permanganate (Condy's crystals) in 7 litres (12 pt) water. Spray at once.

Copper hydroxide

This is preferable to copper oxychloride, which contains chlorine. Treats many fungal diseases on ornamentals and vegetables.

Garlic spray

Garlic is an effective fungicide, but it is also an insecticide and insect repellent, so use with discretion. Useful for fusarium wilt, brown rot and curly leaf.

Black spot on rose foliage.

Botrytis (grey mould).

Lime sulphur
Treats fungus and lichen

Seaweed spray
Sprayed monthly, this feeds and protects plants against brown rot, black spot, curly leaf and other fungal and bacterial diseases.

Sodium bicarbonate (baking soda)
Use for powdery mildew on grapes, cucurbits, pansies, roses and other ornamentals and black spot on roses. Mix 1 litre (35 fl oz) water and 1 teaspoon each of baking soda and cooking oil together with a squirt of pure, soft-soap mixture to aid stickability.

This mixture works best if the leaves are hosed first to wash off as much of the covering of powdery spores as possible, as these tend to prevent the spray wetting the leaf surface properly.

Fighting the good fight
The old adage that prevention is better than cure is never truer than when applied to garden pests, weeds and diseases. The following is a checklist summary of the ways in which we can effect a resistance movement by helping to build health into our plants.

- Ensure that soil is well drained.
- Provide plenty of air circulation around plants.
- Ensure plants are not overcrowded.
- Ensure plants are well fed and watered.
- Choose plants that are suited to climate, soil and location.
- Include as many disease resistant strains as possible.
- Ensure soil is conditioned and well fed with organic materials.
- Never water from overhead – fungus love wet foliage.
- Prune out tomato laterals and perform cutting back activities on all plants only on dry, sunny days – never on wet, humid days. Wounds will then heal quickly, thus preventing entry of the spores, fungi and bacteria that cause disease.
- Seal major pruning wounds on trees and shrubs instantly with an appropriate preparation.
- If you've had to dig out, cut back or prune a diseased plant, sterilise your tools by dipping them in a bucket of disinfectant before using them on another plant.
- Use benign preventative sprays such as Bordeaux mixture, Burgundy mixture and copper hydroxide in hot humid weather or at the first sign of disease, preventative traps for insect pests, and appropriate non-toxic pesticides when a pest reaches unacceptable levels.
- No matter how hard it might be, learn to live with an acceptable measure of pests and disease.
- A tidy garden is a healthy garden – remove dead or decaying plants and garden debris on which diseases will form and feed, and piles of rubbish, old pots etc in which pests will hide.
- If, with the best care you can give it, a plant persists in disease or pest infestation it is probably unsuited to your specific conditions and location. Harden your heart and remove it.

Finally, when a plant is weakened by pests or disease, try to look at the plant as a whole. Generally speaking, a healthy plant will repel disease and withstand a certain amount of insect attack with its own built-in defence mechanisms. If you have a serious disease or pest problem treat these, but try to discover why the plant/crop is so vulnerable. Is it unsuited to cultivation in your climate, soil and location? Does it need more or less water/feeding/sun/shelter, etc? The answer may be quite straightforward and save the time and labour you are otherwise investing in struggling on with an unsuitable or stressed-out plant.

Genetic engineering

Some plants can be genetically engineered to produce their own insecticide. Genetic engineering can also be used to repel pests. For example, snowdrops (*Galanthus nivalis*) make a protein that deters sap-sucking insects from eating them. Scientists have identified the gene that makes this protein and implanted it into crops such as potatoes, tobacco and wheat. The mechanism by which this works is still under research but, because it repels pests rather than killing them, it is less likely that they will become resistant.

Among many other discoveries, chemical companies are currently producing herbicide tolerant and insect resistant soybeans, brassicas, flax, tobacco, tomato, petunia, alfalfa, soy bean, forest trees, sunflowers, wheat, cotton and canola (rapeseed oil). They claim that these crops will drastically reduce wastage through pest infestation and diseases, the resultant increasing crop yields helping to feed the burgeoning world population.

In theory this is an eminently logical solution, but genetic engineering is in its infancy and we cannot yet tell the long-term effects. Chemical companies argue that such crops will reduce the need for chemical spraying and reduce carbon dioxide emissions through reduction in usage of agricultural and horticultural machinery.

But how will the changed chemistry of the plants affect both the plants and the people who eat them, and how quickly will the pests become resistant to agents such as Bt? Will 'copy genes' incorporated into a plant 'escape' and transfer to another species with unwanted consequences?

Joy Bergelson, professor of ecology and evolution at Chicago University, recently discovered that a weed that was altered by scientists to resist a herbicide developed a 20 times greater ability to pollinate other plants and to pass on its traits. The results of Bergelson's study raise the possibility of superweeds impervious to weedkillers being created from weeds crossed with brassicas, soy or maize altered to be resistant to specific pesticides. It also substantially highlights the probability of irretrievable 'transgene escape' or the spread of certain traits from one genetically modified plant to another.

Final thoughts

It would be unrealistic, in view of world population, to imagine that we could entirely do without chemicals, but we can reduce their usage by employing more benign methods whenever possible. We must also remember that it is a mistake to adopt the attitude that the only safe chemicals are those that come from natural sources such as plants.

As we've seen, substances such as derris dust and pyrethrum are harmful to both good and bad insects, and to fish and to some aquatic organisms. Some of the most noxious chemicals (digitalis, strychnine, cocaine) and deadly poisons are obtained from plants. It is wiser to take the median view that whenever we can replace a chemical herbicide or pesticide that is a registered poison with a plant derivative one offering low toxicity, we must do so.

Healthy gardens certainly don't happen by accident. They result from a combination of positive factors: sound and sensible horticultural practice, the way in which the garden has been managed in the previous and earlier seasons, the soil quality and site conditions, the weather in any particular season, judicious use of chemical sprays with biological pest and disease control – and not a little measure of good luck.

Excuses to use if pests, weeds and diseases are overwhelming your plot:
- The butterfies love those nettles!
- We breed the aphids as food for ladybirds.
- Dandelions make such delicious wine!
- That's our wildflower/conservation garden.
- The children do so love making daisy chains.
- Oxalis is such an effective ground cover.
- You mean you've never eaten ground elder?

CHAPTER FIVE

COMPANION PLANTING

Companion planting is not a new concept. For many centuries before the widespread use of chemical pesticides, gardeners of ancient civilisations observed that certain plants attracted beneficial insects and that others, such as herbs with pungent perfumes, repelled insect pests. They also recorded observations about the effect of one group of plants upon another; for example, how potatoes and tomatoes planted together inhibit each other's growth, or how tomatoes, cabbages, beets, carrots and parsley planted together give bumper crops.

There is, however, a good deal of myth and magic about companion planting. The important thing is to experiment and see what combinations work for you. I've been a nasturtium fan since the plants scrambled of their own accord through my potato and tomato plots and raced up the French

Opposite and above: Examples of compatible planting combinations. Some plants attract beneficial insects while others repel insect pests.

bean poles. That season I had the best blight-, disease- and pest-free crops ever. The following year the same crops planted without the insect repelling nasturtiums succumbed to blight and infestation by whitefly, green beetles, aphids and other monsters that exist only to break the gardener's heart. Now both nasturtiums and edibles are ceremoniously sown together because this example of companion planting really does work for me. This season I'm also experimenting with allowing the plant to scramble up through apple trees, having read that it repels codling moth. This planting combination certainly makes an appealing sight, and so far shows every sign of being efficient.

Allelopathy
Horticultural scientists, anxious for a scientific explanation for why some plants, particularly vegetables, can make bad neighbours, refer to the phenomenon as allelopathy, and define it as 'growth inhibition as the consequence of the influence of one organism on another'. Plants can

Companion planting in the vegetable garden can increase crop yields and deter pests.

inhibit the performance of another. Aware that certain plants can disadvantage each other, horticulturists have realised the corollary to this is that compatible planting combinations could increase crop yields without recourse to chemical fertilisers and pesticides.

This is often noticed in the vegetable garden where, despite the best of care, a crop will fail to thrive; yet planted with different neighbours at the other end of the bed it will give bumper crops. Carrots and onions are an excellent example of compatible crops. If you try to plant too many onions in the one area they will starve each other and the total yield will drop. But you can fit a whole planting of carrots in the same area at the same time. Onions have shallow surface roots whereas carrots have deep tap roots, so the two plants don't have to compete for light and air. Carrots fork and go all to leaf with little root if their diet is too rich; onions are gross feeders and take up all the extra nutrients. Onions deter carrot fly, and carrots deter onion fly.

We also know that marigolds, dahlias, salvias, and asparagus, for example, give off chemical secretions from their roots that are effective in controlling nematodes, the soil worms that are a nuisance to both crops and ornamentals.

In a self-sustaining environment a wide variety of plants grow naturally in close communities. They don't grow in rows or as a huge number of one kind as in monoculture systems. The greater the diversity of plants the closer the balance between beneficial predatory insects and the undesirable pests on which they feed. So we accept that companion planting together with crop rotation provides specific benefits to fruit, vegetables, herbs, and ornamentals. The Elizabethan method of 'barrier planting' alternates a row of vegetables with a row of their specific companion herb or flower – for example, nasturtiums between brassica clumps to control aphids; alternate rows of garlic and chives between rows of lettuce; and peas, rosemary, thyme, hyssop and sage between other edibles to repel undesirable pests and attract beneficial insects.

I've always felt that the phrase 'companion planting' is a little limiting – a better phrase would be companion planting and crop compatibility since both practices comprise the whole. The aim of both techniques is simply to provide the best

exude phytotoxin, referred to as allelochemicals, that can kill other plants in a number of ways, such as reducing their cell division or nutrient uptake, and thus reduce competition.

A classic example is the black walnut. Although some plants can be grown successfully under this tree, many others, including apples, azaleas and most subtropical vegetables, quickly sicken and die. Most pine trees also produce undergrowth suppressing toxins, and couch (twitch) growing among crops noticeably reduces yields. It is recognised that the exudations from grass roots stunt the growth of fruit trees, particularly apple and pear, which are rarely happy when planted in a lawn

Good companions

We now know that the essential growth substances – root excretions, oils, minerals and perfume – exuded by one plant or crop can directly

Vegetables and their companions

Vegetable	Latin name	Good companions	Poor companions
Asparagus	*Asparagus officinalis*	parsley, tomato	onion
Aubergine	*Solanum melongena*	pea, tarragon, thyme	
Bean, French	*Phaseolus vulgaris*	beetroot, borage, cabbage, carrot, cauliflower,	chive, fennel, garlic,
Bean, broad	*Vicia faba*	marigold, squash, strawberry, sweetcorn, tomato	leek
Beetroot	*Beta vulgaris*	cabbage, kohlrabi	runner bean
Broccoli	*Brassica oleracea*	bean, celery, chamomile, dill, mint, nasturtium, onion, oregano, potato, sage, rosemary	lettuce, strawberry, tomato
Brussels sprout	*Brassica oleracea*	bean, celery, dill, hyssop, mint, nasturtium, potato, sage, rosemary	grape, strawberry, tomato
Carrot	*Daucus carota*	bean, leek, onion, pea, radish, rosemary, sage, scorzonera, tomato, wormwood	dill
Cauliflower	*Brassica oleracea*	bean, beetroot, celery, chamomile, dill, hyssop, mint, nasturtium, onion, oregano, potato, sage, radish, rosemary	strawberry, tomato
Celeriac	*Apium graveolens*	bean, cabbage, leek, onion, tomato	
Celery	*Apium graveolens*	bean, cabbage, leek, onion, tomato	
Corn	*Zea mays*	bean, lupin, melon, pea, squash	
Courgette	*Cucubita pepo*	bean, mint, nasturtium, radish, sweetcorn	potato
Cucumber	*Cucumis sativus*	bean, broccoli, celery, Chinese cabbage, lettuce, pea, radish, tomato	sage
Horseradish	*Armoracia rusticana*	potato	
Kohlrabi	*Brassica oleracea*	beetroot, onion	bean, pepper, tomato
Leek	*Allium porrum*	carrot, celeriac, celery	broad bean, broccoli
Lettuce	*Lactuca sativa*	beetroot, cabbage, clover, pea, radish, strawberry	
Marrow	*Cucurbita pepo*	bean, mint, nasturtium, radish, sweetcorn	potato
Melon	*Cucumis melo*	corn, peanut, sunflower	
Onion	*Allium cepa*	beetroot, cabbage, carrot, lettuce, potato, strawberry, tomato	bean, pea
Pea	*Pisum sativum*	aubergine, carrot, cucumber, lettuce, radish, spinach, sweetcorn, tomato, turnip	
Pepper	*Capsicum*	basil, carrot, lovage, marjoram, onion, oregano	fennel, kohlrabi
Potato	*Solanum tuberosum*	bean, cabbage, lettuce, onion, petunia, marigold, radish, sweetcorn	apple, pumpkin, tomato
Pumpkin	*Cucurbita moschata*	bean, mint, nasturtium, radish, sweetcorn	potato
Radish	*Raphanus sativus*	bean, cabbage, cauliflower, cucumber, lettuce, pea, squash, tomato	grape, hyssop
Spinach	*Oleracea*	aubergine, cabbage, celery, onion, pea, strawberry	
Squash	*Cucurbita moschata*	bean, mint, nasturtium, radish, sweetcorn	
Turnip	*Brassica rapa*	pea	

environment for growing vegetables and flowers by selecting the correct plants as neighbours. The quick reference tables throughout this chapter provide lists of good and bad companions.

How companion plants work

Repellent and attractor plants fall into seven categories according to their attributes. These plants are able to do one or more of the following:

- attract predatory beneficial insects
- both attract beneficial insects and act as host plants
- mask the scent of plants that are being targeted by pests
- actively repel pests
- kill pests as spray concentrations
- kill or control fungal diseases and bacteria
- accumulate and store essential nutrients in their foliage.

Some plants are so versatile that they can combine several of these virtues – in addition to beavering away attracting, repelling, or storing nutrients,

they may also be used to make benign plant-derivative sprays.

Acquisitive plants

Some companion plants are 'accumulator' plants – that is, their roots draw valuable trace minerals and nutrients from the soil and store them in their leaves. This makes them valuable for mulching and composting. Underplantings of both nasturtiums and comfrey make the best of companions

Crop compatibility: nasturtiums repel brassica pests and help prevent club root.

for fruit trees, as they not only repel insect pests, they also provide rich nutrients as they die back.

Super scenters

We appreciate the effect richly scented flowers have upon people, but we don't always realise the profound effect of their perfume on insects and other plants.

Their pungent or sweet-smelling exudations are given off in the form of volatile oils, which surround the plant in an invisible cloud of minute, airborne droplets of essential essence. These are believed to chemically stimulate and enhance the growth of other plants, at the same time both repelling insect pests and attracting insects that are beneficial. Lavender is just one example of a 'super scenter'.

Masqueraders

Some scented plants may act as 'masking plants', their volatile oils emitting odours so strong that they mask the scent of the plants the pests want to devour, repelling or deflecting them to less susceptible specimens. Cabbage white butterflies are strongly attracted to the herb hyssop and to mustard (*Brassica nigra*) and will abandon cabbages if these plants are planted in adjacent clumps or borders. Also emitting pungent perfumes, pyrethrum, coreopsis, asters, chrysanthemums, garlic, lavender, chives, wormwood and cosmos all act as pest repellents.

Pest confusers

All strongly scented culinary herbs and flowers can be used as 'pest confusers' either by planting them close to the 'victim' plants; by cutting their leaves to mulch tender new transplants; or by steeping them in water to make organic insecticides. For example, a handful of the leaves of feverfew or wormwood give an excellent insect repellent mulch, and both make repellent sprays.

Pest repellent plants

Basil: The basils (*Ocimum* spp) are truly the gardener's friend – bees love them, aphids, fruit-fly, white fly and the house fly loathe them. Loving the sun's trapped heat, they are especially effective in the greenhouse, where greenflies and whiteflies often build up to unacceptable proportions. Underplant tomatoes and beans with basils for bumper insect-free crops.

Borage (*Borago officinalis*) improves the flavour of curcubits and tomatoes, protects strawberries against mildews, and deters pests such as stink bugs and flea beetles from cucurbits. The plant also serves as an attractant for aphids, which might at first seem like an excellent idea for not growing it – but see how you feel when the borage next to your dwarf beans is liberally adorned with the pest, while your beans remain totally unscathed! Since borage self sows readily, remove the pest-infested plants and burn them as soon as new seedlings appear.

Spider flower – perfect pest-attractor
The best companion plant I've found for attracting plagues of green and brown sap-sucking beetles is *Cleome spinosa*, the 'spider flower'. The pests congregate in huge numbers on these plants instead of chewing other treasures to bits. I plant clumps alongside pathways, and if the infestations of beetles become unacceptably high, I reduce their numbers by shaking them off the plants onto the pathways, where they are dealt to by treading them underfoot!

Marigolds give off chemical secretions which repel soil nematodes and many insect pests.

Calendula (*Calendula officinalis*): Pot marigolds keep whitefly away from tomatoes and beans and deter aphids.

Chervil (*Anthriscus cerefolium*): Protects lettuce against aphids, mildew, snails and slugs; also deters ants.

Chives (*Allium schoenoprasum*): Particularly beneficial as companion plants to roses, helping prevent black spot and mildew. Like garlic, deters aphids and a wide range of other pests.

Dill (*Antheum graveolens*): Annual but self sows. Attracts bees and beneficial insects, repels carrot fly, red spider mite, white cabbage moth, slugs and snails.

Garlic (*Allium sativum*): Garlic (and other members of the onion family) have been valued since ancient times for their insect repellent properties and the noisome herb is now made into a wide range of benign pesticides. Used as a spray, garlic makes the foliage of plants unpalatable to chewing insects, and grown as plants, confuses the white cabbage butterfly, aphids, carrot fly and other pests by masking the scent of the target plants. Garlic and chives make excellent companion plants for roses and other ornamentals since they discourage fungus diseases and mildews.

The active ingredients of garlic are complex organic sulphides, which can kill or repel a range of pests – aphids, woolly aphids, bean fly, stink and horned bugs, crickets, grasshoppers, locusts, red spider mite, sawfly larvae (including pear and cherry slug), scale, snails, slugs, thrips, mealy bugs, leaf miners and wireworms. It is also deadly to caterpillars, especially those of cabbage moths and butterflies.

Garlic is also an effective fungicide, and if used as a spray at fortnightly intervals will help prevent blight on potatoes. Double strength garlic sprayed on fruit trees at leaf fall and bud swell will decrease the chances of bacterial infections and curly leaf, and will stop the spread of brown rot. (See recipe later in this chapter.)

Marigolds (*Tagetes tenuifolia*): Repel aphids, cabbage white butterflies, pumpkin beetles, cutworm, spider mites, and onion maggot above ground and nematodes under ground.

Nasturtiums (*Trapeolum majus*): Come in dwarf and climbing varieties. Set among cabbage family plants, celery and cucumbers, they will repel beetles, aphids, and caterpillars and improve the flavour of cucumber, radishes and zucchini. Nasturtiums repel woolly aphids but they attract the black variety – a good reason for planting them because, like borage, they act as a decoy plant. Again this is lateral thinking – it's better to have legions of the black pest on the nasturtiums than on the cabbages!

Tansy (*Tanacetum vulgare*): Grows to 1.4 m (4½ ft). Contains an oil, tanacetum, that has strong insect repellent qualities. Deters ants, aphids, fleas, flies, fruit fly and moths.

Other pest repellent plants well employed in our gardens to promote biological pest control would include brassicas that are left to flower, parsnips, carrots, parsley, angelica, dill, fennel, red clover, thyme and coriander. Not only repellent to pests, but also attractive to predatory beneficial insects are bergamot, dill, mints, spearmint, yarrow, artemisias, Michaelmas daisies, daisy species and cosmos.

horticulture and agriculture is practised. The predatory insects it hosts help control white butterfly and aphid pests.

Phacelia (45 cm/18 in) is a beautiful plant with filmy foliage and fluffy blue flower heads freely borne over an extended period. It attracts that most voracious of predators, the hoverfly. The adult female needs to eat pollen to bring her eggs to maturity and be assured of colonies of aphids on which to feed the larvae. The hoverfly resembles a honey bee in shape, but displays brilliant metallic colours. Adult flies have a short tongue, so in addition to phacelia – which is their favourite food – it is advisable to arrange other suitable plantings such as marigolds, poached egg flower (*Limnanthes douglasii*), and 'baby blue-eyes' (*Nemophilia*). Hoverflies will also eat aphids, scale insects, small caterpillars and caterpillar eggs, which makes them deserving of bed and breakfast in any garden!

Phacelia also attracts other predatory insects such as lacewings, ladybirds and praying mantises. The lacewing preys on aphids, mealy bugs, thrips, scale insects, moth eggs and mites, including those of the red spider. The food fetish of that other most beneficial insect, the praying mantis, includes caterpillars, aphids and leaf hoppers.

Phacelia – the ideal host

Beneficial insects not only prey on insects pests, many also ensure a high rate of cross pollination and thus increased fertility in the garden. A valuable host plant on which beneficial insects may feed and breed is *Phacelia tanacetifolia*, which is used in countries where sustainable

Herbs and their companions

Herb	Latin name	Good companions	Poor companions
Anise	Pimpinella anisum	bean, coriander	carrot
Basil	Ocimum basilicum	bean, cabbage, tomato	rue
Borage	Borago officinalis	strawberry, tomato	
Caraway	Carum carvi	pea	fennel
Chamomile	Chamaemelum nobile	cucumber, mint, onion	
Chervil	Anthriscus cerefolium	carrot, radish	
Chive	Allium schoenoprasum	carrot, grape, parsley, tomato	bean, pea
Coriander	Coriandum sativum	anise, potato	fennel
Dill	Anethum graveolens	cabbage, lettuce, onion	carrot, tomato
Fennel	Foeniculum vulgare		bean, caraway, coriander, dill, tomato
Garlic	Allium sativum	carrot, rose, tomato	bean, pea, strawberry
Hyssop	Hyssopus officinalis	cabbage, grape, plants in general	radish
Lemon balm	Melissa officinalis	tomato	
Lovage	Levisticum officinale	bean	
Marjoram	Origanum majorana	plants in general	
Mint	Mentha	cabbage, plants in general	parsley
Oregano	Origanum vulgare	cabbage, cucumber	
Parsley	Petroselinum crispum	asparagus, carrot, chive, tomato	mint
Rosemary	Rosmarinus officinalis	bean, cabbage, carrot	potato
Rue	Ruta graveolens	rose	basil, cabbage, sage
Sage	Salvia officinalis	cabbage, carrot, marjoram, strawberry, tomato	cucumber, rue
Savory	Satureja	bean, onion	
Tansy	Tanacetum vulgare	blackberry, pepper, potato, raspberry	
Tarragon	Artemisia dracunculus	plants in general	
Thyme	Thymus	cabbage, plants in general	
Yarrow	Achillea	plants in general	

Hosts and attractor plants for beneficial insects

Many of the predators that live off insect pests can be attracted to the garden by providing host plants on which they may breed and feed. Their presence will never rid the garden of pests, but it will keep them at controllable levels. The beneficial predatory wasps referred to are *Encarsia formosa*, which parasitise the eggs of aphids, caterpillars, greenfly, whitefly and other insect pests. Many of the beneficial insects referred to are attracted to almost all the plants listed below.

Common name	Latin name	Insect attracted
Amaranth (pigweed)	*Amaranthus*	ground beetles
Anise	*Pimpinella anisum*	beneficial wasps
Bergamot (bee balm)	*Monarda didyma*	bees, hoverflies, beneficial wasps and others
Borage	*Borago officinalis*	bees, hoverflies, beneficial wasps, ladybirds and others
Brassica (flowers)	*Brassica* spp	hoverflies, lacewings, ladybirds, beneficial to insects
Buddleia (butterfly bush)	*Buddleia davidii*	butterflies, bees, beneficial to insects
Carrot (flowers)	*Daucus carota*	bees, hoverflies, lacewings, beneficial wasps and others
Catmint	*Nepeta cataria*	bees, hoverflies, lacewings, beneficial wasps and others
Celery (flowers)	*Apium graveolens*	beneficial wasps
Cerinthe	*Cerinthe major*	bees, hoverflies, beneficial wasps, lacewings, ladybirds, beneficial to insects
Chamomile	*Chamaemelum nobile*	hoverflies, beneficial wasps
Chervil	*Anthriscus cerefolium*	hoverflies, beneficial wasps and others
Cleome	*Cleome bassieriana*	host plant to insects pests such as greenshield and bronze beetles, which congregate in on these plants and are easily destroyed
Clover	*Trifolium*	ground beetles; parasites of woolly apple aphids
Coriander	*Coriandum sativum*	all beneficial insects
Cosmos	*Cosmos atrosanguineas*	lacewings, hoverflies, ladybirds, beneficial wasps and others
Dandelion	*Taraxacum officinale*	beneficial wasps
Dill	*Anethum graveolens*	bees, hoverflies, beneficial wasps, beneficial to insects
Fennel	*Foeniculum vulgare*	hoverflies, praying mantis and other parasites
Gaillardia	*Gaillardia* spp	beneficial wasps, ladybirds, hoverflies, lacewings and others
Goldenrod	*Solidago*	diamondback moth parasites, all beneficial insects
Hawthorn	*Crataegus*	hoverflies, beneficial wasps and others
Ivy	*Hedera helix*	hoverflies and beneficial wasps
Lavender	*Lavandula* spp	bees, beneficial wasps
Limnanthes (poached egg plant)	*Limnanthes douglasii*	hoverflies, lacewings, beneficial wasps, bees and others
Marigold	*Tagetes*	hoverflies
Marjoram and oregano	*Origanum* spp	all beneficial insects
Milkweed	*Asclepias*	several parasites
Mint	*Mentha*	hoverflies, and several wasps and other beneficial insects
Mustard	*Brassica hirta*	various parasites
Nemophilia (baby blue eyes)	*Nemophilia* spp	hoverflies, lacewings, ladybirds, beneficial wasps, bees and others
Parsnip flowers	*Pastinaca sativa*	hoverflies, beneficial wasps, lacewings and others
Peanut	*Arachis hypogaea*	predatory spiders on *Ostrinia furnacalis*
Phacelia	*Phacelia tanacetifolia*	attracts all beneficial predatory insects
Ragweed	*Ambrosia*	parasites for oriental fruit moths and strawberry leaf rollers
Sedum	*Sedum* spp	bees, butterflies, ladybirds, beneficial wasps and others
Soybean	*Glycine max*	trichogramma wasps
Spurry	*Spergula arvensis*	several insects that prey on cabbage pests
Stinging nettle	*Urtica dioica*	many beneficial insects
Strawberry	*Fragaria*	parasites of the fruit moth
Sunflower	*Helianthus*	lacewings, beneficial wasps
Tansy	*Tanacetum vulgare*	ladybirds
Yarrow	*Achillea*	ladybirds, predatory wasps

Attractor plants for beneficial predatory insects

Some of the more common plants that attract beneficial predatory insects are balm of Gilead (*Cedronella canariensis*), calendula, cerinthe major, catmint, chives, cosmos, coriander, dill, elder, eucalypts, fennel, garlic, chives, gaillardia, hyssop, lavender, lemon ironwood, marjoram and oregano, melaleucas, mints, mustards, onions, parsnips, phacelia, perilla, rosemary, savory, sunflowers, tansy and turnips.

See above for a full list of attractor and host plants for beneficial insects.

Anti-fungal and anti-bacterial plants

These include allocasuarina, basils, chamomile, chives, elder, garlic, garlic chives, horseradish, horsetails, hyssop, lilac, melaleuca, nettles and tomato. Interplant these with any species that are prone to fungal diseases; for example, roses, grapes, cucurbits.

Companion planting and crop compatibility – scientific fact or fiction? Personally I bow to the secret, silent alchemy of plants. May your garden be a companionable one!

Borders of pungent herbs mask the scent of crops irresistible to pests.

Pest deterring plants

One alternative to using pesticides is to use plants that repel, kill or otherwise deter pests. Observe which pests are most troublesome in your garden and plant the appropriate repellent plants. The plants marked with an asterisk fulfil the dual role of repelling undesirable pests and attracting beneficial insects.

Plant name	Latin name	Claimed effects
African marigold	Tagetes erecta	Reduces nematodes, aphids, caterpillars
Alfalfa, or lucerne	Medicago sativa	Reduces corn wireworms
Anise	Pimpinella anisum	Deters aphids, fleas, reduces cabbage worms
Artemisia	Artemisia spp	Repels slugs and snails, biting and chewing insects
Basil	Ocimum basilcum	Controls variety of pests including greenfly, whitefly
Bean (flowers)*	Phaseolus	Reduces corn armyworms; attracts beneficial insects
Black nightshade*	Solanum nigrum	Reduces Colorado beetles; poisons larvae; attracts beneficial insects
Borage*	Borago officinalis	Attracts bees; reduces Japanese beetles on potatoes and deters tomato hornworms; attracts aphids away from valued plants
Broccoli	Brassica oleracea	Reduces striped cucumber beetles
Calendula	Calendula officinalis	Deters whitefly, greenfly, aphids
Chamomile	Chamaemelum nobile	Repels thrips, cabbage white butterflies
Caper spurge	Euphorbia lathrus	Deters moles
Carrot	Daucus carota	Deters onion flies
Castor bean	Ricinus communis	Controls moles, mosquitos and nematodes
Catnip*	Nepeta cataria	Deters ants, aphids, Colorado beetles, darking beetles, flea beetles, Japanese beetles, squash bugs, weevils, attracts beneficial insects
Celery	Apium graveolens	Deters cabbage butterflies
Chervil	Anthriscus cerefolium	Deters aphids, slugs and snails
Chilli peppers	Capsicum spp	Made into spray kills and repels many insect pests
Chive	Allium schoenoprasum	Cures blackspot on roses; deters Japanese beetles, aphids; discourages insects from climbing fruit trees
Chrysanthemum	Chrysanthemum coccineum	Reduces nematodes
Citronella	Cympobogon spp	Oil is used as general insect repellent
Clover	Trifolium	Deters cabbage root flies
Coriander	Coriandum sativum	Deters Colorado beetles
Corn	Zea mays	Reduces striped cucumber beetles
Dandelion	Taraxacum officinale	Repels Colorado beetles
Dead nettle	Lamium album	Deters potato bugs
Dill*	Anethum graveolens	Repels aphids and spider mites, attracts bees and beneficial insects
Dog bane	Plectranthus ornatus	General insect repellent
Elderberry	Sambucus	General insect repellent
Eucalyptus	Eucalyptus	General insect repellent
Fennel	Foeniculum vulgare	Deters aphids
Feverfew	Tanacetum parthenium	General pesticide, deters wide range of insects
French marigold	Tagetes patula	Deters Mexican bean beetles, nematodes, aphids
Garlic	Allium sativum	General insect repellent, deters Japanese beetles, caterpillars
Horseradish	Armoracia rusticana	Deters Colorado beetles
Hyssop	Hyssopus officinalis	Repels fleas, insect larvae; attracts cabbage white butterflies and caterpillars; reduces Colorado beetles

Odiferous feverfew daisy, *Tanacetum parthenium*, repels pests.

Plant name	Latin name	Claimed effects
Johnson grass	*Sorghum halepense*	Reduces Willamette mites on vines
Lavender cotton	*Santolina chamaecyparissus*	Deters corn wireworms and southern rootworms
Leek	*Allium ampeloprasum*	Deters carrot flies
Marigold	*Tagetes*	Reduces nematodes, cabbage pests, aphids
Marjoram and oregano	*Origanum* spp	Deter pumpkin beetles, cabbage white butterflies, onion maggots
Melalencas	*Myrtaceae* spp	Oil repels many insects
Mints	*Mentha* spp	Repels cabbage white butterflies, aphids, beetles, woolly aphids, ants, mosquitoes
Mustard	*Brassica nigra*	Reduces aphids; attracts cabbage white butterflies and caterpillars
Nasturtium	*Tropaeolium majus*	Reduces aphids, cabbage worms, Colorado beetles, woolly aphids, deters squash bugs and white flies
Neem	*Azadirachta indica*	General botanic insecticide; repels wide variety sucking and chewing insects
Onion	*Allium cepa*	Deters Colorado beetles, carrot flies
Parsnips	*Pastinaca sativa*	As spray is toxic to fruit flies, house flies, red spider mites, aphids
Peanut	*Arachus hypogaea*	Deters *Ostrinia furnacalis*
Pelargoniums	*Geranium* spp	General insect repellent
Petunia	*Petunia*	Repels Mexican bean beetles, potato bugs and squash bugs
Pot marigold	*Calendula officinalis*	Deters asparagus beetles, tomato hornworms, aphids, white cabbage butterflies and caterpillars
Potato	*Solanum tuberosum*	Deters Mexican bean beetles
Pyrethrum	*Tanacetum cineraiifolium*	Broad spectrum
Quassia	*Quassia amarama*	As spray kills aphids, caterpillars, pear and cherry slugs, sawfly larvae, spider mite and thrips
Radish	*Raphanus sativus*	Deters cucumber beetles, root flies, vine borers and many other pests
Ragweed	*Ambrosia artemisiifolia*	Reduces flea beetles
Rue	*Ruta graveolens*	Deters beetles and fleas
Rosemary*	*Rosemarinus officinalis*	Deters bean beetles, cabbage moths, carrot flies, and many other insects
Rye	*Secale*	Reduces nematodes
Sage*	*Salvia officinalis*	Deters cabbage worms, cabbage moths, and root maggots
Santolina	*Santolina chamaecyparissus*	Repels insect pests
Savory	*Saturega*	Deters Mexican bean beetles
Scorzonera	*Scorzonera hispanica*	Deters carrot flies
Southernwood	*Artemisia abrotanum*	Deters cabbage moths, carrot flies
Soybean	*Glycine max*	Deters corn earworms, corn borers
Spurry	*Spergula arvensis*	Reduces aphids, caterpillars and root worms
Sudan grass	*Sorghum sudanense*	Reduces Willamette mites on vines
Tansy	*Tanacetum vulgare*	Deters many insects including ants, aphids, fruit flies, cabbage worms, Colorado beetles, Japanese beetles, squash bugs
Thyme*	*Thymus vulgarus*	Deters cabbage loopers, cabbage worms, whiteflies
Tomato	*Lycopersicon lycopersicum*	Deters loopers, flea beetles and whiteflies on cabbage
Wormwood	*Artemisia absinthe*	General insecticide; deters mice and other rodents, slugs and snails
Yarrow	*Achillea millefolium*	Repels flies, ants, mosquitoes

CHAPTER SIX
ORGANIC EDIBLE GARDENS

Gardens are always evocative. My passion for edible gardening was nurtured in childhood when a well stocked plot of vegetables was as important to my family as fresh air and sunlight. My parents were firm believers in the old adage 'one for the birds, one for the bugs, and one for me', and all produce was grown in good home-made compost without recourse to toxic sprays or chemical fertilisers.

Today, we're faced with issues so grave they seem a world away from the natural simplicity of life in that garden. Although economic necessity is still an important consideration, it is more concern for our family's health in this age of chemical agriculture and genetic food engineering

Above: Homegrown crops are free from genetic modification and chemical residues.
Opposite: Healthy soil, healthy plants, healthy people! Food grown without recourse to chemical fertilisers and sprays.

that makes us determined to remain positive and try to grow our own food, or locate sources of organic produce.

We're now well aware of the dangers of consuming crops grown by chemical means, but just what are genetically modified (GM) foods and what risks do they pose?

Food and our future
What is genetic engineering?
For hundreds of years all food plants have been improved genetically by plant breeders to give better yield, growth, colour and taste. This has been done mainly by hybridisation of plant materials – by crossing plant species so that the new plant inherits the best of both parents.

Genetic modification focuses on the genetic codes of plants – the order in which the nitrogenous bases of DNA are arranged in the molecule.

Certified organic produce guaranteed free from genetic modification.

These genetic codes are the blueprint for every separate living organism. The characteristics of every plant, from its ability to grow and fight pests to its nutritional value, are defined by these genetic units or codes. For example, natural mutations determine a plant's ability to evolve to suit a particular niche, such as hot, arid or cold, wet soils.

Genetic engineering is the process of artificially transferring genes specific to one type of organism into another. Thereby scientists want to transfer desirable qualities from one organism to another, for example to make a crop resistant to a pest or herbicide. They have also begun to introduce genetic material from some types of fish, insects and animals into food plants such as tomatoes and potatoes.

Potential benefits and present problems
As mentioned in chapter 4, giant biotechnical companies argue that genetically modified (GM) crops will increase food yield and thus help to feed a world that will contain eight billion people by 2050. At face value, this objective seems difficult to fault, but the issue poses us with an urgent problem of the present, rather than of the future.

Fearing worldwide consumer resistance and huge financial losses once controlling legislation is introduced, biotechnology companies are taking a low profile approach to their large scale release of GM foods, meaning that virtually untested and unlabelled, huge quantities of these foodstuffs are already flooding global markets.

Scientists admit that the unforeseen consequences of GM foods could cause serious damage to human health and the environment. In Britain, researcher Dr Arpad Pusztai has presented evidence that genetically modified foods have damaged the immune system of rats. British scientists believe that certain native birds, animals and plants could be wiped out by genetically modified agriculture. Geneticists Dr John Fagan and Mae Wan Ho describe genetic engineering as 'the biggest single danger facing humanity'. Like the wonder chemicals of the 1940s, it is being unleashed without rigorous testing. And it could create new toxins, superviruses and contamination of natural crops by the escape of pollen from modified plants.

Understanding the dangers
Worldwide concern over genetically modified crops revolves around four key issues. The safety of the food itself, the risk of modified material escaping into other plants (trans-gene escape), the problems of labelling so that consumers have the choice to refuse such products, and the enormous economic power that genetically modified techniques give large multinational companies.

The danger inherent in trans-gene escape is the possibility that pollen from GM crops will contaminate non-modified plants; for example, the pollen from herbicide-resistant crops has the potential to create herbicide-resistant 'superweeds' through uncontrollable cross pollination. This would necessitate increased usage of chemical control and subsequent increased contamination of water and food. There is also the risk of the spread of diseases across species barriers.

We understand that genetic engineering could have the potential benefit of helping feed tomorrow's world, but we're also aware that it could pose the greatest danger of any technology yet introduced. Unlike chemical and nuclear contamination, gene pollution can never be cleaned up; genetic mistakes are passed to all future generations of a species. There is no way of recalling or containing a genetic modification. Once it has 'escaped' it can never be retrieved. In this instance, man cannot escape from the consequences of his own ingenuity, and the consequences are incalculable.

Unlabelled foods

In March 1999, the FDA of America reported that 60 per cent of foods on supermarket shelves all over the world are already genetically modified. They contain genes derived from, or artificially copied from fish, animals, insects, viruses and bacteria. They have not been adequately tested and as yet thousands are unlabelled.

Lack of international legislation and testing regulations at present means that manufacturers throughout the world can introduce GM ingredients into foods without assessment of the risks and without informing the consumers. The danger exists that food manufacturing consortiums will race for profit before the public, wary of uncontrolled genetic produce, exert pressure for clear identification and labelling of all such foods.

While it is necessary to keep an open mind about the possible potential benefits of genetically modified food and seeds, it is a gross infringement of human rights to be denied, through absence of labelling and clear identification, the knowledge that gives us the ability to choose what food we put into our bodies. Currently only certified organic produce is guaranteed to be free of genetic modification.

Scary New World

There are about 20 food crops that supply 90 per cent of the world's food (FDA, USA, 1998). These crops are now being genetically engineered and patented. Already world trade in seeds and food crops is becoming dominated by a few multinational biotechnological companies such as gene giant Monsanto Chemicals, who have bought hugely into world seed markets and now have a stranglehold on grains such as soya, corn and wheat. Their object is to own the genes that boost productivity, the distribution of seeds and the seeds themselves – which farmers are not allowed to sow without paying Monsanto – and to engineer crops resistant to herbicides that are owned exclusively by Monsanto, such as 'Round Up Ready Soy'.

This presents a compelling case for growing our own food and for saving our own seeds which we know have not been treated with fungicides or pesticides or subjected to genetic modification.

Heirloom seeds

In the book *Saving the Seed*, author Renée Vellve tells us:

Before plant breeding became a science and an industry it was an art: seeds were continuously selected and saved. Every house had its seedstore and every village its particular bean or barley year after year. And generation after generation the seeds were handed down as part of the family treasure. They were also given as wedding gifts, exchanged for different varieties across village boundaries, and placed in tombs when elders died.

Safeguarding the future of endangered cabbage or turnip varieties may lack the dramatic appeal of rescuing rare wild flowers or giant pandas, but saving seeds from our own plants grown by chemical-free sustainable methods is vitally important. Such seeds are not the produce of an agri-chemical monoculture seed industry, but seeds that have been grown organically in unpolluted soils and harvested by hand. By saving them we ensure they

Saving our future with the seeds of the past.

remain in the genetic pool for producing better varieties and for the use of future generations. Many varieties of vegetables and grains are disappearing around the world. Commercially grown seeds are often hybrids and unsuitable for saving, they become 'Terminator' seeds, because the gardener must buy new every year.

In addition, biotechnology companies generally show little interest in selecting and saving seed with traits such as superior taste, nutrition and natural resistance to disease. In sustainable horticulture it is believed that seeds saved from plants year after year produce better crops because the plants adapt to their specific microclimate. To achieve this it is important to be strict about saving seed each year and from only the strongest and healthiest of plants.

The modern commercial seed industry also shows little sign of a transition towards organic seed production. For this reason, growers today can rarely use organic seeds because sufficient quantities of proprietary patented lines are unavailable, or extremely expensive. Seeds for our foodstuffs actually face a future filled with more synthetic chemicals than ever before. Apart from being raised by chemical means, the seeds are then treated with insecticides and fungicides prior to sale to farmers and gardeners.

Seed savers

Fortunately, there are still small private companies, collecting, growing, multiplying and selling the seeds of older hardy fruit and vegetable varieties raised by organic methods. The plants, treasured for their hardiness, disease resistance, high nutritional values and good flavour, originate

Genetic treasures: vegetables grown from hardy heirloom seeds.

from seeds grown for hundreds of years by our ancestors and from those imported into New Zealand, Australia and America by early settlers of all nationalities.

We are fortunate that these companies have realised the value of antique edible plants and are working to ensure their survival as part of their country's history, to ensure their availability for future generations and to preserve them as a national resource both for cultivation and genetic diversity. By growing as much as possible of our own hardy, flavoursome and nutritious food from these seeds, we support the small companies that work to harvest them in the face of giant corporations, and in doing so we help perpetuate the species.

It is beyond the scope of this chapter to list the wide range of hardy heirloom fruit and vegetable seeds available to the home grower, but following are lists of international suppliers offering stock. Seeds available include those of hardy antique varieties of fruiting trees, tomatoes, potatoes, saladstuffs, peas, beans, peppers, brassicas, cucurbits, root vegetables, and many unusual foodstuffs, as well as herbs and flowers.

Today our society relies on 150 out of a possible 80,000 food plants (*Organic Horticulture*, Henry Doubleday Research Association, UK, 1998). New Zealand and Australia must import some 75 per cent of their food crop seeds from America and Europe. Only three per cent of the variety of food plants that our grandparents and great-grandparents ate in 1900 are still available today. Since 1920 we've lost 90 per cent of our vegetable seeds, 85 per cent of our fruit varieties, and our flowers are vanishing too. Once lost they are extinct. Irretrievable.

Collecting and storing seeds

Collecting one's own organically grown seed is as simple as tucking the seeding head into a waxed paper bag and securing it with a tag. Though polythene bags have the advantage of being waterproof, they're unsuitable because they prevent airflow and create seed rotting condensation. The best time for seed collection is mid-morning on a dry day when the dew has evaporated. When all the seeds have dropped, remove the bag, and clean the seed.

Wet cleaning is used for those plants that carry their seeds in moist flesh such as tomatoes, rock melons, cucumbers and pumpkins. Scoop the seeds out into a fine sieve, standing it in a container of water (this way you don't lose smaller seeds!) and rub them vigorously until loose flesh is removed. Uplift the sieve, drain off excess water and then turn the seeds onto a plate or paper and place in a warm airy place, turning occasionally to dry naturally for about 10 days.

Dry cleaning is used for seeds maturing in a dry capsule, pod, husk or case, such as peas, beans, sweetcorn, popcorn, maize, radish, lettuce, carrot, onion, beet, okra and many garden flower seeds. Once the plant has gone to seed, it may be pulled up and hung over a catching receptacle or sheet indoors, or the dry pods may be harvested individually.

Place the seeds in an airtight container labelled with the name of the plant, date of seed collection, and store. Most garden seeds will last a year or two simply by keeping them in a cool, dry dark place. Others will last from three to six years or longer. An alternative method for long term storage is to put them in the fridge or freezer in an airtight waterproof container. Put a piece of garlic, rue or pennyroyal in your seeds if shelf stored to inhibit bugs and fungi.

Sowing the seeds

Large seeds such as those of cucurbits, beans and corn do better if they're sown directly into enriched soil worked to a fine tilth, while the small seeds of lettuces, onions and tomatoes are better started in seedling trays.

However, if you live in a cold climate and want to start your seedlings off early, then you'll need to start them off in containers. For best results use a fine seed-raising mix, or make your own by sieving home-made compost and adding peat and fine pumice, in equal quantities. Other mixes might include some good sieved soil, with a lightening component such as peat moss, well-rotted leaf humus or mushroom compost and some sharp river sand. The fertility does not have to be high, and manure and compost content should be well matured.

If you can't make your own mix and have no recycled containers because you're starting from scratch, commercially prepared seed-raising mix and a wide variety of seedling containers are available from garden centres.

For sowing the seeds of larger plants I like to use peat pots, or milk/cream cartons that can then be planted straight into the ground together with the mature seedlings. This prevents root disturbance, and the pot quickly rots allowing roots to penetrate surrounding soil.

Highly recommended for sowing smaller seeds are reusable cell tray containers with multiple compartments. This avoids wastage and overcrowding, and cuts out the time-consuming and tedious process called 'pricking out' – transplant-

Suppliers of heirloom seeds

New Zealand
Koanga Gardens, RD 2 Maungaturoto, Northland.
Tel: ++64 9 431 2145. Fax: ++64 9 431 2901.
Kings Seeds (NZ) Ltd, PO Box 283, Katikati.
Tel: ++64 7 549 3409. Fax: ++64 7 549 3408.

Australia
Kings Seeds (Aus), PO Box 975, Penrith 2751,
New South Wales. Tel/Fax: ++61 2 477 620 901.

USA
Seedsavers Exchange, 3076 North Winn Road,
Decorah, Iowa 52101. Tel: ++1 319 382 5990.
Fax: ++1 319 382 5872.
W. Atlee Burpee & Co, 300 Park Ave.,
Warminster PA 10974. Tel: ++1 215 800 888 1447.
Email: burpeesc@surfnetwork.net

UK
Heritage Seeds, Henry Doubleday Research
Association, Ryton Organic Gardens, Coventry,
CV8 3LG, UK. Tel: ++44 1203 303517.
Fax: ++44 1203 639229.

Today's seedlings
are tomorrow's
crops.

ing seeds to larger pots whereupon they flop and faint or expire from shock! With cell trays each seedling plug is eased straight out into the soil when the time is right.

To prepare the containers, fill almost to the top with seed-raising mix and flatten it lightly with a board. Remember to water the mix before the seeds are sown or they may end up washed into one corner or out altogether!

When the seed bed is fine, flat and moist, with eager anticipatory fingers you can spill flowers, fruit and vegetables across its face. If the seeds are mere specks, use tweezers to place them, or sprinkle them in fine sand and run the mix into furrows. Sprinkle only the finest covering of mix over the top. (With misguided generosity I used to smother my seeds beneath a blanket of mix, for which they repaid me by failing to germinate, rotting and never being seen again.) Finally, moisten the surface of the seed bed with a hand sprayer and cover with board, glass or polythene.

Place containers where the temperature is warm enough to promote germination. If you haven't a greenhouse, a cold frame, table top or window ledge in a warm sunny position will do. Check the seeds for germination, remove covers immediately when germinated, expose them gradually to full light and keep well moistened with a hand sprayer.

Laying out the beds

You're now in no doubt that part of the lawn must become a vegetable plot, or you need to adapt your existing edible garden for increased food production by sustainable methods, and have already started by sowing in containers an exciting diversity of the best of the modern hybrid seeds together with an intriguing selection of heirloom varieties.

While they grow, find a pencil, paper and drawing board and read on before taking to boot and spade to prepare a vegetable plot to receive them!

The site

Successful vegetable gardening requires a site offering maximum sunshine and protection from prevailing winds – in other words a clever combination of exposure and enclosure. The simplest ground layout for a vegetable garden is a square or rectangle divided into four or more beds. The site is best divided up into individual beds of such a size that they do not need to be walked on, which compacts the soil.

Pathways

Ideally, it should be possible to do all sowing, weeding and harvesting from the path that surrounds each bed. Pathways providing easy working and wheelbarrow access are vitally important between beds. Suitable mediums include bricks, pavers, concrete slabs, gravel, pea shingle, pebbles, and bark.

Enclosures

Traditional enclosures include brick walls, dwarf hedges, picket or wooden fences, cordons of fruit or vines trained on wires or frames, and stands of soft fruit bushes.

In addition to providing shelter, solid enclosures offer the additional bonus of providing support for climbing edibles. This increases the productive surface of the garden, since vertical planting is practised. Less permanent plantings like melons, squashes and cucumbers are easy to train on netting, frames, trellises, or against a solid vertical support.

English box, *Buxus sempervirens,* or the quicker growing *Lonicera nitida* are the traditional dwarf hedges for enclosing vegetable gardens. Both grow easily from cuttings, so don't be daunted by the fact that you may need some 500 plants for your hedges! When the cuttings are rooted plant them 15–20 cm (6–8 in) apart.

General management

Sustainable management of the edible garden involves the use of the raised bed and no-dig systems and mulching, together with the building of soil fertility with organic materials as detailed in

Once a lawn, now a productive vegetable garden!

chapter 3. Plants are kept healthy with benign pest and disease control as outlined in chapter 4, and with companion planting as in chapter 5.

Maintaining continuous produce and maximum yields

- Maintain a high state of soil fertility with regular dressings of organic nutrients so that plants can be grown at the greatest possible density.
- Prolong the growing season by staggered sowing of early, middle and late varieties. Glut is fine if you have time for and enjoy freezing, jamming, juicing, saucing, pickling and pureeing. But the culinary possibilities of the contents of your vegetable plot all maturing at once are limited and your family may not appreciate becoming slave labourers.
- If you haven't a greenhouse, build a basic cold frame, make or purchase inexpensive polythene cloches and have replacement plants ready for those that have cropped.

Harden off in a sunny sheltered corner before planting out. Protect early season seedlings with the cloches, cover cloth or recycled plastic bottles and containers.

- Interplant larger, slow to mature vegetables with 'catch crops' – smaller, quick to mature vegetables such as salad stuffs, oriental vegetables and dwarf beans – which may be planted under or between larger vegetables and used as 'fillers'. They maximise soil space and help prevent weed formation.
- Grow as many vegetables as possible vertically to maximise space; for example, beans, peas, cucurbits.
- If your soil is heavy or poorly drained use timber or bricks to raise the beds.

Crop rotation

Crop rotation ensures that repeated crops of one variety do not take out the same nutrients and minerals from the soil each year so that eventually the crop starves and fails. Growing the same plants in the same soil each year also encourages a build up of insects, viruses and disease spores that afflict one type of vegetable, so the more often crops are rotated the healthier both the vegetables and soil will be.

Crop rotation and high soil fertility ensure bumper crops.

Rotation plan

Year 1

Bed 1: Grow root crops (salsify, parsnips, carrots, beetroot). Do not add lime or manure this area.

Bed 2: Sow potatoes. Add plentiful manure but no lime.

Bed 3: Grow other crops (celery, onions, peas, cucumber, pumpkins, sweet corn, salad crops). Check soil acidity and add lime if necessary. Manure well.

Bed 4: Plant brassicas (cabbages, broccoli, kale, Brussels sprouts, cauliflowers, radishes, turnips, kohlrabi). Dress with lime, but only add manure if soil is short of organic matter.

Year 2

Bed 1: Sow potatoes.
Bed 2: Grow other crops.
Bed 3: Grow brassicas.
Bed 4: Grow root crops.

Year 3

Bed 1: Grow other crops.
Bed 2: Plant brassicas.
Bed 3: Grow root crops.
Bed 4: Grow potatoes.

Year 4

Bed 1: Grow brassicas.
Bed 2: Grow roots
Bed 3: Grow potatoes
Bed 4: Grow other crops.

Year 5

Same as year one.

Space in this volume does not allow a separate section on vegetable varieties and their cultivation requirements. There are many excellent books on the subject, and those recommended in the bibliography at the end of this book detail both stalwarts of the vegetable plot and new and exciting gourmet and miniature varieties. They also advocate sustainable and chemical-free edible gardening.

CHAPTER SEVEN
NO-SOIL AND SMALL-SPACE GARDENS

Above: Tiny road-front garden planted entirely in troughs and pots.

If your space for a garden is an inner-city court-yard, an urban 'pocket handkerchief', or a 'no soil' balcony, verandah, roof top or patio – read on!

The appeal of a small, attractive and easily maintained garden is universal, but for many gardeners urban location and the constraints of space make it a necessity. World population has increased hugely during the twentieth century; when its present 7 billion people doubles in the year 2050, space for living will already have diminished dramatically, placing us irrevocably in the age of the small garden.

It has been said many times that the garden is another room of the house. The value of this additional living space is important to us all, but it is of vital importance to urban dwellers who are surrounded by noise, dust, pollution, traffic and crowds of people. The garden is our refuge, our secret retreat, a place of green and peace created by our own hands. It is an oasis of calm where we can hide from the noise and bustle of the world outside; where we can shed the heavy cloak of stress and strain placed upon us by the pace and competition of modern living

Whether the garden is a tiny, walled inner-city courtyard, a roof garden, a collection of pots on an apartment balcony, the patio of a retirement unit, or the suburban dweller's modest backyard, the therapeutic value of this precious space is unparalleled. We can still practise sustainable gardening here, enjoy the satisfaction of saving and sowing our own seeds and watching them germinate, and tend and harvest organically home-grown salad greens, fruit and vegetables.

No matter how small the space, with clever planning and planting, it will allow us to sit in sun or shade, read a book, eat al fresco meals with family and friends, and watch our children at play. We can even make our own compost, run our own home worm farm, dry the laundry and create discreet places to screen dustbins, tools and toys just metres from the door.

In short, the small garden must offer as many, if not all, the facilities of the large garden. The challenge is to become fiendishly clever at methods of fitting them all in!

Fences screened with climbing plants insulate urban dwellers against city dust and noise.

We need to ensure that every centimetre of space is utilised in the most attractive, economical and efficient manner possible. The almost fail-safe method of doing this is, as always, measuring up those precious centimetres, transposing them as metres onto graph paper, then deciding what you and your family want from your garden. Chapter 11 offers instruction on designs for low maintenance sustainable gardens to help you plan zones and areas. The 'ground' rules for gardens large and small are exactly the same, and also apply whether you're creating a new garden or revamping an existing one.

The foundation

Plantings of small trees, flowering shrubs with evergreen and variegated foliage, versatile conifers, ornamental grasses, bulbs and a few plants with striking architectural form or bold leaves will help to create a basic framework that will maintain year round interest. Raised beds for the edible garden fit well around the edges, or down one side, leaving the central area free for play and entertaining facilities. Reserve one small shady corner as a utility area for compost making, worm farm, tool storage, etc.

Going up the wall

A basic advantage of many small gardens is that they're usually enclosed by walls, hedges and fences, which not only creates a delightful sense of privacy and seclusion, but also provides instant structural features for space-saving vertical gar-

---

High society
Climbers and twiners suitable for containers:
Actinidia kolomikta, Hydrangea petiolaris, Solanum jasminoides, Bougainvillea glabra, Ipomea spp, *Thunbergia elata, Campsis radicans, Jasminum* spp, *Trachelospermum jasminoides, Clematis* spp, *Lonicera* spp, *Cobaea scandens, Mandevilla laxa, Vitis* spp, *Eccremocarpus scaber, Passiflora caerulea, Wisteria sinensis, Hedera* spp.

Pillar roses of restrained habit:
Red: 'Danse de Feu', 'Climbing Alec's Red', 'Paul's Scarlet', 'Guinee'.
Silver-pink: 'Ash Wednesday'.
Pink: 'Cornelia', 'Ballerina', cerise-pink 'Parade'.
Salmon pink: 'Compassion', 'Phyllis Bide', 'Abraham Darby'.
Yellow-gold: 'Golden Showers', 'Windrest', 'Golden Wings', 'Graham Thomas'.
Apricot-gold: 'Buff Beauty', 'Lady Hillingdon', 'Crepuscle'.
White: 'Climbing Iceberg', 'Sombreuil'.
Mixed pinks, lemons, dark rose: 'Mutablis'

Year-round interest plants:
Ivies, *Hedera colchica* 'Sulphur Heart', *H. helix* in variegated forms; *Lonicera japonica* 'Halliana', *Cotoneaster horizontalis* and other cotoneasters; *Cytisus battandieri*.

dening – as supports for climbing plants. In paved city courtyards where little soil is available, both flowering and edible climbing plants may be grown in containers, planter boxes or raised beds. Walls and fences screened with climbing plants help insulate urban dwellers from the noise and dust of the city and help create privacy and shelter.

Ornamental climbers, roses, climbing vegetables such as beans, peas and cucurbits, and espaliered fruit may all be grown vertically, leaving precious ground space free for plants of a more terrestrial nature.

Pollution tolerant

Since many small gardens are in inner-city locations, they're subject to industrial or urban pollution.

Winter specials:

Chaenomeles, Garrya elliptica, Jasminum nudiflorum, Camellia x *williamasii.*

Spring specials:

Teucrium fruticans, Forsythia suspensa, Clematis spp.

Summer and autumn specials:

All climbing roses and honeysuckles; *Schizophragma integrifolium*; vines such as *Vitis vinifera* 'Purpurea', *Clematis viticella* hybrids, *C.* x *jackmanii* hybrids, *Campsis radicans.*

Of restrained habit: the pillar rose 'Ballerina'.

Here is a list of true survivors of restrained growth habits:

Ceanothus spp: Hardy mound forming ground cover, or shrub. Blue flowers.

Chaenomeles: Many species available. Deciduous shrub, colourful flowers, attractive branches.

Cistus spp: 'Rock rose'. Small hardy shrub, prolific flowers. Drought tolerant.

Cotoneaster spp: Attractive small leafed shrub, colourful berries.

Elaeagnus spp: Hardy evergreen shrub, glossy green/variegated leaves.

Forsythia spp: Spring flowering shrub, golden-yellow flowers.

Ilex spp: Holly. Hardy evergreen tree, glossy/variegated foliage, red berries.

Malus spp: Small trees, attractive blossom and edible fruits.

Philadelphus: 'Mock orange'. Hardy deciduous shrubs, richly fragrant white blooms.

Prunus spp: Small trees, attractive blossom in spring, some with edible fruit.

High-rise gardens

Gardeners living in high-rise tower blocks must make their gardens on the roof or on a small balcony. Bold groupings of containers holding evergreen shrubs and conifers as well as colourful flowers provide both a basic structure and a screen providing shelter and privacy.

A simple water feature will impart a sense of tranquillity on a roof or balcony garden, and has the added virtue of bringing light and a reflection of the sky down into a small area, which gives an illusion of space. A wide, shallow container will maximise reflection.

With soil-less roof or balcony gardens, container planting makes all things possible. Choice of container shape is important. Although the selection of rounded pots is infinite, with space at a premium in these elevated situations, square or rectangular containers that interlock or stack for vertical planting optimise available space. Lower, square-bottomed containers are also desirable in roof gardens because they present a firmer base to withstand potential high winds – wind-proof plants are a good idea too! (See section on container culture later in this chapter.)

Support for climbing plants that give shade and shelter may be provided by firmly bolted-

On the tiles: a delightful roof garden.

down trellises, or arches attached to stout frames and fixed to the roof joists. The weight of soil and containers, the degree of local wind and its effect on the structures and plantings will need careful consideration.

Shade, shelter and seclusion

In our world today air pollution can be a serious problem, particularly for those living in large cities. Trees play a major role in purifying the air we breathe. The tiniest of gardens usually has room for at least one small multi-purpose specimen tree that will provide an edible crop, flowers, shade, beauty and privacy. The fruit trees now available as dwarf hybrids fulfil this purpose admirably.

Choosing an ornamental specimen tree that will not grow too big often poses a dilemma for the small-space gardener. The list below gives a selection of small- to medium-sized trees that are generally hardy to many soils and climatic conditions. When planting, keep surface rooting trees away from drives and drains and avoid tall trees that may shoot up to touch overhead power lines.

Deciduous trees for smaller gardens

(Key: G.R. – growth rate, D. – dimensions)

Acer spp: G.R. medium, D. 1–6 m (3–20 ft). Beautiful palmate leaves, fine form, brilliant autumn colour. Many colours available. Protect from drying winds.

Aesculus carnea: pink horse-chestnut. G.R. slow, D. 7 x 6 m (23 x 20 ft). Dramatic lobed foliage, pink candle-like flowers. Prefers cool climates, moist soil.

Albizzia Julibrissen: silk tree. G.R. fast, D. 4–6 m (13–20 ft). Ferny leaves, attractive branches, pink silky flowers held aloft. Tolerant of both hot and dry conditions.

Betula pendula: silver birch, many spp, some pendulous. G.R. fast, D. 1.5–5 m (5–16 ft). Graceful branch structure, silvery trunks. Tolerant wide range soils and situations.

Koelreutia paniculata: golden rain tree. G.R. medium, D. 3 x 2 m (10 x 6½ ft). Yellow summer flowers, golden autumn leaves. Tolerant climatic extremes.

Laburnum spp. 'Golden Chain': G.R. fast, D. 4 x 2 m (13 x 6½ ft). Pendulous yellow flowers in spring. Cool moist conditions. Seed pods poisonous.

Magnolia: many spp. G.R medium–large, D. 2–7 m (6½–23 ft). Showy large tulip-shaped winter flowers. Tolerant wide range of conditions.

Malus: crab apple. G.R. medium. D. 3 x 2.5 m (10 x 8 ft). Artistic oriental branch structure, colourful flowers before leaves, ornamental berries and fruit. Tolerant wide range of conditions.

Nyssa sylvatica: G.R. slow, D. 5 x 3 m (16 x 10 ft). Scarlet in autumn. Prefers moist soils.

Prunus: flowering cherries, almonds, peaches and plums; many spp. G.R. medium, D. 3–6 m (10-20 ft). Beauty of form, blossom and foliage. Edible fruit some species.

Pyrus sacilifolia 'Pendula': weeping silver pear. G.R medium, D. 2–2.5 m (6½–8 ft). Beautiful small tree with weeping silver foliage, small ornamental flowers in spring. Well drained soils.

Robinia pseudocacia 'Frisia': G.R. medium D. 4–6 m (13–20 ft). Golden foliage throughout season. Hardy most soils.

Sophora japonica 'Pendula': Chinese pagoda tree. G.R. medium. D. 3 x 2 m (10 x 6½ ft). Fine outline tree, low weeping branches, resembling upturned glass in shape. Most soils, not too dry.

Sorbus: 'rowan' or 'whitebeam', large genus. G.R. medium. Small to medium trees, white/cream flowers, abundant berries in red, orange, pink, yellow, white. Recommended spp – *S. acuparia, S. vilmorinii, S. cashmiriana, S.* 'Joseph Rock' (autumn colour, amber berries). Hardy.

Evergreen trees

Acacia: wattle (jasmine/mimosa), many spp. G.R. fast, D. 6 x 4.5 m (20 x 15 ft). Attractive foliage, golden-yellow winter flowers. Tolerant wide range soils, dry hot climates.

Agonis flexuosa: willow myrtle. G.R. fast, D. 5 x 4 m (16 x 13 ft). Small leaves, willowy habit, small white flowers, new foliage pink. Hardy.

Brassaia actinophylla: Queensland umbrella tree. G.R. medium, D. 5 x 2.5 m (16 x 8 ft). Large elongated glossy 'umbrella' leaves. Exotic tree for temperate areas and containers.

Callistemon salignus: bottle-brush tree, G.R. medium, D. 5 x 4 m (16 x 13 ft). Showy pink young growth, deep red, pink bottle-brush flowers. Hardy to wide range conditions.

Cordyline australis: NZ cabbage tree. G.R. fast, D. 4 x 1 m (13 x 3 ft). Excellent landscaping accent tree or container specimen. Tall bare trunk, spiky sword-like foliage, dramatic clusters of berries. Green, purple, variegated, black forms. Hardy to most soils and climates.

Conifers: many spp. Attractive small trees of diverse shapes, forms and colours. Hardy most climates.

Ilex spp: holly. G.R. slow, D. 4 x 3 m (13 x 10 ft). Deep green or variegated glossy foliage, polished red berries. Hardy.

Photinia serrulata: Chinese photinia. G.R. fast, D. 3 x 3 m (10 x 10 ft). Vibrant coral new foliage over glossy green. Clusters of smoke-like white-pink flower heads, hardy most soils and climates. Good hedging plant.

The small-space vegetable plot

No matter how small the plot, growing chemical free fruit and vegetables is an important part of the sustainable gardener's philosophy. The immense versatility offered by containers affords the small-space potagist the pleasure of having home-grown vegetables, herbs, flowers and even dwarf fruit trees. All beds should be of the raised, no-dig design (see chapter 3) for ease of management and working access.

Bite-sized container crops

Almost all vegetables can be grown in containers. Many gardeners grow herbs in pots, but even a crop such as potatoes can be grown in a 10-litre (2-gal) plastic bucket, a cut down dustbin or an old barrel. Aware of ever diminishing garden

In this small-space potager, raised beds of enriched soil provide maximum crop yield.

space, seed companies are concentrating on hybridising vegetable varieties that are smaller in growth habit, but big on yield. There is now an exciting international range of gourmet baby vegetables and dwarf varieties at our disposal.

Carrots, cauliflowers, radishes, beetroots, dwarf beans, aubergines, courgettes, curcubits, capsicums and chilli peppers, onions, oriental greens and brassicas comprise only a few of these smaller edibles. Standard forms of capsicums, chillies and aubergines grow on compact bushes that rarely exceed 1 m (3 ft), thus making highly decorative and prolific plants for containers or small spaces. Tomatoes now come in an amazing variety of sizes, and these are especially successful in tubs, pots or commercial grow-bags.

Among the root vegetables, traditional stalwarts such as carrots, beetroots, radishes, parsnips and kohlrabi now come in globe-rooted forms, which may be sown in shallower troughs and thinned out in the normal way.

An alternative no-dig system for restricted spaces is to use 200-litre (44-gal) drums or piles of

Large vegetables require deep troughs.

tyres (excellent for growing potatoes (plant vertically!); large slatted wooden crates, such as those used to transport pumpkins, watermelons and other vegetables, or old packing crates, which can often be purchased cheaply from removal firms. Filled with the no-dig soil recipe (see chapter 3) they can be abutted to form 'beds' of different types of vegetables, or used singly as space-saving instant beds in any position. Wooden crates will disintegrate eventually; however, not only have they been of great use to you for a limited time, but they've also been recycled in a useful manner instead of being burnt or dumped.

Most curcubits require a pot about 30 cm (12 in) in diameter and 30 cm deep; they will require a trellis or some support to climb up. A grouping of three or four dwarf bean bushes or six climbing varieties planted in a large container (40 cm x 60 cm/16 x 24 in) at the foot of a teepee frame or in a small bed will crop prolifically if picked regularly. Vertical cultivation of vegetables leaves precious ground space free for the underplanting of other crops, or for the grouping of smaller pots containing herbs and companion plants beneath.

Larger varieties of the taller capsicums, tomatoes, cauliflower, broccoli, marrows, pumpkins and other curcubits need large pots 40–60 cm (16–24 in) cm in diameter and 35–40 cm (14–16 in) deep. Old half barrels, built-in planter boxes or fibreglass water tanks (remember to insert drainage holes) hold small groupings of larger vegetables such as cauliflowers and single plants of sprouting broccoli which, with regular picking, will crop over a long period.

A universally popular broccoli for growing in small spaces is 'Raab', and a grouping of one each of an early, middle and late season variety will give almost year round crops even in the container garden.

Standard cauliflowers are a large vegetable that take a long time to mature, but two universally popular dwarf varieties are 'Alpha' and 'Idol', which may be grown in medium-sized containers or in small beds just 15 cm (6 in) apart. They should be harvested when the heads are tennis ball sized.

Pots or troughs about 15 cm (6 in) in diameter and 15–20 cm (6–8 in) deep are suitable for smaller vegetables and herbs. Most bought troughs are 20 cm (8 in) wide and vary in length from 30 to

Small-space success

Here are a number of ideas to help you get larger and better crops and sustained yield from the space you have available

- Position your edible garden where it will receive both shelter and the maximum amount of sunshine.
- Grow as many vegetables as you can vertically to maximise space.
- Choose varieties that suit your own soil and region.
- If your soil is heavy or poorly drained, use timber or bricks to raise your beds.
- Stagger your sowing and planting for a continuous supply of crops.
- Grow vegetable varieties that have been bred for small spaces or container growth.
- Increase soil fertility with home-made or commercially prepared organic liquid fertilisers, manures and composts.
- Keep pests and diseases at bay with a strict hygiene routine.
- Grow beans and peas in a teepee style for all-round exposure to light.
- Ask your nurseryman to recommend prolific cropping dwarf varieties.

Pots of good taste: rocket lettuce and radicchio (chicory) planted with marigolds.

- Use cloches and cold frames both early and late season to extend growing periods.
- Above all remember that containerised crops need máximum sunshine.
- Regular watering, and feeding to maximise yield and harvesting.

90 cm (1–3 ft). These may be used for more shallow rooting vegetables such as self blanching celery, saladstuffs, oriental brassicas, beetroot, kales, silver beet and spinach. Chinese greens are compact in growth habit and mature quickly, which makes them excellent container subjects.

Beet and spinach plants are ideal for container and small space cultivation since they are shallow rooted and have vertical growth habit. For big healthy plants which may be cropped on the 'pick and come again' basis, grow one to a pot, approximately 30 cm x 25 cm (12 x 10 in) or space 30 cm (12 in) apart in nitrogenous rich soil. They require regular watering in dry weather to prevent bolting.

Cultivating the small edible garden

Exactly the same rules apply as for the huge vegetable garden! Intensive vegetable production in a tiny area requires beds of well conditioned soil that has been enriched with organic manures and materials. Choose a sunny sheltered site. Dense planting provides ground cover to maximise moisture retention, and vertical planting maximises ground space for vegetables of a more terrestrial habit. Sow 'catch crops' between larger varieties and practise crop rotation.

Up and coming

Even with a 'no soil' or pocket handkerchief vegetable plot, continuous crops can be had by successive sowing of seeds in smaller pots to replace plants that have been harvested. Plan for continuity of produce by setting aside space for a nursery area for young plants to replace those which have been harvested. With replacement seedlings the growing season can be as extended and the crop yield can be as fruitful as that from a medium-sized garden potager.

Protective coverings
Mini-cloches and row cloches

To protect replacement seedlings in pots early in the season make a mini-cloche. Take a length of number 8 wire and bend it into a loop that is about the same diameter as the pot top, making sure you have left a leg long enough to push into the soil, compost or potting mix. Draw a plastic bag over the loop of wire and tie it to the pot with string or large rubber band.

To make a simple cloche for a row of vegetables, bend lengths of number 8 wire to the desired depth – that is, with enough space to allow the plants to develop. Push the wires into the soil at regular intervals and then thread an elongated sheet of clear polythene over and under them to ensure firm coverage. Tie the ends loosely. Simple and inexpensive cloches such as this protect tender seedlings against slugs and snails as well as the vagaries of the elements.

A basic cold frame

You will require a number of pieces of planking, depending on the desired size and height of your frame. The rear wall should be built higher than the front to accommodate taller seedlings. The side struts will need to be angled to meet the lower front wall. The cover may be constructed of glass or a length of heavy-duty clear polythene attached at either end to a light batten. An even more basic design would be a square or rectangle of four planks of wood with an old window or piece of glass hinged onto or resting on top.

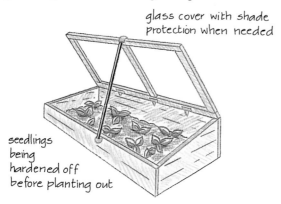

glass cover with shade protection when needed

seedlings being hardened off before planting out

Design for a basic cold frame.

Container culture

The small space gardener has an enormous range of containers at his or her disposal, composed of wood, plastic, terracotta, concrete, wire and basket ware. Whatever the material, the container must be strong enough to withstand frequent watering and moves; they must be complementary to the plants they display and the situations they furnish.

Containers have revolutionised landscaping design and are said to be the single most popular garden accessory. They are absolutely indispensable to the small plot gardener! As long as the plants are watered and fed well with organic liquid manure, containers allow gardens to be created in soilless situations – patios, decks, verandahs, bricked courtyards or concreted backyards. Almost anything can be planted in a pot, except for plants with deep tap roots.

The secret of successful container gardening lies in taking time to choose the right sized pot for the plant, in using a good quality mix, and in incorporating water-retaining crystals and slow release fertiliser granules in the potting medium.

Never use neat garden soil in a container. Even if it is compost enriched and conditioned, it will dry out and become compacted very quickly.

Also immensely valuable for containerised plantings are the potting mix saturating agents that are added at the time of planting, or sprinkled on the surface of the pots later. These are different from the water retaining crystals; the saturating agents help the mix retain moisture and slow its passage through the roots of the plant so that they have longer to absorb water. I was sceptical about these agents at first, but they are efficient, and it's a joy to see the precious water you pour into the top of the pot stay there, instead of running straight out of the bottom!

Hanging baskets

Hanging baskets and window boxes also allow the sustainable gardener to maximise space in a small garden. But to be successful, they too must be planted with the correct materials. Avoid cheap potting mix that dries out quickly and choose lightweight mixes especially formulated for planters. They will also contain water storage granules and slow release fertiliser pellets. Because hanging baskets and window boxes require watering daily, nutrients wash out of the mix quickly. The pellets will ensure some four months supply of food. An organic liquid fertiliser or liquid tea applied weekly as a booster will ensure long-lived floriferous plants.

Remember to hang hanging baskets well away from windows – high winds could prove lethal!

No soil? No problem! Try container culture.

Herbs, vegetables and salad stuffs are often grown on window sills or built-in window boxes, which may be made of plastic or wood – remember that the latter can become very heavy when fully planted and wet, so secure them strongly. Most troughs for window boxes or rows of plantings should have a planting depth of at least 50–60 cm (20–24 in) to accommodate root growth.

Try an edible basket of perennial lettuces or spinach with 'pick and come again' leaves, or some parsley, sage and basil, or a kitchen window box containing dwarf tomatoes, trailing courgettes, spring onions and herbs, or whatever takes your fancy. Hanging gardens? The sky's your limit!

Grow-bags

Grow-bags are flattish polythene sacks of potting mix and compost with the addition of water retention granules and slow release fertiliser granules. They are designed to lie flat on the ground so that rows and blocks of plants or seedlings can be sown directly into them. To disguise the polythene, group smaller pots of companion plants such as marigolds, nasturtiums or herbs around the base. Grow-bags are excellent for no-soil gardens on patios, verandas or roof tops, since they can be disposed of when crops are finished and do not present storage problems like containers. I've grown tomatoes in them with great success.

Potted trees

The availability of jumbo-sized pots, crates and barrels in a variety of materials enables the container gardener to incorporate fruit trees into the planting scheme. Even inner-city dwellers can luxuriate in spring blossom and home-grown fruit from the wide variety of grafted and dwarf fruit trees available from good nurseries. Young fruit trees, whether in containers or garden beds, may also be trained in the espalier method against wire frames or walls to provide maximum cropping in minimal space.

Mobile containers

One of the great advantages of container gardening is that plants can be moved easily, but a soil-filled container can weigh heavily. If you have a no-soil garden situation it is worth considering mounting all but the smallest containers on simple trolleys made of a flat piece of wood fitted with four furniture castors and a rope handle; this can help to avoid back injury. Tilt one side of the container, push the trolley under, then ease the other side of the pot on. Garden centres offer a range of custom-made devices on wheels for this purpose. Most are made of strong plastic-coated wire and are relatively inexpensive. The mobility of a container garden means that plants can be rotated, and groupings rearranged, so that the display is always at peak perfection. Tender plants can be

Potmobile.

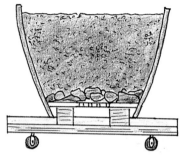

moved to sheltered sites or indoors. If this is impracticable, wrap the container in frost or shade cloth.

Recycle

Keep extra containers on hand so that new seedlings will be developing to replace crops which are being harvested. If storage space is short, use polythene planter bags which squash flat when not in use. It is possible to recycle the old mix from finished crops but it should be treated before being used again. Add commercially prepared compost, slow release fertiliser granules and water retaining granules, but if you do not wish to mix your own, garden centres offer several commercially prepared agents for revitalising used potting mix.

Liquid feeds

A good new potting mix or well manured and conditioned soil should provide your vegetables with all the nutrients they need, but crops in containers require frequent watering, and this causes nutrients to wash out quite quickly. These can be replaced with liquid fertilisers such as fish or comfrey emulsion every fortnight or so, or with sheep pellets.

Horticultural suppliers also offer a comprehensive range of organic fertilisers and foliar feeds, such as seaweed-based liquid plant foods for ferns and foliage, and foliar feeds for general purposes, flowers and fruit, and roses. There are also super-organic and super-seaweed blends, and blood and bone formulas. Another good organic foliar feed is a concentrated fish fertiliser. I use this particular variety because the smell deters pests and it is not too high in nitrogen. Take care with nitrogenous preparations – they are fine for leafy plants and vegetables, but will promote lush foliage at the expense of flowers and fruit in other varieties.

The manufacturers of many commercially prepared foliar fertilisers offer a 'feeder set' which contains a pack of plant food, a clip-on hose connector and a feeder jar. There is no mess or complicated mixing; the handy feeder jar is clipped straight onto the end of the ordinary garden hose and the plants are fed and watered at the same time.

Apartment dweller's guide to composting

Pierce drainage and aeration holes in the base and sides of a lidded plastic bin and raise it just above the ground by standing it on several blocks of wood or half bricks. Fill it with the chopped roots and stalks of any spent crops and all organic kitchen waste, adding sprinklings of complete fertiliser or commercially prepared manure pellets between layers.

Cover the mixture and let it lie for a month or so (turning it once weekly) until the plant material rots into compost. If you stand a container beneath the drainage holes at the base of the bin to catch the seepage, this may be diluted with water and used as a liquid manure. With this method you can make compost in a very small area or in a corner of a shed or garage.

No excuses

As space for living diminishes, the small garden under sustainable management becomes even more important. Also, since economic circumstances often dictate that both partners in the home must work fulltime, a small, low maintenance garden leaves time for enjoyment and relaxation, as well as a private place for periods of personal space and calm in our frenetic everyday world. The many aids to small plot and container cultivation means there's no excuse for flowers, fruit and vegetables grown in tiny spaces not to come up smiling with rude good health and smothered with abundant crops!

CHAPTER EIGHT
PRACTISING PERMACULTURE

Above: This ancient New Zealand pohutukawa hosts a natural ecosystem of plants, birds, insects and small animals.

The three-fold ethics of permaculture are: care of the earth, care of the people, and sharing the surplus. Cooperation with our environment, not competition, is the basis of all our actions. The basic life ethic recognises the intrinsic value of every living thing and its vital place in the ecological chain. We work with and for nature and not against it.

'Aha,' you may say, 'it's very well to want to care for the earth, but it's very difficult to know where to start in our everyday lives, especially if we're city dwellers.' However, with the exception of keeping larger domestic animals, the basic principles and practises of permaculture are very similar to those of sustainable gardening. They may be practised to perfection if you have a lifestyle block, but many can be easily instituted in the average urban garden. A system can be adapted to suit our individual situation and can offer us the starting point towards embracing the ethics of permaculture in our own domestic gardens.

We know that sustainable agriculture, horticulture and land use is the key to our survival in the new millennium. We understand that industrialised modern farming systems are mostly unsustainable because they rely on unrenewable fossil fuel energy, quick-fix chemical fertilisers, degradation of land through deforestation, soil erosion, and salination and chemical pollution of soil and water. Unsustainable agriculture and horticulture places great stress on the environment and on everything in our ecosystem. We are taking everything from the land and giving little back

Permaculture is a design system for creating sustainable human environments; if we attack and plunder nature, we attack ourselves and ultimately destroy our environment.

Mutual benefit
Permaculture is a coined word derived from two words: permanent and agriculture. The principles on which the system is founded are simple universal truths. To discover these truths we've only to look at the ecosystem of an ancient forest, which has survived for thousands of years without any help from man. Natural ecosystems are made up

William Ricketts' carved figures in the Dandenongs in Victoria, Australia, symbolise the ethics of permaculture – the union of man and nature.

Within an ecosystem such as this, a diverse range of elements are interconnected to meet each other's needs perfectly, and there is always a zone pattern.

Guilds and zones

Under the permaculture system, each area of the garden, no matter how small, is referred to as a guild. A guild does not stand alone and separate. Each flows into the other and each is located so that it has a symbiotic relationship – to interact, help and be part of the other. Permaculture guilds bring plants, animals and human beings into close and mutually advantageous association.

The guilds are designed under a simple zoning system. This starts with zone zero – the house. It is the centre of activity and should be designed to suit the occupants' needs, to be energy efficient and to be as low maintenance in style as possible.

Many homes are now being built not of timber but of natural materials native to the area; for example, mud- and clay-brick houses, which are warm in winter and cool in summer, and which integrate harmoniously with their natural landscape.

The ideal permaculture system harnesses energy from renewable biological sources which can be recycled on site – wind, water and sun power. This includes fuel and human energy. However, for many of us, the constraints of geographical situation and climate do not allow this. Only those of us fortunate enough to have sufficient land can use wood grown on a sustainable basis (immediate replanting after felling) to heat our homes and cook our food. But what we can all do, whether rural or city gardeners, is to save power and energy by installing solar heating devices on our homes, and utilising water in the most efficient and economical manner possible.

Energy efficient planning is crucial and it is important for designers of modern homes and their occupants to know how to harvest, use and store solar energy and to use and conserve water wisely. Many of the homes coming off architects drawing boards for the twenty-first century will be designed with alternative water storage systems and with composting toilets.

Modern composting toilets bear no resemblance to the malodorous old 'long drop', are efficient and aesthetically pleasing, and are widely

of millions of elements – trees, shrubs, birds, mammals, insects, fungi, and people, and this diversity is essential for their survival.

Each element within each ecosystem has many roles and is supporting a number of other elements. Each large tree provides homes for a multitude of birds, insects, plants and other creatures. It provides leaf mould to compost the forest floor, which, in turn, supports creatures that eat decaying vegetation, and nourishes the seedlings that spring up to regenerate the ancient forest. The forest itself provides shelter to man and provides him with wood for building homes and fuel for cooking.

used in permaculture and sustainable systems for manure. They are becoming an increasingly popular feature in holiday and rural homes. (Composting toilets are discussed separately in chapter 9.)

Getting started

So where do we start? We'd like a small orchard. The fruit trees need nutrients, fertiliser and pest control. We supply both by putting in a companion planting system beneath the trees, together with a few pest-patrol chickens – and ducks if we're rural dwellers. The poultry needs feeding – the plants and pests feed them. We need a small pond for the ducks. The water area, no matter how large or small, and with or without ducks, gives us pleasure to behold; it will quickly attract an eco-system of insects, plants and animals of its own as part of the harmonious whole. The system is already becoming energy efficient, because we are employing agents other than ourselves to do the work. They are natural agents, each helping and interacting with the other.

Nothing exists alone. Everything has its own intrinsic value and is part of a whole. Permaculture attempts to bring all the elements together as a sustainable whole.

Small-space permaculture

I'm often asked by owners of modest townhouse gardens if it is possible to design and manage their gardens under the permaculture system. The answer is most certainly 'yes'. Let's recap briefly on the basic tenets of sustainable gardening recently discussed, because they are closely allied with those of permaculture. These basic tenets are as follows:

- Enrichment and nourishment of the land with organic fertilisers and conditioners.
- Low toxicity pest, disease and weed control.
- The recycling of all materials that once possessed life, so they may give it again.
- The employment of companion planting systems to attract and host beneficial predatory insects and repel undesirable pests.
- The employment of plant materials suited to climatic situation and geographical location.
- The employment of hardy and disease resistant plants.
- Avoidance of monoculture and establishment of diverse planting systems.

Permaculture brings animals and humans into close association.

- The growing of chemical free fruit and vegetables.

All these principles can be practised in a garden of any size, in any location and under all climatic conditions. The smallest garden can have an 'orchard' of dwarf fruit trees in containers or espaliered along fence lines, or keep a couple of chickens in a moveable ark. On more rural properties the permaculture system will entail the addition of orchards, beehives, small animals – ducks as pest patrols, poultry as compost machines and pigs, a goat and house cows wherever possible.

The permaculture system brings all these elements together into a logical working order by zoning them into mutually beneficial and energy efficient units, the guilds. This brings animal, plant and human life into close association. Plants and animals can be used in a variety of ways – to provide fertiliser; to provide insect, weed and pest control; to recycle nutrients; to help soil aeration and for erosion control.

Zoning

Regardless of the size of your land, under a sustainable permaculture system it would be zoned into parts, each determined by the number of times you visit the area, structure, plant, utility or animals daily. In small-space and urban gardens, fruit, vegetables, eggs and poultry and all com-

Vegetable garden and orchard are situated in zones 1 and 2.

posting materials are produced near to the house in zones 1 and 2. On lifestyle blocks, zone 3 would flow on from zone 2, and might produce milk, pork, cheese, yoghurt, honey and further composting materials.

Zoning is designed for ease of management and the saving of human energy. For example, parents with young families would need to visit laundry lines daily, yet this facility is still often hidden away some way from the house; you would visit the chicken house up to 400 times a year to feed the birds and collect the eggs; the vegetable garden is visited daily; but you would visit a fruit tree perhaps only the half a dozen times a year required for its maintenance – spraying and pruning – and to harvest its crop. You would not therefore plan to plant large fruit trees in zone 1.

The following zones can be any shape or size, but will flow each into the other.

Zone 1

Any part of the garden that is visited daily must be in zone 1 for quick and easy access. This zone includes the vegetable/herb garden, utility areas, entertaining/play areas and poultry houses. Edible and other plants requiring water other than rain water will also be in zone 1.

Zone 2

Zone 2 includes orchards. In urban gardens, dwarf trees may be grown in containers or fruiting trees espaliered on walls or along wire fences that fulfil the dual purpose of dividing the garden into zones and supporting the trees. On larger properties, animal houses and animals used for orchard management, outbuildings, the implement shed, compost bins, and the worm farm are also situated in zone 2.

Zone 3

In zone 3 are the bigger fruit and nut trees, the pasture area, and less managed animals like house cows, pigs, sheep, semi-managed birds like turkeys and geese. If you have sufficient land, some areas in zone 3 can be planted in trees that provide firewood.

Zone 4

For rural dwellers, no matter how small the property, under the permaculture system an area of wilderness is conserved, left alone for native bush as habitat and sustenance for native animals. Zone 4 is a place to observe and learn, but not to manage.

In an urban garden, the patch of bush nurtured by the lifestyle block owner would be scaled down to a small semi-wild area in which the following plants might be grown to fulfil the same purpose:

- A patch of nettles (sunk in buckets to control invasive roots) to provide butterfly habitat and liquid manure

- Tall non-invasive grasses, which are allowed to form seed heads to feed birds
- Tall herbs (such as fennel) and any of the beneficial insect attractor plants listed in chapter 5
- Space allowing, a small native evergreen shrub or tree bearing nectar-rich blossom or berries according to season, to attract and sustain beneficial insects and native birds.

Animal farm

Animals are a vital part of the permaculture system. For example, even if you live in suburbia and have only space for a few chickens in a moveable ark, a minute vegetable garden and a few dwarf or espaliered fruit trees, you can manage your garden under the permaculture system.

Each of these have a symbiotic relationship with each other. The chickens – and ducks if you have room for a couple and a small pond – will be fed household scraps and waste materials from the vegetable garden and will forage naturally. In return they will provide you with eggs, destroy weeds and pests and manure the land as they move around the garden, and provide surplus manure that if collected and aged can be used as a compost activator and provide fertiliser and liquid manure for the vegetable garden. If you have room for a small orchard, the chickens will require less feeding as they will free range, keeping down pest levels at the same time.

A few ducks will fulfil much the same purposes as the hens, but they can be messy creatures and are not really suitable for keeping in small

urban gardens. If you really want them to be part of your system, check council regulations regarding whether you may keep them or not.

If you have room to keep a goat, pig or house cow or cows in zone 3, you will have milk, meat, weed control and fertiliser in return for your energy.

The animals, the plants, the land and its owners are working together and benefiting from each other while caring for the land in a sustainable manner. You need not worry about having to manage and live with hordes of animals if you put your garden into a permaculture system, because both the land and the number of animals on it will be carefully planned to co-exist in mutually beneficial dependency. You need only maintain a few of each to do a perfectly good job.

Fowl play

Chickens and ducks can be used for multi-purpose functions in quite small areas. They help control invasive grasses and weeds, eat slugs, snails and bugs, supply eggs, meat and manure. Another excellent way to use your poultry in the system is to set aside one or two metres adjacent to the hen house for fencing off as a composting yard. Keep this topped up with hay, weeds and any other vegetative waste you can spare to a good depth. Let the poultry out into the 'yard' and leave them there for part of the day before they're employed on free-range pest control duties. They'll love scratching about in the vegetation, eat weed seeds and add rich manure to the composting mix. You can rake the mix up when mature and spread it as a rich composting mulch on beds and into the compost heap. The most convenient place for this 'compost yard' will obviously be near the edible gardens and orchard where the organic matter can be spread directly on the beds or used as mulch.

Hens are very easy to keep on smaller urban properties, but if you want a rooster too, you'll need to consider neighbours! His 'timekeeping' can otherwise make you very unpopular.

As with any animals there are practical considerations to keeping hens. How will you feed and shelter them and protect them from weasels,

A small wilderness area, even in the urban garden, will provide habitat and sustenance for wildlife.

stoats and vermin? How will you keep them confined only to the areas in the system that you want them and out of the vegetable and flower gardens? What sort of fencing can you provide? Give thought to what sort of birds you need. Do you want them for eggs, and meat, and for breeding, or just for eggs and as foragers?

There are many breeds to choose from – ring up your local poultry breeder's association and ask for advice. The attractive 'Barred Rocks' are a sturdy breed; they're quiet, lay well and are heavy enough for table birds. Some breeds are much more placid than others: bantam hens (excellent for small-space systems) and the beautiful white Chinese silkies make first class mothers and will sit happily on other birds' eggs.

'Chookmobiles'

You can still maintain a mini-compost yard if you're an urban permaculturist, but your chickens must live largely in a moveable ark. Wheel the 'chookmobile' up to the yard and let the hens out for an exercise period late each afternoon. They'll go back into the ark to roost of their own accord and you can shut them safely in again.

Feeding

In permaculture and sustainable management systems each element is geared towards self-sufficiency. If you need to feed your poultry purely on bought-in feed, in effect you've lost a link in the chain because your eggs and meat (although free-range) will cost you a good deal of money. Also, commercial feeds invariably contain both antibiotics and hormone growth booster products.

If you need to give your poultry and pigs supplementary feed in order to rear chemical-free food, choose organically raised poultry grain in addition to forage foods. Your local biodynamics association will provide details of suppliers.

Although you want to keep your poultry to work in zones 1 and 2, it's best to always feed them in a specific area away from the house. Never feed them at the back door. They'll be indoors before you know it! Let your poultry out in the morning after they've laid so you do not have to waste time and energy hunting for the eggs.

Hen health

As a general rule in both urban and rural situations, it's wise to keep only a small number of birds – enough to suit your purposes – and to look after them well. Although the principle is to make the birds work for you, they will repay you handsomely for that little bit of extra care. A handful of happy, healthy birds will lay well and work the land efficiently – a mob of unmanaged scrawny specimens will soon degrade rather than enhance it.

If your hens are mostly confined to a moveable ark, provide a container of diatomaceous earth for

Happy, healthy birds will lay well and work the land efficiently.

a dust bath, or make sure the hens have access to a soft soil area to rid themselves of parasitic pests.

To help them digest their food well, and to form strong-shelled eggs, add crushed egg or oyster shells and grit to their feed. Use crushed garlic or garlic oil in water containers to keep intestinal worms under control.

It is possible even in urban gardens to plant a selection of forage shrubs and trees in zones 2 and 3 to help feed the poultry. A good mix of species will provide hard seeds that fall in early summer, berries that mature in late summer to early autumn and large seeds from autumn to spring. In addition to the traditional orchard fruits you could plant small trees and shrubs with berry fruits such as guava, cape gooseberry, elderberry, tree lucerne, gooseberry, currants etc, acacia species, native trees, and many more.

Keeping ducks

Ducks are as valuable as hens in the permaculture system, but they need to be chosen with care. They need to be good layers and foragers, of placid temperament so that they don't fly away, and able to be confined if necessary behind simple low fences. Khaki Campbells, Indian Runners and Cayugas are the types most suited to domestic gardens, but I have slight reservations about the Indian Runners – they're somewhat territorial and will frighten off neighbours' children with all speed! Both the Cayugas and Campbells are good layers and foragers, but the latter often mate with wild ducks and their offspring invariably fly away as soon as they're mature. Apart from the provision of a small pond, ducks require much the same management and feeding as chickens.

Piggy paradise

It is beyond the scope of this volume to relate the finer points of porcine husbandry, but in the permaculture system a pig's needs too are relatively simple: plenty of food, a clean pen with a floor that will drain dry quickly after being hosed down, a dry warm house, a forage area and some supplementary feeding. You will need access to a good supply of food and vegetable scraps or your venture into pig farming will not be economically viable! A type of pig suitable for a small scale permaculture block is the kunekune pig, which is small, placid and an excellent forager. Pig manure

Pigs and permaculture are perfect partners!

needs storing and aging well, and the employment of some of your composting worms to help process it.

Top trees

Under the permaculture system, trees are chosen carefully for their multi-purpose sustainable values. They must earn their space in the system by being aesthetically pleasing while offering practical values such as shade, shelter or erosion control, and should also be productive – that is, they must bear some kind of edible crop suitable for animals and humans. An example might be the use of the tree *Acacia longifolia*. Tolerant of a wide range of climatic conditions and soils, it provides shelter for human beings, animals and more tender plants; it creates wind breaks and frost protection, and mulch and compost are produced from its prunings. Its roots are nitrogen fixing and its leaves provide fodder for animals. The flowers supply pollen for bee fodder and the tree plays host to beneficial predatory insects. Its millions of seeds provide food for free-range poultry and wild birds. It makes excellent firewood, is quick growing and its root system is good for breaking up heavy soils.

Many other species of trees offer multi-purpose attributes such as these, so in a permaculture system where every inch of the land is managed sustainably to interact with adjoining zones, choose your tree or trees with care. (See chapter 12 for more details on suitable trees.)

The home orchard: a sustainable cornucopia of plenty.

The fruits of your labour

Planning the home orchard is a luscious, mouth-watering idea, and, of course, if organically managed it will be a sustainable cornucopia of plenty.

Choose your site carefully. This is especially important in the urban garden where every inch of space counts. Check that the orchard site will fit into the permaculture zoning plan. If you choose your fruit trees wisely, you'll have crops to harvest almost year round, so you'll probably visit the home orchard once daily. This means the orchard would need to be close to the house in zone 2 or 3. In a permaculture design plan you would normally have your lawn, flower garden, herbs and vegetables adjacent to the north side of the house in zone 1, and the orchard extending from that into zone 2. Other considerations include the soil quality of the site, and whether it has both adequate shelter and exposure to sunlight. A north facing site in the southern hemisphere and a south facing site in the northern hemisphere is essential for maximum fruit production. Take into consideration existing trees and pasture.

Shelter is an essential requirement for an orchard – you'll be picking very few fruit from the trees if they are blasted by gale force winds as soon as their fragile blossoms open or if tiny fruit are torn from the trees as soon as they form!

Less is better

Give thought to how you will manage your orchard, especially if you're an urban permaculturist and have to be out at work all day. How much time you have to spend developing and maintaining it will help you determine its size and the number of trees you can realistically look after. One of the golden rules of both the permaculture and sustainable garden system is that a small number of happy, well cared for healthy plants or animals will reward you far more than a larger number of wasteful specimens. You'll be happier and more relaxed too. The recommended size of a home orchard which two adults could comfortably look after would be a maximum of a quarter acre (1000 m^2) and comprise no more than eight trees. You're the designer!

The right plant for the right place

When choosing fruit trees make sure that they are suited to your soil and geographical location. Resist the temptation to purchase luscious-sounding trees from specialist catalogues, as they are likely to turn up their toes and die, despite TLC, after the first season. The reason for this has little to do with the quality of your husbandry, but lies rather more in the fact that the trees were commercially raised in paddocks of warm, free draining volcanic soil that happened to be much to their liking. When transplanted to cold wet clay, despite your Herculean efforts to improve it, they simply can't cope.

Topography and soil type

Time given to studying the lie of your land and your soil type and quality is time well spent. In just one small area you can have a number of naturally occurring features – a hollow of cold wet soil, a hot dry bank, frosty areas, frost free areas, warm free-draining soils, patches of shade or partial shade and areas of full sun. The potential to grow a diverse range of trees from subtropical through to citrus and Mediterranean to traditional temperate climate specimens will depend largely on these natural conditions and your soil fertility. Match your tree to the area! The fertility in the soil in your sustainable orchard will be conditioned by ground-cover plants rich in nutritious materials and by the droppings of poultry. When practising permaculture techniques in your garden, you'll learn how to nourish your land and plants with compost, liquid manure, and green crops and use the crop rotation principles already discussed in this book.

Putting it together

Once you've decided on this humdinger of a site for your orchard, list all the factors you'll need to create to put it under the permaculture system. You'll need appropriate shelter, underplanting of food sources such as comfrey for the hens and ducks, and host plants and food for beneficial predatory insects (e.g. phacelia, borage and forget-me-nots). You'll also need repellent plants for insect pests, and weed suppressant and nutritious ground covers such as comfrey and clovers. Additional flowering plants for the orchard floor include hardy bulbs, which will delight humans with colour and scent, and provide food for insects during winter. When the bulbs' foliage dies back in spring it will make a weed suppressing and nutritious ground cover over the roots of the trees. You'll be creating a bee embroidered herbal and floral lei of diverse plants beneath your fruit trees. (Refer back to chapter 5 for listings of other suitable plants.)

Underplanting of appropriate companion plants beneath fruit trees ensures a high rate of fertility, cross-pollination and bumper crops.

The sustainable orchard with all its edible and flowering underplanting is very different to the traditional style of a neatly mown orchard surrounded by straight rows of sheltering trees. Many gardeners are initially worried by the 'messiness' and cheerful chaos of this exuberant self-supporting tapestry, until they begin to understand how it works – that it is, in short, an ultimate ecosystem! Fruit trees and grass are very bad companions because grass roots exude chemicals that inhibit both their growth and yields.

So go for diversity: think chickens, ducks and birds foraging, firewood, butterflies, predatory insects, hedgehogs, flowers, scent and beauty – a diverse combination of essentials contributing to a successful and sustainable whole.

Topical tropicals

If you're fortunate enough to be able to plant subtropical trees, like the ancient forest they'll soon create their own lush 'jungle' and will cover the ground with their own bio-mass of nourishing fallen leaves, twigs, fruit and branches. You will,

Persimmon: vibrant foliage and luscious fruit.

of course, need to live in a temperate zone to do this, or have very good shelter and an adequate source of rainfall, and sunlight in winter. Subtropicals require a warm, sheltered north facing slope or site in the southern hemisphere and a warm south facing site in the northern hemisphere. Trees for the subtropical orchard include avocado, bananas, babaco, casana, casiiroa, cherimoya, guava, pawpaw, passionfruit, tamarillo and macadamias.

Regrettably for the urban permaculturist, dwarf varieties of tropical fruit trees are still not generally available. The alternative is to choose one or two ordinary-sized favourites according to space available and allow them to fulfil the role of multi-purpose trees, providing crops, shade, shelter, and aesthetic appeal.

Seasons of plenty

Ensure that you choose a selection of trees which will crop over a long period, rather than all at the same time, and study catalogues to find out whether the varieties you choose are good for eating fresh, for cooking, freezing and preserving. And once again, look for dwarf varieties if you're a small-space gardener. Another important consideration when choosing fruit trees is to remember that some species such as plum and pear need other varieties to assist with cross pollination. Take advice from your local nursery. It goes without saying that you need to give most earnest consideration to disease resistant varieties, provided they are suitable to your soil and climate.

Fencing

You'll need to give consideration to fencing both your orchard and edible gardens for the management of animals you want to keep in – or out! On lifestyle blocks a good method is to use a heavy quality but unobtrusive Hurricane netting with a single strand electric wire at the base and top to keep out rabbits, possums and larger domestic animals. In urban gardens, if poultry are not confined to an ark, simple trellis screens, wood panels or wire fences will keep them where you want them to be.

Under the permaculture system, animal pests such as rabbits, hares and possums are recycled as dog and cat food, and as rich fertiliser via the compost heap or buried in the ground near fruit trees and shrubs. Shot or humanely trapped, they are a problem turned into a sustainable resource. They are culled of necessity to save native trees and plants from destruction and to prevent other ani-

Masses of plum blossom promise a fruitful harvest.

mals and birds from starvation by depletion of food sources. They are returned to the land to replace what they have taken out.

Pen, paper and permaculture

As with all good garden landscaping, the golden rule if you're converting an existing garden or creating a new one under the permaculture system is to plan everything on paper before you start, and then to start small. Develop the areas nearest the house first and when you are managing them easily, expand out and into the other zones.

The first task is to draw a plot plan of the site, incorporating existing features such as boundary, access, walls, fences, land contours, utilities, location of existing shrubs and trees, easements, driveways and the site orientation of your home.

Consider the climate; though this cannot be changed, with careful planning it will be possible to modify some of its effects with structures or plants to create shade or sun traps, or to direct wind movement. The range of temperatures will also determine the position and range of plants you can grow, and will determine the siting of both utility and leisure areas. (Refer to chapter 13 for further details on landscape planning.)

Every permaculture design is unique because everybody's house site, soils and climatic conditions are different. They will dictate the amount of space available and the sort of fruit trees you can grow, and everyone will choose to grow different vegetables and rear different animals. Permaculture designs evolve to suit the size of the site and the needs of the designers; they're about taking one step at a time, adding one more zone at a time, finding out through experience how best the system works for you.

We began this section by asking ourselves how best in our daily lives we might care for the earth. Our answer is that in both city and country gardens, in developing clean, ethical horticulture we take a giant step towards ensuring its survival.

Sustainable gardening is a way of doing something significant about the greenhouse effect, soil degradation, the ozone layer, fossil fuel depletion, genetic diversity, wilderness preservation, reforestation, recycling – just about every major environmental issue! All our journeys will be different, but the destination is the same: sustainability, self sufficiency and satisfaction.

Local colleges and polytechnics run frequent courses in permaculture and horticulture – an excellent project for winter evenings. Enrol now!

CHAPTER NINE

THE WATER EFFICIENT GARDEN

As sustainable gardeners it is essential that we know how to conserve water, how to use the water we have in the most efficient and economical manner possible, and how to water our plants efficiently. A quick splosh with the hose is criminally wasteful of water and totally inefficient.

Rain water is the circulatory system of the earth, running through lakes, rivers and oceans in an intricate network of veins and arteries, sculpting the earth's face and providing sustenance for all forms of life.

Water is evaporated into the atmosphere from oceans, lakes and rivers, from the soil surface and from vegetation. Transported from place to place in clouds and precipitated back to earth as rain, snow, sleet or hail, it flows across and through the earth, often stored in natural underground reservoirs.

Over 97 per cent of the world's water is in oceans and is too saline for most purposes. Of the 2.7 per cent that is fresh, more than three-quarters is locked either in glaciers or polar ice. Another large portion is locked too far beneath the earth's surface for easy withdrawal. This means that of all

Above: Without water all plant and animal life would cease to exist.
Opposite: Low-maintenance groundcover reduces lawn area and subsequent water use.

the earth's fresh water only 0.36 per cent – that found in lakes, rivers and steams – is easily accessible and available for human use.

Without water vapour in the air, the skin of all living creatures would crack and harden and their lungs would shrivel painfully. Without water vapour chilling in the atmosphere to form rain and snow, the earth's surface would be a barren desert. The vast ocean reservoir, which covers about 70 per cent of the earth, is the ultimate source of most of the water present in the air or found in, or under the land surface.

We are dependent on this water for subsistence, for protection, for industrial energy, for processing materials, for low cost transportation and for countless forms of recreation. We use it for drinking, bathing, agricultural and horticultural irrigation, cleaning and washing our homes and clothes, for running factories and washing cars, and for many other aspects of everyday life.

Without water we would be helpless, we would cease to exist.

Past and present
In times past, when people had to fetch and carry water, the average individual daily consumption

Without water we would cease to exist.

Some rural dwellers have to buy tankers of water during drought periods.

One option more forward-looking councils are considering is to require that new homes with septic tanks have some form of in-built recycling system. Some commercial enterprises are also making the move towards treating wastewater and sewage on site, giving an alternative to septic tanks. The systems used are marketed under somewhat formidable names like BioCycle Aerated Waste Water Treatment (AWTS), Home Bio-Cycle Aeration Plants, or Ecotank Aerated Water Recycle System. Basically they work on the principle of treating all household waste in a four chambered aerobic tank system, using the active bacteria of the sewage to assist with the break-down process. Household water is thoroughly treated to become a clear odourless liquid clean enough to irrigate the garden. Provisions for different garden sizes and consideration of site contours, soil and water-table levels are part of the package, as are compliance with particular regional specifications.

These systems are suitable for most households not connected to a public sewerage system, and are particularly useful for lifestyle blocks, holiday homes and rural dwellings. As property owners we are only too well aware of our need to seek sustainable ways to purify and recycle household water. However, systems such as these are still expensive and are not yet readily available to the average household.

Expanding cities, increased pollution, global warming and drastically changing weather patterns are straining the availability, quality and cost of water. It has already become man's most finite resource. We've reached the stage where every litre of water we save is priceless; each litre we don't use is one litre less to be purified, stored in reservoirs and dams, and distributed, and this leads to lower water treatment costs.

There are social, environmental, political and financial factors to consider also. Building dams and reservoirs costs billions of dollars and swallows up large, otherwise productive land masses. If we take vast amounts of water from lakes and rivers, we endanger aquatic and animal life, and diminish the natural scenic and recreational enjoyment of these environments. It is therefore obvious that we must become more conscientious about how we use the water in our existing storage systems.

was about 10 litres (18 pt). In our modern world we're used to unlimited supplies of water at the turn of a tap, and don't even notice when we allow several litres to flow down the drain while cleaning our teeth. In ancient Persia, wastage of water was an act punishable by death!

On average, as individuals we now consume about 300 litres (66 gal) per day for domestic use – 100 litres (22 gal) more than we used 40 years ago. Thirsty domestic appliances such as dishwashers and washing machines consume a great deal of this water. Drainage systems designed to cope with the households of decades ago are now struggling under excess loads because of these appliances, and local councils are becoming increasingly aware of the need to study methods of recycling domestic water. Despite the fact that the problem is exacerbated by overloaded septic tanks, as yet there are unfortunately few actual wastewater recycling systems available to the average property holder.

The water efficient garden

As gardeners, we have a particularly vital role in conserving water since it is estimated that a horrifying 60 per cent of the water consumed by the average home is poured onto the blessed plot! We can drastically reduce that figure by planting and designing gardens that are less water hungry (see chapter 10); we must institute storage, recycling and irrigation systems that will use water efficiently and economically.

We can store rainwater in tanks, learn how to recycle water, and possibly consider, where appropriate, the installation of the composting toilets discussed later in this chapter. Using a rainwater tank will help to conserve water by providing an additional source for the garden and other outside uses. Because of air pollution, rainwater collected in the cities is unsafe to drink unless filtered and purified.

Much of the water we use in our homes can be recycled for garden use, but at present this tends to be rather a labour of love until technology offers the average householder simple but efficient ways of managing greywater water recycling systems such as those shortly discussed.

The water efficient garden is the garden of the future.

Soil and water

Water falling onto the soil, either by natural rainfall or by irrigation, is categorised either as runoff water, gravitational water or capillary water.

Runoff water

Runoff water is water that washes off the soil without soaking in. It isn't wasted because it goes on to flow into creeks and rivers, but it has the disadvantage of washing away topsoil and causing erosion on steep or sloping terrain.

This is why gardens designed on hillsides must be terraced and well mulched, so that moisture is held and conserved.

Gravitational water

A large volume of the water falling onto soil is drawn down into the subsoil by gravity, or it seeps away into springs and streams. Different soils determine the rate at which gravitational water drains away – sandy and volcanic soils drain quickly, whereas heavy or clay soils hold the

Attractive combinations of low water requirement plants in a hot arid area.

water much longer. If gravitational water is retained too long, it fills the pore spaces in the soil and this affects aeration, causing the roots to 'suffocate' and the plant to die. As gravitational water moves down through the earth it can also decrease soil fertility by leaching soluble plant nutrients from the soil.

Capillary water

This is the water of most significance to plants and soil. It is the water held in the smaller pore spaces of the soil after gravity has drained excess water away. The free movement of capillary water distributes it through the earth making it available to plant roots and moving it towards the soil surface to keep it moist.

'Field capacity' is the term used to assess the amount of water left in the soil after gravitational water has drained away. We know that different soils will have different field capacities depending

Water is an essential element for all living things.

Plants and water

No other compound or element is as essential to the proper functioning, growth and reproduction of a living plant than water. It acts as a support for its tissues and for all the physiological life processes. Photosynthesis, respiration and enzyme activity occur in water solution, and plant minerals and nutrients are extracted from the soil and carried via water throughout the plant's entire system.

When the soil dries out a plant wilts, because it has exhausted its capacity to withdraw moisture from the area of its root circumference. In hot dry weather when water loss from leaf transpiration (giving off of water vapour through foliage cells) is high, the water in the soil immediately surrounding the roots is soon exhausted. Since water moves only slowly from moister surroundings, either the roots must struggle to grow towards a damper area of soil, or new water must be supplied either by rainfall or irrigation if the plants are to survive.

In most plants, the soil below the 'dripline' – the outer edge of the foliage – is the region of most active root growth and feeding. Water drips from the plant's leaves onto this area of soil during rainfall, and as the plant grows in diameter, the leaves and the dripline extend in an ever increasing circle. When watering any plant – tree, shrub or perennial – we need to water the entire dripline surrounding the plant. If water is applied in one spot, the roots will only be encouraged to develop in this one area.

Choosing an irrigation system

If you're snarling that you've barely enough water to put through the hose, consider it proven fact that watering with a hose is time and labour intensive, inefficient and wasteful. Less than 50 per cent of water is actually utilised by the plants, the rest lost to run off and evaporation. A basic irrigation line can result in between 80–90 per cent efficient water usage giving a saving of 30–40 per cent over hose application.

When towed through a garden, the average garden hose functions as a crude but effective scythe; it will flatten flower beds, decapitate vegetable plants, and knock down your containers like ninepins as it writhes across the patio like a love-sick snake. That is when it is not tying itself into sanity-threatening knots.

So let the children go shoeless to school. Fall behind on the mortgage repayments and put in an irrigation system to create a garden that is both

Opposite: Irrigation systems use water economically and efficiently.

water efficient and low maintenance in design and management.

In designing and operating an irrigation system the aim is three-fold:
- to provide the additional water plants need when rainfall is insufficient;
- to utilise the amount of water available in the most economical and efficient manner possible;
- save water, time, labour and cost.

Forward planning

The first thing to do when planning a garden watering system is to visit garden centres and study the systems and equipment available to learn which type will best fulfil your needs. The wide range available, starting from simple do-it-yourself (DIY) kits, will knock your eyes out and confuse you utterly, so it's back to the drawing board before you buy! Using graph paper, draw in the property boundaries. Use a scale of 100:1 for standard urban blocks, or for larger properties a scale of 200:1.

Next, measure and draw in the location of all fixed details such as paved areas, driveways, paths, walls, sheds and buildings. Mark the location of all taps, tanks, downpipes and any other sources of water. You may not intend to use all these sources as a start, but if you have a developing garden you may want to install and add to your irrigation system gradually.

Accurately measure beds, borders and lawns so you can begin assessing how many metres of irrigation piping, joints, drippers, sprinklers or risers, etc, will be needed. Check your external tap types to ensure you buy correct connectors – those marketed as 'universal' will often fit everybody's tap except yours!

Armed with your plan, get a reputable firm to give you advice on the system that is right for you. Almost all DIY irrigation kits come with comprehensive instruction booklets.

Water storage systems

As most rural folk are aware, the water required for domestic and horticultural consumption is often not available from a mains supply. It is necessary to 'harvest' rainwater from the roof and run it directly into the garden by means of diversion pipes from gutterings, or store it in a tank until required. Recycling domestic water is another option.

There are several important aspects to be considered before investing in a tank. The first is cost, which will vary according to the material it is made of. Tanks are manufactured from galvanised steel, fibreglass, concrete and ferro-concrete and each has its own particular merit.

Galvanised steel tanks

These tanks are economical, light to transport and easy to install; but they can be subject to corrosion, which will eventually limit their life. Better quality steel tanks have a laminated polymer PVC type lining, which gives a 15-year guarantee.

Fibreglass tanks

Tanks made of fibreglass are corrosion resistant and offer a life expectancy of at least 20 years, but they cost almost twice as much as those made from galvanised steel. They're light to transport, easily installed and are just becoming available in environmentally sympathetic colours.

Concrete and ferro-concrete

These tanks are the most expensive and cost more to transport and install, but their life is indefinite. The largest transportable concrete tank is 22.5 kilolitres (4947 gal), and the largest transportable ferro-concrete tank is 34 kilolitres (7476 gal). If two or more tanks are used, interconnection should be arranged to ensure maximum turnover of water.

Recycling water

The water efficiency of your home can be improved by recycling waste water and diverting it for use in the garden. Recycling will diminish the flow of waste water that hard-pressed treatment plants have to process, at the same time saving water and your money, and helping your garden through times of drought. Recycling wastewater can be as simple as carrying one 10 litre (18 pt) bucket of bath water out to water a shrub or your containers. However, it is appreciated that recycling water by hand is not easy and idealism must be balanced with realism. Carting buckets of water from house to garden is time consuming and tiring, and your family's best overall contribution to water conservation would be to use it as sparingly and as conscientiously as possible at all times.

Recycled waste water is usually considered under two headings: greywater and blackwater. Greywater represents about 60 per cent of water used inside the home and is that which comes from bathing, washing dishes, laundry, etc. Blackwater is the water that comes from the flushing of toilets.

Shades of grey

If you decide to utilise greywater, it is essential to consider whether it contains harmful substances. Most soap and liquid detergents should cause plants no problem. Many washing powders contain sodium salts as bulking agents, but at normal dilution rates they should be safe. Environmentally friendly brands of laundry and dishwasher detergents use potassium salts rather than caustic sodium salts and are biodegradable.

A more potential problem is that many chemical based domestic detergents and cleansers contain boron, a crystalline metalloid element. Boron is toxic to human beings and boron toxicity in plants is manifested by stunted growth and a 'scorched' appearance. Take special care with water from the dishwasher also – detergents for this purpose often contain caustic soda and toxic chemicals harmful to both people and plants. So give some thought (see chapter 4) to the ingredients of your household cleansing agents and opt for biodegradable products made from vegetable oils and plant derivatives.

Provided environmentally sympathetic cleansers have been used, greywater from bathroom and laundry can be diverted straight into the garden. Kitchen waste water and that from dishwashers may require some treatment to remove grease and food particles. With all greywater the object is to keep the pathogens or bacteria count down.

Black water – think before you flush

Many currently acceptable practices in Western society are both wasteful and environmentally destructive. The flush toilet and the modern sewerage system are both. We have allowed our prejudices to create a situation where a staggering 30 per cent of our drinking water is now used to flush toilets and create major environmental problems downstream.

In his book *The Toilet Papers*, California State architect Professor Sim Van der Ryn described the process thus:

Mix one part of excreta with one hundred parts clean water. Send the mixture through pipes to a central station where billions are spent in a futile attempt to separate the two. Then dump the effluent, now poisoned with chemicals but still rich in nutrients into the nearest body of water. The nutrients feed algae, which soon use up all the oxygen in the water, eventually destroying all aquatic life that may have survived the chemical residues. All this adds up to a strange balance sheet; the soil is starved for the natural benefits of human manure that go down the toilet . . . so agri-business shoots it up with artificial fertilisers made largely from petroleum. These synthetics are not absorbed by the soil and leach out to pollute rivers and oceans. Our excreta – not waste but misplaced resources – end up destroying food chains, food supply and water quality in rivers and oceans . . . How did it come to pass that we devised

Using greywater in the garden

The following pointers will help you get the best use of recycled water for your garden:

- Waste water can be diverted over a wide area from a drainpipe outlet through a number of hose lengths clipped together with Y-shaped joints.
- If you're using hose outlets from bathroom, laundry or kitchen to divert greywater directly into the garden, simple filter systems to remove food particles, hair and other waste can be made by tying on small bags of fine meshed cloth at the hose ends – similar to the filter bag in a top loading washing machine. They will require emptying now and again – I tip mine straight into a compost bucket.
- Greywater is *not* suitable for soak hose or micro-jet irrigation systems as the small particles of waste will build up and block emitters or water holes.
- If greywater is to be used to irrigate vegetable gardens, restrict its application to the soil around and under plants. It should not touch above-ground edible fruit and foliage – tomatoes, corn, broccoli, cauliflower, etc. Don't apply it to the soil around leafy salad-type vegetables and *never* water any food-bearing plants from above with it. Take particular care that greywater does not splash onto crops such as lettuces, spring onions, radishes, or other vegetables that are to be eaten raw and might become contaminated with waste materials in the water.
- On the whole, greywater is best used for ornamental plants and precious fresh water supplies conserved for edibles.

Ensure that recycled water does not contaminate edible fruits.

- Regular, light top-dressings of compost or vegetative mulches on areas receiving greywater will deter flies seeking tiny food scraps and facilitate quick and natural decomposition of waste residues.
- Disperse greywater over as many garden areas as possible, avoiding a concentration in any one single site.
- When available rotate fresh water with greywater for irrigation to aid in leaching the soil of possible contaminants.
- Waste water is best used on mature plants, which can tolerate possible impurities, rather than on seedlings or immature plants.
- Greywater is alkaline, so try not to use it too frequently on acid-loving plants such as rhodos, azaleas and citrus. It is safe to use greywater for lawns, fruit trees and most other trees and shrubs.

such an enormously wasteful and expensive system to solve such a simple problem? Excreta is one of the few substances of material value we ever return to the earth . . .`

The use of human excreta as a natural fertiliser is an emotive and difficult subject in the Western world. Somehow, we've never relished the thought of using human excrement as a fertiliser, despite the fact that Asia has been using it since ancient times. We pump billions of tonnes of rich organic sewage annually into the seas, making it one of our planet's worst forms of pollution.

But our thinking is changing. Companies in a number of Western countries have set up processing plants to process sewage into organic soil conditioners. In beef and dairy farming countries such as Australia and New Zealand, compost produced from human waste is being used in pasture trials with dramatic results. Paddocks treated with the fertiliser grew more and bigger clover, were lush and green, and their earthworm populations

Polluted natural water sources could ultimately destroy life on earth.

exploded! The compost is said to be ideal for hay and silage production and appropriate in use for any rural horticultural venture.

Composting toilets

Viewed only as an aberration of 'greenie' society a few years ago, composting toilets are now becoming popular in both suburban and rural homes – and in some areas are replacing septic tanks. They are an excellent option in areas where water is scarce, where reticulated sewerage schemes are unavailable, where water tables are high and/or where conventional effluent disposal methods are difficult.

Composting toilets in appropriate situations are now also recognised as a valuable environmental advantage. Since they do not require flushing, they save enormous amounts of water, and they produce excellent organic fertiliser. For those of us in less urban areas who have more individual responsibility for our waste materials, consider, if appropriate, the installation of a modern composting toilet in addition to the water conservation practices already considered.

There are a number of efficient, aesthetically pleasing and reasonably priced types readily available, which turn human waste into a usable garden resource.

Loo life

A composting toilet pan works by separating body solids from urine. The solids fall straight into an aerated composting container, while the urine is drained off into a urine tank or into a greywater system filtered through gravelled drainage channels.

The body solids are decomposed with the help of fresh air, natural heat and micro-organisms, and the addition of tiger worms or compost worms (see worm farms, chapter 3.) The decomposition is an efficient natural process and over a period of time the mass transforms into organic compost. Only 10 per cent of the input volume remains after the natural process of decay has taken place inside the composting container, so that an average household would remove waste as compost only once a year.

By separating the urine from the solids, the decomposition process is accelerated. Urine is rich in nitrogen, phosphorus and potassium and is bacteria free. It is an excellent activating agent for the compost heap. Old urine is caustic and highly ammoniac – as such it can be used as non-chemical control for weeds and invasive grasses.

The difference between the infamous and malodorous old 'long drop' toilet and the modern composting toilet is that the former worked on an anaerobic – no air – principle. Anaerobic composting releases hydrogen sulphide and methane, which give off the characteristic bad odours; they also work at much lower temperatures, thus there is not enough heat to destroy pathogens in human waste.

The commercial composting toilet, which is as smart and streamlined as any traditional model, works on an aerobic system with oxygen moving throughout the whole mechanism. Carefully designed ventilation ducting systems create forced air draught movement drawn from the bottom of the heap up through roof vents. Aerobic decomposition is fast, has minimal odour and creates higher internal temperatures than anaerobic composting thus efficiently destroying bacteria.

Obviously composting toilets can only be employed in appropriate situations, but urban development has reached a stage where dramatic changes are necessary in our attitude to and practices of waste disposal in areas connected to public sewers. Otherwise the critical levels of pollution in our oceans and natural waters, which have already rendered countless aquatic species extinct, could ultimately destroy all animal life on earth.

CHAPTER TEN

XERISCAPING – CREATING THE DROUGHT RESISTANT GARDEN

Above: Xerophytes – low water requirement plants.

Having accepted that water is our most finite source, we recognise the need to rethink our ideas on garden design. In Australia, for example, the driest populated continent, incalculable water is used to maintain public and private gardens that feature water-hungry tracts of traditional English lawns and herbaceous borders. England's 'soggy sceptred isle' produces more than enough water to ensure the survival of gardens of this style. But if we insist on keeping to this tradition in the southern hemisphere and the USA, where water in many areas is scarce, not only are we willfully helping to deplete world supplies, but we are also denying ourselves the opportunity to design gardens and grow plants suited to our own natural environments. Many of our indigenous plants are beautiful, unusual and self sufficient, being perfectly adapted to the climate and fluctuations in rainfall.

Though it is certainly a good idea to stop wasting time, money and water by bunging in roses and rhododendrons in situations that are least likely to suit them, this doesn't mean that we're restricted to growing only native plants. We have at our disposal a huge variety of exotic plant species that will adapt well to having less water.

In the United States, drought resistant garden landscaping is called xeriscaping, and is defined as the practice of water conservation by the application of appropriate horticulture. This simply means designing gardens planted with drought resistant plants called xerophytes. This style of gardening has been widely adopted by many other countries, especially those with hot arid areas. Once established, this style of garden requires little maintenance or watering. Inspired by dry, pebbled Australasian river beds, English plants expert Beth Chatto transformed an old car park on her UK property into an outstanding gravel garden planted with xerophytes.

A successful xeriscape involves the following seven simple principles, most of which are also essentials of both sustainable and low maintenance gardening:

- Appropriate design for predominating climate.
- Conserving soil moisture by conditioning soil with organic materials to make it more moisture retentive and by using mulches to lessen surface evaporation.
- Reduction of turf areas.
- Installation of appropriate irrigation systems.
- Selection of drought tolerant plants grouped according to their water requirements.
- Maintaining water reserves by recycling and using rainwater storage systems.
- Provision of shelter against drying winds and hot sun.

Laying down the lawn

In reassessing our ideas on both water efficient and low maintenance garden design, lawns are top of the 'reconsider' list, since they may easily be replaced with attractive alternatives.

I'll admit that I'm as fond of the sight of a tranquil expanse of unbroken lawn as the next gardener. But how many lawns are actually in good enough condition to justify the fact that they're expensive, labour intensive, time-consuming features that require constant watering and maintenance? How much of your existing lawn does your family actually utilise?

Plan to reduce your lawn size to the minimum that will satisfy your family's needs; and if you're sowing a new lawn, choose drought resistant seed. This can thwart El Niño's attempts to dehydrate your precious patch of ancestral greensward to a lunar landscape of desert-like cracks punctuated by wisps of what look like wizened coconut matting. In addition to selecting a drought resistant grass mix, it's equally important to choose the correct seed to suit your family's needs. As well as scorching horribly, fine velvet lawns soon disappear beneath the onslaught of kids, dogs, balls, tricycles and climatic extremes.

Mixes available are usually blends of the following grass seeds:

- Rye and clover mix – this is cheap, but clover doesn't make a good lawn.
- Fescue and browntop mix – this makes fine lawns, but only in sheltered or cooler regions.
- Turf type rye grasses – these are fast growing hardy lawns, but require more mowing.

Before you decide to concrete the lot, be reassured that mixes of tall fescue grasses usually sold under trade names such as 'Mow-It-Less', or 'Drought-breaker', make hard-wearing, shade and drought resistant lawns. And just coming onto the market are new 'dwarf' grass blends that grow to a certain height and no more. Why didn't someone think of that 40 years ago!

Keep the lawn healthy and attractive by mowing weekly with mower blades at a height of 2 cm (1 in) and no lower. When a lawn is shaved like a skinhead weeds will soon re-infest it and the grass will die back in the first drought period. In countries such as Europe and America turf is left to grow longer – an excellent practice for hot dry areas. The longer top growth protects root systems and allows seed heads to form providing a continual supply of newly germinating grass plants to replace older ones.

If you must water your precious patch, deep water once weekly – light sprinklings with the

'Bowling-green' lawns are wasteful of water, time and energy.

Alternative lawns: pebbles, gravel, timber decks, or paved entertaining areas offer an excellent alternative to labour-intensive lawns.

hose only encourages a shallow root system, which will fry in hot sun. Mow without the catcher and leave clippings on the lawn as a mulch during drought periods.

Alternative lawns and hardscaping

Reducing or replacing lawn areas is one of the priority design principles behind establishing a water efficient garden. A sweep of attractively laid red brick, pavers, pebbles or shingle may require more expense initially than a bag of lawn seed, but the consequent savings in water, labour, maintenance and mechanical energy is enormous. It is said that the first signs of spring in the suburbs is the two-stroke symphony of lawn mowers burning petrol, oil or electricity. Consider countries such as India, China, the Middle East and Japan – huge tracts of the globe's face where gardens are designed to suit the limitations of climate, location and environment. Because of population density, scarcity of space and water, lawns are rarely part of oriental design. Tranquillity and a sense of space, even in the smallest of areas, is achieved by the use of open expanses of fine gravel, pebbles or sand.

No-mow grass and ground covers

On the whole, alternative lawns are neither as hard wearing, water saving or low maintenance as one might think. The surface can look ragged, will need watering in summer, will not stand up to heavy foot traffic, and may die back and look sparse and bare in winter. Replacement of turf areas with hardscaping materials is usually the better option.

If you absolutely can't live without a patch of green verdant luxury, no-mow Mercury Bay weed, *Dichondra repens*, is the most common hardy alternative to turf grass. Although it takes up to two years to establish, it eventually forms a

'Soft fall' play areas

If you've a young family then you'll obviously need to incorporate a 'soft fall' play area in your plan. Instead of struggling to maintain a small lawn, study the design of childrens' play areas when you next visit public parks and gardens.

Sand pits, water trays, paddling pools, pathways for tricycles and ground space beneath swings and climbing frames are invariably covered with hard wearing padded and reinforced artificial turf, or pressed layers of fine bark. This type of play space is safe and practical, and combines well with adjacent adult entertainment areas which may be paved as courtyards and patios, or designed around timbered decking.

Mesophytes – medium water-use plants.

thick evergreen carpet of kidney-shaped drought tolerant evergreen leaves. It also looks attractive interspersed with paving slabs in a chequerboard or similar pattern.

Thymes Square

It is possible also to sow aromatic lawns of thyme or chamomile, *Chamaemelum nobile*, which release delightful perfumes when trodden underfoot. Lawn chamomiles come with double or single flowers (these can both be dried to make relaxing camomile tea), but the variety 'Treneague' is non-flowering. *Thymus serpyllum* creeps over flat surfaces, *T. pulegiodes* 'Aureus' has foliage variegated green and gold, and *T. coccineus* produces a magnificent carpet of scarlet flowers. But be aware that the flowering thymes are beloved of bees – something of a hazard to bare feet in summer!

The downside to aromatic thyme or chamomile lawns is that neither will withstand heavy foot traffic and both will require painstaking weeding until they're well established. Chamomile will require mowing initially to help it thicken and will need watering during summer to prevent patches dying out. The gaps can be filled with divisions from mature plants, but this can end up being labour intensive.

Creepy-crawlies

A number of hardy creeping ground-cover plants can also be used to create alternative lawns, but not all are completely drought tolerant and the same intolerance to heavy foot traffic applies.

Ground-cover plants might include species such as *Ajuga, Cotula, Fuchsia procumbens, Hedera,* drought resistant blue-flowered *Isotoma fluviatilis, Leptinella, Orthiopogan, Parahebe, Pratia, Schizocentron, Viola hederaceae* (which requires moisture but is lovely in small patches), and any other crawling plants that will form a dense weed-supressing mat. When choosing, check for frost and cold hardiness if you suffer severe winters.

Designing and planting

A low water requirement garden doesn't mean you have to have a backyard full of cacti and yuccas! Design plans for less water hungry beds, borders and shrubberies feature plants from any of the following groups:

- drought hardy trees and shrubs, including fruiting varieties suited to environment
- trees and shrubs employed as shelter belts
- plants of bold architectural form
- xerophytes – drought resistant plants, including silver-foliaged species
- hardy natives
- ornamental grasses
- ground-cover plants
- bulbs

A list detailing suggested plants within these categories is included at the end of the chapter. They're suitable for use in both drought tolerant and low maintenance gardens. Bear in mind, however, that although many are also cold tolerant, they're not necessarily frost hardy. If you live in an area that enjoys long hot summers but suffers freezing winters, then xeriphytes like succulents and cacti are not suited to the grand design.

A garden incorporating varieties of plants that can survive mainly on natural rainfall is not only water efficient but is also less labour intensive – assuming the plants have been placed initially in conditioned, well-mulched soil, or planted with ground covers to prevent surface evaporation.

Whether you're designing a water efficient garden from scratch or redesigning an existing one, the following vital points should be considered:

- the path of the sun, both in summer and winter
- the prevailing winds in all seasons
- provision of shelter from drying or salt laden winds
- availability of existing shaded areas
- any sloping land
- type of soil and water retentive capacity

If you're revamping an existing garden, you'll have a pretty good idea about all these factors; if you're starting the garden from scratch, try to resist the temptation to rush out and start digging. Ideally you should first try to observe how these factors affect your outdoor living space over the full four seasons. The boggy shallows you had earmarked for a watergarden may become a concrete pan during summer, and the area you had visualised as the outdoor entertainment area may be plunged into dense shade or be subject to screaming winds in autumn and winter.

The three zone plan

For availability of watering and ease of maintenance it's wiser to group trees and shrubs together (as in the zoning plan that follows) rather than in isolated pockets. This is far more efficient than struggling to irrigate a whole garden when only a few plants really need water.

If you're redesigning, try to be strong enough to harden your heart and remove all inappropriate plants – swap them with friends for less water hungry specimens or resite them in grouped plantings. If you can spare the water and can't bear the thought of not growing at least some of your favourite, but more thirsty plants, fruit and vegetables, then zone your garden according to

Hydrophyte – high water use plant.

water requirements. This simply means grouping plants with similar water needs together – low water use plants (xerophytes), medium water use plants (mesophytes) and high water use plants (hydrophytes).

Give thought to the siting of plant zones; obviously the high water requirement plants will need to be nearer the house and a water source so that you can look after them easily, and where they'll benefit from the more sheltered environment. Planning the high water requirement zone nearer the house also means that recycled water, or roof rainwater diverted into a storage tank, is easily accessible for feeding the thirstiest area. It's important also that this zone is not already invaded by the moisture-robbing roots of mature trees or shrubs.

Plants for the three water zones
Low water zone plants – xerophytes

Selections of plants for hot dry areas with little shelter might include Australian and New Zealand natives such as flaxes (phormiums), cabbage trees (cordylines), ornamental grasses, leucospermums, proteas, banksias, acacias, grevilleas, yuccas, cacti, aloes, bromeliads, succulents, herbs, plants with silver foliage, lavenders, daisies, climbers such as bougainvillea and fruit trees such as olives and dates. It can also includes hardy bulbs and ground covers.

Some like it hot – Xerophytes

How do drought resistant plants conserve water? Plants lose an enormous amount of water during transpiration, so many have evolved ingenious techniques for conserving water, which ensures survival in hot dry climates. Features of xerophytes which help them to conserve water include:

- small leathery leaves
- a thick waxy cuticle and thick protective outer layer of skin
- sunken foliage pores
- small compact cells
- extensive root systems
- water storage cells, either in the leaves or the stem
- foliage covered with fine silver moisture trapping hairs
- extra fibrous supportive tissue in foliage skin. When the stomata (sunken foliage pores) close due to dehydration, the loss of water to transpiration can be reduced to almost nil. The extra fibrous stem supportive tissue prevents the dehydrated wilt we see in water hungry plants.

Medium water zone plants – mesophytes

Include the hardier vegetables (pumpkins or potatoes grown in straw), herbs, hardier fruit and nut trees, grape vines, and trees and shrubs. Choose the latter from a selection with evergreen, variegated, grey, red and gold foliage for year-round variety of colour, shape and form. Bulbs and ground covers can also be included in this zone.

High water zone plants – hydrophytes

This zone might include a small lawn, perennial and shrub borders, vegetable garden, most fruit trees and most exotic ornamental shrubs, including roses. For the water efficient vegetable garden, the raised no-dig beds system detailed in chapter 3 is designed for maximum ease of working, watering and moisture retention.

How much water?

It's difficult to give hard and fast rules, because everyone's soil, climatic conditions, garden design and choice of plants is different. However, watering guidelines are based on three things: type of root systems, the moisture retaining capacity of your soil, and, assuming you have chosen plants with low water requirements, the adaptations they have evolved to survive dry situations.

Plants with deep extensive root systems and those that are able to store moisture (cacti, succulents, aloes, etc) are able to survive on very little water; plants growing in quick draining sandy or volcanic soils require more frequent watering for shorter periods; plants growing in heavier soils, which take longer to wet, retain moisture over longer periods and require less watering overall. Plants that are growing in mulched soil require much less water than unmulched soil.

Rely as much as possible on natural rainfall and when you water, do so at regular intervals, say once a week or once a fortnight. Having learned your soil type and its moisture retentive capacities, water deeply and thoroughly to a depth of 30 cm (12 in) rather than more frequently and lightly.

Frequent light waterings are dangerous, because they only wet the surface of the soil, encouraging roots to grow upwards in search of moisture. The water evaporates quickly and the soil dries out, leaving the roots to fry. If you are watering with an irrigation system, you'll soon learn precisely how long to leave the sprinklers or soaker hose on to give a deep soaking.

Surviving the seasons

If you live in an area with long, hot, dry summers, but can manage to provide enough water for a small vegetable garden, try to work with the weather patterns to conserve water. Plant specific water hungry crops such as salad stuffs, cabbage, celery and carrots during the cooler, wetter months of the year. Less thirsty vegetables that can withstand the hottest months with minimal watering might include potatoes grown in straw or barrels, pumpkins, chilli peppers, capsicum, zucchinis, strawberries, asparagus and garlic.

If you need to transplant seedlings or plant tender young plants during hot weather, invest in some rolls of lightweight cover or shade cloth and leave it draped lightly over them until the flowers start to form. Remove it at this stage, or you'll prevent beneficial insects from pollinating them and get no crops! Shade cloth will give young plants a much better chance of survival by protecting them from the sun's scorching rays, by masking them from insect pests and by helping to conserve moisture in the soil.

Fruit trees

Remember that fruit trees and bushes should be integrated into the tree and shrub category so that the reward for self sacrifice in axing the lawn is home-grown produce. Place them in the high water requirement zone as detailed above – or if you live in an absolute desert, there are many dwarf varieties of fruiting trees, including citrus, bred specifically for growing in containers. These are especially valuable in countries suffering extremes of heat in summer and cold in winter. The containers can be moved into shelter for protection during colder months and watered during the hot season.

Properly planted in a tub of good quality potting mix incorporating generous proportions of water saturating aids, liquid retention crystals and slow release fertiliser, you may still enjoy fruit in return for minimum labour and water consumption.

Low-thirst plants

The list of low-thirst plants for water efficient gardens which is provided at the end of this chapter is by no means exhaustive, but suggests groups from which drought tolerant plants may be chosen. Although chosen for hardiness, like most plants many will perform better if some watering is possible, but they won't wilt and expire without it. Most will tolerate light frosts, but they are generally suited to temperate areas and will require some protection in colder climates.

Eye-catching combinations of drought-defying plants.

Plant trees and shrubs between autumn and spring when soil moisture levels are high, and conducive to quick root development. Smaller specimens establish more quickly than larger ones. If you plant during the summer months your plants will be entirely dependent on the copious amounts of water you'll need to give them to nurse them through. They will survive as long as you don't allow them to dry out, but they will do little in the way of establishing root growth. Group fruit trees together in the medium water zone area in a position of full sun and away from competition from other plants. Mulch heavily between specimens using thick layers of overlapping newspaper, and top-dress with bark or vegetative mulch.

Mediterranean plants such as cistus, lavenders, oleanders, silver-leafed plants, olives and many herbs perform well in dry gritty soils. Many of the drought tolerant plants listed at the end of this chapter are also suitable for inclusion in low maintenance gardens.

Gardens in the sun

The permutations for creating attractive plant association by combining selections from each group of drought-defying plants are endless. The dry garden is not just a dull old dustbath of cacti and succulents, but one created with plants presenting petals and foliage of exciting and contrasting colours, texture, form and shape – all blooming at different times for year round interest.

Xeriscaping is the system of employing drought busting plants appropriate to low water zones, of working with natural conditions instead of trying to beat them into submission. It is a system for creating gardens in the sun.

Drought tolerant plants

Key: D – deciduous C – climber E – evergreen EF – edible fruit F – flowering (given only where blooms are conspicuous enough to be ornamental) MS – many species R – recommended S – shrub T – tree

Tough trees

The following trees are suitable for planting in dry areas:

Abies, firs (MS. E.)

Acacia, spp, wattle (T-S. F. E. MS.) R. – *A. baileyana, A. conferta, A. decora, A. fimbriatia,*

A. floribunda, A. spectabilis, A. vestita.

Albizia, silk tree (T. D. F.)

Azara microphylla, vanilla tree

Bauhinia spp (T. F.) R. – *B. alba, B. carroni, B. purpurea*

Casuarina spp, she-oak (T. E.) R. – *C. stricta* and *C. torulosa*

Cordyline australis, cabbage tree (T. E, F.) R. – *C.* 'Purple Tower', *C. albertii, C. nigra.*

Conifers (MS. E.)

Dryandra (T-S. F. E.) Drought resistant, hardy to poor soils

Eucalyptus spp (T. E.) Over 600 species – choose garden-sized varieties. R. – *E. dumosa, E. erythrocorys, E. erythronema, E. ficifolia, E. forrestiana, E. grossa, E. kruseana, E. lansdowneana, E. leptophylla, E. nutans, E. torquata, E. woodwardii*

Ficus carica, fig (T. D. EF.)

Gleditsia tricanthos, honey locust (T. D.) R. – *G.t* 'Emerald Cascade', *G.t.* 'Rubylace', (reddish-purple), *G.t.* 'Sunburst' (golden)

Jacaranda mimosifolia (T. F. D.) Large gardens only

Junipers (M. S. E.)

Juglans regia, walnut (T. EF. D.) Large gardens only

Macademia ternifolia (T. EF. D.) Include in medium water zone

Nerium oleander, oleander (T. F.) Toxic to humans and animals if ingested

Olea europa spp, olive (T. MS. EF. E.)

Punicea granatum, pomegranate (T. F. D. EF.) Highly ornamental flowers and fruit

Pyrus sacilifolia 'pendula' (D.)

Robinia pseudocacia spp, (T. D.) R. – *R.p.* 'Frisia' golden robinia

Creative conifers

Listed above in hardy tree-shrub categories, conifers are a vast family of mostly evergreen trees and shrubs bearing leathery textured, blade or needle-like leaves. Their water requirements are modest and they come in an infinite range of shapes, heights and colours making them invaluable for providing the garden with year round interest. They require little pruning and except in areas of hot humidity suffer few diseases and pests. Colours range from many shades of green,

Vibrant bougainvillea thrive in a sun-drenched Mediterranean garden.

silvery-blues, through copper-bronzes to rich golden yellows and creams.

Stately dark green or golden conifers such as pencil pine, *Cupressus sempervirens, C. s.* 'Gracilis', or *Thuya pyramidalis* rising singly or in groups form bold architectural statements among specimens of softer rounded or weeping forms. There are many low growing prostrate conifers which provide excellent ground cover.

Palms

Tough drought tolerant palms include *Washingtonia, Brahea armata, Butia capitata, Jubaea Chilensis* and *Chamaerops humilis* (European fan palm). Although not strictly palms, cycads are drought tolerant palm-like plants.

Phormiums (flaxes)

Not strictly a tree or a shrub, versatile, drought resistant and cold-hardy phormiums offer the landscaper both softly weeping or broad upright, sword-like foliage for dramatic accents. The genus comes in colours, sizes and heights to suit every situation. Many have bi- or tri-coloured foliage ranging through cream- and yellow-striped greens, apricot-pinks, scarlet-pinks to purple-bronze-blacks. The cabbage tree, *Cordyline australis*, has all the attributes of the phormiums and makes a striking small landscaping specimen.

Shrubs

Artemisia spp (MS. S.) Finely cut, dissected silver foliage

Agryanthemum frutescens, marguerite daisies (MS. S. F.)

Banksia spp (T-S, MS, E. F.) Bold plants with striking foliage and dramatic flowers. R. – *B. coccinea, B. collina, B. ericifolia, B. grandis, B. integrifolia, B. marginata, B. serrata*

Brachyglottis (*Senecio* spp) (S. F. E.) Daisy flowers, water-conserving felted foliage

Berberis spp (S. D.) Cultivars with attractive lime green, purple or gold foliage

Callistemon spp, bottlebrush (T. S. F. E. MS.) R. – *C. citrinus, C. linearis, C. phoeniceus, C. rigidus, C. viminalis*

Cassia artemisiodes (T-S. F.) R. – *C. eremophila, C. phyllodenia*

Chamaecyparis (T-S.E. MS.) Conifers of diverse form, colour and size

Cupressus/Cupressocyparis (T-S. E. MS.) Conifers of diverse form, colour and size

Cistus purpureus, rock roses (S. MS. F .E.)

Coprosma spp (S. E. MS.) Hardy shrubs with glossy, often variegated foliage

Convolvulus cneorum (S. F. E.) White chalice flowers, silver foliage

Cotoneaster spp. (MS. S. F. E.) R. – *C. cornubius, C. lacteus, C. franchetti, C. pannosus, C. salicifolius.* Masses tiny flowers followed by colourful long lasting winter berries

Cytisus spp, broom (S. E.) R. – *C. albus, C. x racemosus, C. scoparius*

Dodonaea viscosa, ake-ake (T-S. F. E.) Attractive purple foliage

Euryops pectinatus (S. F. E.) Silver-green foliage, yellow daisy flowers

Feijoa sellowiana, guava (S. E. F. E.)

Genista spp, broom (S. F. E.) R. – *G. pendula alba, G. lydia, G. pilosa*

Grevillea spp (S. MS. F. E.) R. – *G. alpina, G. banksii, G. baueri, G. caleyi, G. juncifolia, G. juniperina, G. lavandulacea, G. noelli, G. rosmarinifolia, G. sericea, G. speciosa, G. stenomera*

New Zealand cabbage trees and flaxes are well suited to dry soils.

Sun seeker: flamboyant Hawaiian hibiscus hybrid.

Hakea spp (MS. S. E.) R. – *H. leucoptera, H. lorea, H. multilineata, H. nodosa, H. petiolaris, H. purpurea, H. sericea, H. sauveolens, H. victoria.* Large and spectacular pin cushion flowers of yellow or orange

Helianthemum nummularium, sunrose

Hibiscus spp (S. semi-deciduous MS.) *H. syriacus* is hardiest. *H. rosa-sinensis* and *H. schizopetalus* will thrive in medium water zone. Hawaiian and Fijian cultivars are bold and flamboyant but not frost hardy

Hydrangeas (S. D. F.) Handsome foliage, large blue, pink, white, mauve flower heads

Juniperus spp, juniper (T-S. E. MS.) Versatile conifers in many shapes, sizes, colours

Lagerstroemia, crepe myrtle (S. D.) Colourful flowers and autumn foliage

Leptospermum spp, tea tree (T-S) R. – *L. flavescens, L. citratum, L. scoparium*

Melaleuca spp. (T-S. F. MS. E.) R. – *M. adnata, M. armillaris, M. erubescens, M. genistifolia, M. incana, M. linariifilaia, M. nesophila, M. nodosa, M. pulchella, M. squamea, M. thymifolia, M. uncinata*

Olearia spp (S. F.) Daisy flowers, wax coated foliage

Osmanthus fragrans (S.) *O. heterophyllus*

Picea (T-S. MS. E.) Spruces of diverse size, colour and shape

Philadelphus coronarius, mock orange (S.) Fragrant white flowers, glossy foliage. R. – *P.* Virginal, *P.* Belle Etoile

Plumbago auriculata, plumbago (S. E. F.)

Pyracantha spp (S. E.) R. – *P. rogersiana, P. coccinea, P. augustifolia*

Pelargonium spp, geraniums (MS. S. F.) Aromatic evergreens, colourful flowers

Pittosporum spp (MS. F. T-S. E.) R. – *P. crassifolium, P. ralphi.* Lemon scented blooms

Protea spp (MS. E. F.) From S. Africa and Australia, require light sandy soils. Include *Leucadendron, Leucospermum, Mimetes, Serruria* and *Grevillea.* Striking foliage, colourful and dramatic flowers/bracts. R. – *P. barbigera, P. compacta, P. cynaroides, P. eximia, P. neriifolia, P. nana, P. repens, P. scolymochephala*

Rosa spp, roses (MS. EF (hips) F. S. D.) R. – *Rosa rugosa* and *R. harisonii* in dry zones, many others for medium water zones

Tamarisk aphylla, (T-S. D.) R. – *T.* 'Pink Cascade', *T. rubra, T. hispida, T. parviflora*

Telopia speciosissima, waratah (S. E.) Architectural foliage, vibrant dramatic flowers

Thuja (T-S. E. MS.) Conifers of diverse colours, sizes and forms

Vitis spp, grape (C. D. EF.)

Westringia fruticosa, coast rosemary (S.)

Perfect perennials

Acanthus mollis (bear's breeches). Glossy architectural foliage, tall flower spires

Achillea spp (yarrow). Select non-invasive varieties

Agapanthus spp. Tall perennial with long strappy foliage, large globe heads of blue, white or violet flowers

Armeria (thrift). Grass-like clump forming mats throw up 6 cm (2½ in) tall pompom flowers

Clivia spp. Most useful evergreen perennial with striking red/orange/gold flowers, lustrous strappy leaves. Will tolerate hot, dry shade but will scorch in direct sunlight

Coreopsis spp. Annuals and perennials bearing golden yellow daisy flowers

Dianthus spp. Pinks and carnations with richly fragrant flowers and silver foliage

Echinacea purpurea (cone flower)

Echinops (globe thistle). Striking blue-grey/white ball-shaped flowerheads

Echium vulgare (known as viper's bugloss in northern hemisphere). Attractive to beneficial insects. Considered a noxious weed in some areas of Australia. Upright self sowing plant with white, lavender or pretty mauve-pink flowers. *E. fatuosum* is a hardy shrub-like perennial with bold blue flower spikes

E. piniana. Biennial forming attractive rosette of leaves during first year and throwing up long-lasting stunning 3 m (10 ft) flower spikes of electric blue in the second. *E. wildpretti* bears coral pink blooms

Eryngium spp (sea holly). Bold spiny flower heads with bluish metallic sheen

Gaillardia grandiflora (blanket flower)

Helichrysum apiculatum (everlasting daisy)

Heliotrope ('cherry-pie'). Richly fragrant purple flowers

Hemerocallis (daylily). Strap-like foliage, colourful and exotic lily-like flowers. Evergreen and deciduous species

Iris spp. Many varieties suitable for low water zones

Limonium (statice). Everlasting flowers of white, pink, blue, lavender

Linum spp (flax flower)

Nepeta fassenii (catmint). Aromatic silver green foliage, lavender-blue flower spires

Papaver orientale (oriental poppy)

Penstemon. Bears spires of colourful bell-shaped flowers over many months

Rudbeckia hirta (gloriosa daisy)

Salvia spp (MS.)

Stachys byzantina. Felted silver foliage, mauve flowers

Thymus spp (MS.)

Silver threads

Always useful in the garden and excellent in containers, silver leafed plants become invaluable in hot dry summers. Their drought resistant soft grey foliage breaks up and lightens massed greens, and provides the perfect foil for bold flower colour. Often natives of hot Mediterranean countries, but reasonably cold hardy, silver plants require well drained soils (especially in winter) and positions in full sun. They're available in all shapes and sizes, from trees to ground covers. Garden-sized trees include the delightful weeping silver pear, *Pyrus sacilifolia* 'pendula', silver

Sun-loving oriental poppy.

birches, olives, the blue cedars, junipers and the smaller conical conifers.

Highly recommended medium-sized shrubs include the *Artemisia* family – the cultivars 'Lambrook Silver', 'Powis Castle' and *A. ludoviciana* 'Silver Queen', all bearing beautiful, finely dissected silver foliage. A welcome recent addition to the Artemisia family providing an attractive spreading ground cover is *A.* 'Broughton Silver'. Few plants can trace their Mediterranean origins with such clarity – Artemisias were planted by the roadsides by the Roman army so that soldiers could pack their sandals with aromatic sprigs to soothe feet sore from marching!

Other attractive shrubs include, the 'sweet pea bush', *Podalyria calyptrata* (2 m/6½ ft) which has silky silver leaves and lavender-pink flowers. Small to medium shrubs include feathery cotton lavender, *Santolina chamaecyparissus,* and *Convolvulus cneorum* with wonderful shiny aluminium-grey foliage and white chalice flowers. A personal favourite is *Pyrethrum* 'Silver Lace', whose name describes its lace-like foliage perfectly and which smothers itself in small daisy flowers throughout summer.

A blue flowered shrub which clips well into topiary shapes or hedges is silver germander, *Teucrium fruticans.*

Recommended silver-foliaged ground covers include *Stachys byzantina,* 'lambs ears', with soft furry leaves, dwarf lavenders, prostrate rosemary, low growing *Artemisia* 'Valerie Finnis', and

Architectural grandeur: globe artichoke.

Cerastium tormentosum, which forms a creeping mat of platinum-white. The crawling yellow ever-lasting daisy *Helichrysum argyrophyllum* has glitzy silver leaves, *H. retortum* has luminous white flowers, and the aromatic *H. augustifolium* is more commonly known as the curry plant. Slightly taller ground cover daisies include the hardy Gazania family with boldly coloured flowers and green or grey felted foliage.

Grey-foliaged bedding plants include the ever popular scented pinks and carnations, the Dianthus family, and dusty miller – *Senecio cineraria* – with platinum silver-white felted and sculptured leaves. An effective and vigorous spreading plant that doubles up as a sprawling mound or climber, *Helichrysum petiolare* has small grey heart-shaped leaves like grey velvet.

For the contrast of upright form choose silver-blue ornamental grasses such as *Festuca glauca*, *Elymus solandri*, or *Poa astonii* with elegant weeping foliage – they're also frost hardy. Blue oat grass, *Helictotrichon sempervirens*, has spiky silver leaves and attractive feathery flowers. More about ornamental grasses shortly.

If knock the eyes out drama is your desire – and you've space – plant one of the giant thistles belonging to the cardoon, onopordum, or globe artichoke families. Bearing deeply dissected felted leaves to 1 m (3 ft) in length, the plants soar to 2 m (6½ ft) and are topped with a huge lavender thistle-like flowers.

For bold architectural form, the flax-like New Zealand astelia, *Astelia chamathica,* with broad sword-like glistening silver leaves is superb. The deciduous plume poppy, *Macleaya cordata,* is also a striking plant with large heart-shaped leaves that look like those of a fig, grey-green above with white undersides that glisten in the breeze. The stems throw up impressive 2 m (6½ ft) stalks topped with long lasting feathery plumes of cream flower heads, which age to smoky bronze.

The verbascums also make dramatic accent plants, throwing up tall flower spikes of pink, purple and yellow from large rosettes of silver-white felted foliage.

Eryngiums (sea hollies) bear striking cone-shaped flower heads with an exciting metallic lustre. A traditional favourite is *Eryngium giganteum,* commonly called 'Miss Wilmott's Ghost' after the famous British gardener.

As underplanting for roses or to provide contrast among other green leafed perennials, try poppies with deliciously frilly flower heads and silver-green foliage, *Lychnis coronaria* with white woolly leaves and magenta flowers, or *L. c.* 'alba' with white flowers.

Easy to grow, silver plants have some of the most beautiful and diverse foliage of all garden plants. I also find them most useful in repeated plantings to add cohesion and to form a unifying principle throughout the garden; which reminds me of the tragic tale of the garden visitor who eyed my prized all-silver garden with gratifying thoroughness, and declared, 'It'll look quite pretty when you get some colour in there.'

Climbers and twiners
Akebia quinata (E. F.) Soft green clover-like leaves, scented chocolate-purple blooms

Billardiera, apple-berry (E. F.) Australian climber with dark green narrow leaves and bell-shaped cream blue-tipped flowers, followed by deep purple-blue berries

Bougainvillea spp. (C. E. MS.) R. – 'Scarlett O'Hara'

Campsis grandiflora, trumpet vine (D. F.) Spectacular flame-orange blooms in summer, attractive glossy foliage. R. – *C. radicans*, *C.* 'Madam Galen'

Gelsemium, Carolina jasmine (E. F.) Glossy dark-green foliage, fragrant yellow flowers

Hardenbergia (E. F.) Winter flowering – massed violet-blue or pink pea-shaped blooms

Hedera, ivy (E. MS.)

Kennedia, Australian coral pea (E. F.) Salmon-scarlet pea shaped flowers

Parthenocissus (D. MS.) Hardy vines offering brilliant autumn foliage

Oetrea (E. F.) Bears arching sprays of massed violet-blue flowers

Solandra, golden chalice vine (E. F.) Huge exotic flowers striped purple. Vigorous

Tecomaria capensis, Cape honeysuckle (C. F. D.)

Vitis (D. MS. E. F.) Edible fruit, some species grown for autumn foliage

Wisteria spp (C.MS. D. F.) R. – *W. floribunda* (Japanese wisteria), *W. sinensis* (Chinese wisteria)

Ornamental grasses

Do you think only of grasses as something that gets up your nose and makes you sneeze in summer? As animal food or just that cursed stuff that grows faster than the wheels of your mower spin? Think again. Ornamental grasses (*Graminaea* spp) are so important they're called 'the hair of the earth' and are treasured on today's garden landscaping scene for their unparalleled beauty and diversity of texture, form, colour and size.

In addition to withstanding freezing temperatures, tussocky grasses have low water requirements and are found in many of the world's most arid areas. As many of the more common drought tolerant plants are at least slightly frost tender, grasses are excellent for areas that have long searing hot summers and freezing winters. Their light airy structure and graceful pendulous habit provide pleasing contrast amongst plants with rounded shapes and foliage.

The list below is by no means exhaustive but will give you an idea of the diversity of ornamental grasses available, and ideas for their use in the dry garden.

Very dry places
Carex spp
Chionocloa spp
Ophiopogon jaburan
Cortaderia spp
Libertia peregrinans
Festucas glauca, scoparia
Helictotrichon sempervirens
Brizia media
Astelia banksii

Exposed coastal or eroded areas
Carex comans
Carex trifida

Carex testacea
Cortaderia
Astelia banksii
Miscanthus sinensis
Acipyhlla spp
Phalaris var. *picta*
Cortaderia selloana

Grasses for ground covers
Carex spp
Dianella spp
Libertia peregrinans
Festuca scoparia
Ophiopogon spp
Brizia media

Cold tolerant grasses
Carex spp
Chionocloa spp
Cortaderia spp
Hakonechloa macra (with protection)
H. m. aureola (with protection)
Miscanthus sinensis

Variegated grasses
Hakonechloa 'aureola'
Molinia caerulea 'variegata'
Alopecurus pratensis 'aureo-marginatus'
Arundo donax 'versicolour'
Arundinaria viridstriata and bamboo spp
Cortaderia spp
Phalaris Aruninacea var. *picta*
Miscanthus sinensis 'zebrinus'
Agropyron pubiflorum

Golden grasses
Phyllstachus aurea, golden bamboo
Acipylla aurea
Aciphylla (coxella) dieffenbachii
Carex elata 'aurea'
Milium effusum 'aureum'
Carex stricta 'Bowles Golden'
Alopecurus pratensis
Aciphylla 'Golden Spaniard'
Libertia peregrinans
Ucinia rubra
Pennisetum cultivars – bronze-toned stalks, rosy-purple flower heads
Briza maxima, Briza media – maroon-red flowers

Water-storing plants

Water-storing plants include agaves, aloes, cactus, succulents, and yuccas. The ultimate arid area garden is of course one that requires no water at all. The striking architectural form of the popular species listed below create distinctive landscaping effects with little effort. Many have the added virtue of multiplying without any help from the gardener!

Many of the lower growing compact succulents, ice plants and cacti also form superb weed and drought-defying ground covers. Dismissed for years as dull and boring, the combination of water shortage and the need for low maintenance gardens has thrust these under-planted and under-valued plants into the limelight. Amazingly versatile, they come in every shape, form and colour from miniature ground covers, through trailing varieties to bold architectural giants.

Aeonium: Rosette forming succulents from the Mediterranean area and North Africa. Mature plants often develop eye-catching multiple trunks topped with large rosettes and may grow to over 1.2 m (4 ft) tall. Foliage is colourful and includes bold purplish-blacks – the dramatic *Aeonium* 'Schwartzkopft' is black. Aeonium bear a profusion of small starry yellow flowers.

Aloe spp: An African genus of rosette forming plants with thick fleshy leaves. Often bear vibrant reddish-orange flowers on multi-headed spikes. R. – *A. vera, A. saponaria.*

Agave: Genus of dramatic larger succulents mainly from south-western USA and Mexico. Form large rosettes of big strappy leaves edged with sharp spines. R. – *A. attenuata, A. americana,* and the attractive variegated *A. victoriae-reginae.*

Beaucarnia: Beloved of landscapers, the pony tail palm or bottle palm from south-western U.S and Mexico is a very distinctive succulent with a head of grassy leaves atop a round bulbous stem. The stem is a moisture reservoir, which expands and contracts as its reserves vary.

Carpobrotus: African genus including *C. edulis,* the common ice plant. Wide spreading ground cover with fleshy succulent leaves and vibrant pink, yellow, red or white daisy-like flowers.

Crassula: Widespread genus of succulents including many different forms and heights. Highly variable foliage forms but most carrying clusters of white, cream or pink flowers.

Cactaceae spp (cactus): A cast of thousands, in every shape, form and size. Flowering sometimes infrequently, but with exotic long lasting blooms.

Drosanthemum: Southern African genus of succulent trailing perennials with pink or purple daisy-like flowers. Superb ground cover.

Echiveria: Rosette forming succulents from Central South America. Available in wide range of foliage colours and sizes. All have similar small red, yellow, or orange flowers on wiry spikes emerging from the rosettes, which are often silver tinged pink.

Sedum: Large genus of succulents, excellent ground covers. Smaller species are mat or rosette forming with fleshy rounded leaves, some resembling jelly beans. Larger species usually have similar foliage but are borne on short trunks. Flowers are commonly pink, pinkish-red or white. R. – *S. spectabile.*

An *Echiveria* hybrid, with its perfect form and subtle colours, looks stunning when teamed with a blue glazed pot.

Sempervivum: Rosette forming succulents from Europe. Foliage varies from tiny to large and strappy and plants bear small flowers of cream or pink. Superb ground covers.

Yucca gloriosa: Genus of rosette or clump forming semi-succulent plants from N. Africa, many with attractively variegated foliage. Some are ground covers but others develop into bushes or small-trunked trees to 1.3 m (4 ft) high. Leaves are often tipped with spines and plants throw up spectacular stalks of creamy-white bell-shaped flowers 1 m (3 ft) tall.

Ground-cover plants

Arctotis spp, African daisy. Colourful ground-cover daisies, many with silver foliage

Artemisia spp. R.– *A.* 'Valerie Finnis', *A.* 'Broughton Silver'

Bromeliads spp. Epiphytes

Cacti, many species

Dimorphotheca pluvialis, Cape daisy. White, pink, lavender flowers, petals on some hybrids elongated and spoon-shaped at tips

Drosanthemum, succulent trailing plant, daisy flowers

Gazania, daisies, dwarf

Helichrysum petiolare, forms silver-grey spreading mound

Agryanthemum, Marguerite daisies. Dwarf cultivars

Carpobrotus edulis, pig-face (MS.)

Centranthus rubra, false valerian

Cotoneaster horizontalis, spreading shrub with attractive autumn-winter berries

Gramineae (MS.) Dwarf ornamental grasses

Grevillea biternata

Lamranthus roseus, ice plant. *L. aureus, L. multiradiatus*

Rosmarinus officinalis prostratus, rosemary

Succulents (MS.)

Thymus spp (MS.) R. – *T. vulgaris, T. praecox, T. arcticus*

Verbenas (MS.)

Bulbs and corms

The term 'bulb' is loosely used to describe a range of plants growing from corms, tubers and rhizomes. Many are especially valuable in the dry garden because of their ability to become dormant during drought periods. They're able to rely on moisture stored in their corms or tubers to see them through to the next rains. Many of the hardy South African bulbs such as nerines and amaryllis, which are inactive during summer, burst into flower with the arrival of the autumn rains.

Allium, ornamental onions

Amaryllis, belladonna lily. Large pink or white trumpet shaped blooms, 50 cm (20 in) stems

Babiana, member of iris family. Strap like leaves and violet-blue flowers

Colchicum, large pink, mauve or white flowers appear in late summer before foliage

Chionodoxa, small starry blue flowers on 15 cm (6 in) stems

Crocosmia masonorum, C. paniculata. Orange, rust-red flowers on arching stems

Haemanthus, bold orange-red flowers appearing before broad strappy leaves

Freesia, richly fragrant flowers of many colours in early spring

Fritillaria, pendulous bell-shaped flowers, green, yellow, purple, prettily freckled

Ipheion, small star-shaped lilac-blue flowers over low growing glass-like foliage

Ixia, starry flowers of bold colours on 50 cm (20 in) stems

Lachenalia, spires of pendulous tubular flowers of golden-orange

Liriope muscari, dark strap-like leaves, spires of thickly clustered purple flowers

Nerine, spider lily. Tall stem topped by massed tubular flowers, white, pink, red

Ornitholgalum, clusters of white star-like flowers atop tall stalks

Rhodohypoxis, forms low grassy clump, profuse waxy pink, white starry flowers

Romulea, crocus-like flowers, deep pink, red, over grass-like foliage

Sparaxis, white, pink, orange, purple-red starry flowers on 30 cm (12 in) stalks

Tigridia, jockey's caps. Distinctly shaped pink, red, yellow flowers on 15 cm (6 in) stems

Vallota, Scarborough lily. Clusters large red trumpet-shaped flowers on 30 cm (12 in) stems

Watsonia, tall clumping plant, 1 m (3ft) spires of white, salmon, pink, coral flowers

Zepthranthes (autumn crocus), yellow-eyed white chalice flowers, grass-like foliage

CHAPTER ELEVEN

DESIGNING THE LOW MAINTENANCE GARDEN

I do not envy the owners of large complicated gardens. The garden should fit its master or its tastes, just as his clothes do; it should be neither too large nor too small, but just comfortable…If the garden is larger than he can individually garden and plan and look after, then he is no longer its master but its slave.

Gertrude Jekyll, 1874

An alternative definition offered in my late twentieth century dictionary for 'gardener' is 'A servant employed to tend the garden'. The trouble with gardening is it sometimes seems that no matter how much you do, it is never, ever enough! Little doubt who is servant and who is master. This particular master offers no defined 40-hour week, no long weekends, no sick leave, salary or bonuses, but infinite scope for overtime – all unpaid. When the garden hungers, we bestow food; when it thirsts, we give it water; when it ails we dispense medicine; and when inclement

Above: Successful low maintenance gardens employ a harmonious integration of hardy natives and exotics.
Opposite: This Californian garden combines strong design with plants suitable to its environment.

weather threatens we offer protection. What other 'leisure' pursuit demands 365 days a year servitude – in all weathers?

The sustainable garden is a low maintenance garden so let's define this phrase immediately. First of all, low maintenance gardening doesn't mean spending less time and energy on all the boring jobs like mowing, weeding and pruning. To mow and prune once a fortnight instead of weekly doesn't work – the garden will simply resemble the Amazon just that bit quicker.

An easy-care garden requires a complete change of philosophy and design. It is easy to give good advice to others. My only justification for doing so is that my knowledge has been won through brutal toil and bitter experience! Garden-

Gravel pathways run through beds of hardy natives, exotics, ornamental grasses and succulents.

Try first to identify the garden areas or chores that are most labour intensive, time consuming and irksome. Make a list and ask yourself, Can I eliminate/modify this problem? Can I dispense with the area or project altogether, or if not, how can I make it less labour intensive?

If there is no way to make the area less labour intensive, you have only two alternatives: concrete the whole lot over; or grin and bear it, but grant this particular work area high priority in your overall scheme of things. Go all out to get the area or problem under control, or the project better managed, then be strict about setting aside a specified length of time in your daily/weekly work schedule so that you keep absolutely on top of it.

ing doesn't have to be a pastime that can only be enjoyed by dedicated masochists. Do you control your garden or does it control you? Would you love an attractive easy care garden but don't know where to start? If your answer is 'yes' to both these questions, slow down and read on!

Low maintenance gardening means adopting an entirely new way of gardening whereby the great time wasters – weeding, mowing and pruning – are drastically reduced or eliminated altogether.

I've developed 10 basic rules that will ensure success for those who love their garden but who want a life beyond it!

1. Create an easy-care design.
2. Choose easy-care/certified disease resistant plants.
3. Choose less water hungry plants.
4. Ensure that the plants are suitable to your soil and climate.
5. Give the plants a good growing environment. Adopt no-dig methods.
6. Install automatic irrigation in high water requirement areas, e.g. the vegetable garden.
7. Put ground covers and mulches beneath plants.
8. Reduce or replace lawn areas with pavers and brickwork.
9. Install mowing/edging strips round lawns.
10. Choose compact slow-growing shrubs.

Redundancy list

Following are some time-consuming features that can be reduced, removed or replaced:

Lawn
- Reduce edges that can't be cut with the mower or strimmer and need cutting with shears.
- Replace lawn areas with areas of attractively laid bricks and pavers.
- Reduce number of beds, containers, ornaments and furniture in grassed areas – don't let the lawns be an obstacle course for yourself and the mower. (Refer back to chapter 7 for lawn management ideas.)

Beds and borders
- Reduce wide borders that have to be walked on to reach plants at the back
- Reduce herbaceous borders, which involve a lot of work and look bare for much of the year and beds planted out in labour intensive annuals.

Bare soil areas
- Apply thick organic mulches and plant weed suppressant ground covers.

Plants
- Reduce plantings of invasive self sowing plants.

Bête noirs

My personal devils are kikuyu grass and 'wandering willie' *(Tradescantia fluminensis)* both incumbent in fiendish abundance when we bought Valley Homestead. Kikuyu is the southern hemisphere's equivalent of the northern hemisphere's couch grass, both reproducing with fearful fecundity by underground runners.

In the northern hemisphere and colder parts of America and Australia, the thuggish *Tradescantia* is potted up and cosseted as a houseplant in centrally heated rooms. Given my water retentive New Zealand clay soil and a warm moist climate, its bolting talons root down faster than one can blink. It actually builds up three dimensional layers, scrambles up into trees and shrubs, letting fall canopies of terrifying tentacles that, when they reach the ground, root yet again making a vast impenetrable web. A small shoot accidentally dropped onto the too-hot-to-walk-on driveway lies fresh and perky for days attempting, I swear, to root down even there.

Having signed the pledge against the prettily packaged poisons, I despaired that eliminating wandering willie and kikuyu from garden and farm would be my life's work. By hand stripping one bed at a time over several months I thought I'd gained control. Wrong. Without eternal vigilance they still miraculously reappeared and leapt away again. I decided to balance idealism with realism, bite the bullet and gain control once and for all with a chemical herbicide. I experimented with the herbicide on a small area of each. When they scarcely flinched I knew I'd be trapped on a relentless cycle of chemical 'control' and decided all I'd got left was a complete change of philosophy – if you can can't beat it, make a focal point of it.

Thinking positively, wandering willie creates a dense and not unattractive ground cover beneath trees or on steep shaded banks with arid soil where little else will grow; kikuyu creates tough hard-wearing and drought resistant lawns. However, both require a high degree of control and the smallest shred of either, accidentally transported elsewhere, roots immediately and romps away. Even with my new *laissez-faire*

Tradescantia fluminensis has a mile-a-minute growth habit.

philosophy, I must devote at least one small part of my work schedule daily to controlling their grow-a-mile-a-minute fingers along fence, lawn and border edges so that I remain in control.

I've also learned that with highly invasive weeds such as these it is vitally important not to leave them lying in heaps for removal later. Small pieces left at border edges can survive mower blades and if you use your clippings of invasive weeds as mulch, then you are transplanting them elsewhere with your own hands! I drop noxious and invasive weeds into a stout black bucket as I work – they're then tipped into a water barrel to rot into nutritious liquid fertiliser and sludge.

Although one can do a good deal to discourage thugs such as these, the discipline of little and often is the only way to remain in control and avoid a massive reclamation job every few weeks.

Succulents in containers require little maintenance.

- Reduce plants that need lots of tying and staking.
- Reduce bulbs, which need lifting annually.
- Reduce fast growing plants, which need constant cutting back, and replace with plants of slow, compact or dwarf growth habit.

Hedges
- Reduce hedges to low and manageable height or replace them with fences or trellises.

Scramblers and ramblers
- Replace handsome but rampant climbers with climbing plants of restrained growth habit that require little pruning.

Containers
- Reduce number of containers unless you are a small space gardener, in which case the labour of constant watering and feeding is justified. Alternatively, create exciting container combinations with different varieties of massed succulents. Use the 'potmobile' described in chapter 7 for moving pots about.

Deciduous trees
- Reduce those that tend to drop their leaves all year round (e.g. birches), and try to maintain a balance between evergreen and deciduous trees to minimise leaf clearance labour.

Shrubs
- Replace those of rapid growth habit, which require constant pruning, with others of slow compact growth habit.

Edible gardens
- Reduce large-sized vegetable plots to a number of small beds, which offer easy working and harvesting access from all sides.
- Manage on no-dig raised bed system (see chapter 3).
- Install durable brick or paver pathways with barrow access width.

Watering
- Replace hand held hose watering with an automatic micro-irrigation system (chapter 9).
- Reduce numbers of water hungry plants and replace with drought tolerant specimens (as detailed in chapter 10).

Spraying
Phase out plants that require spraying, because they persist in disease or pest infestation despite the best of care. Replace with plants that are guaranteed certified mildew/pest/disease resistant.

Pests and diseases
Minimise by following guidelines in chapter 4.

Weeding
- Reduce need to weed by planting weed suppressant ground covers and sealing bed surfaces with heavy mulches.
- Purchase a mechanical weeder that uses a gas powered flame or steam to control weeds (see chapter 4).

Designs for living
Low maintenance gardens start on the drawing board, whether you're designing one from scratch or redesigning an existing plot. Before you even put pen to paper, think about your family's lifestyle.

A low maintenance garden should allow time for family hobbies and absences from home, and should not require a body abusing reclamation job each time you return! It should incorporate small or alternative lawn areas, be water efficient, and be planted with hardy plants that will thrive in your climatic and geographic location. The

Design for living: a trouble-free integration of hardy natives and exotics.

plants should be underplanted with weed suppressant ground covers or heavily mulched.

Spend as much time as you can just studying your site. Note which areas are windiest, sunniest, driest, wettest, hottest, most shaded and sheltered, and where the soil is best and poorest. Equipped with pencil and paper ask yourself what you want from your garden and list the features required to fulfil your family's needs. The time given to observing the climatic and topographical features of your section is well spent, because you'll then have a good idea where each facility will be best sited.

Instead of slaving to introduce new features into your plan, let existing natural features of the landscape around your home be part of your grand design. For example you could make a feature of a 'borrowed' landscape of distant views or an attractive tree in your neighbour's garden.

Mapping the site

Once you've decided what design features your lifestyle requires and where they will best be positioned, commit your plans to paper. It's tempting to rush outside, grab your spade and get stuck in, but the paper work really is worth the extra time – mistakes are much easier to correct on paper than on site! Having carefully measured your plot, draw in the existing yard boundaries, and note important existing features such as mature trees, walls, fences, pathways, etc. This is best done on graph paper to ensure that everything is to correct scale on your drawing.

Adding the features

Now take several sheets of tracing paper and experiment with different designs, drawing on the tracing paper on top of the graph paper map of your existing section. Make drawings of individual features – shrubberies, vegetable plot, compost and utility areas, large trees, play and entertaining areas, ornamental pond, etc – on separate sheets. Then cut them out, and move them round the site until you feel they're in the best and most attractive position possible.

As discussed in chapter 10, an important design principle of the low maintenance garden is to reduce lawn areas and plan lawns sown with drought resistant, hard wearing seed or alternative 'lawns' of hardscape materials or ground cover plant.

If you are going to have lawns, avoid 'dotting' individual trees and shrubs about. Mowing and weeding under them is boring and labour intensive. Since they rob the soil and grass of nutrients, such areas rarely look healthy, and they present the problem of trying to find shade and drought tolerant plants to hide the bare patches. The low maintenance garden features trees and shrubs planted together in groups and underplanted with weed suppressing ground covers or well mulched, so that mowing and weeding is unnecessary. A strong framework of taller trees and shrubs will give beds and borders a sheltering foundation framework, shade and privacy. Plan the fore-ground to take smaller more compact shrubs and perennials. Incorporate the no-dig system into your plan (see details in chapter 3).

Easy-care bedding plants

Name	Type*	Notes	Height
Ageratum (floss flower)	HHA	Masses of powder-puff flowers (spring–summer) on bushy plants. For edging choose a compact variety	15–45 cm (6–18 in)
Alyssum (sweet alyssum)	HA	Popular edging plant. Tiny, honey-scented flowers (mid-summer) cover the small-leaved cushions	7.5–15 cm (3–6 in)
Anchusa (bugloss)	HA	Usually grown as a perennial but you can buy the annual *A. carpensis* (blue flowers spring–summer)	45 cm (18 in)
Begonia (bedding begonia)	HHA	Free-flowering plant useful in semi-shade. Flowers (spring–summer) are white, pink or red. Buy in flower.	10–30 cm (4–12 in)
Bellis (daisy)	HB	Single or double daisies (early summer) for edging or containers. Giants have 2 in (5 cm) wide blooms.	7.5–15 cm (3–6 in)
Brassica (ornamental cabbage)	HA	The flat heads of ornamental cabbage and kale have colourful and decorative leaves. All winter display.	22.5–45 cm (9–18 in)
Calendula (pot marigold)	HA	An old cottage-garden favourite with yellow or orange flowers in summer. Use dwarfs for edging.	22.5–60 cm (9–24 in)
Cheiranthus (wallflower)	HB	Wide range of colours (off white–deep red) for spring–early summer flowers. Grow Siberian wallflower for late blooms.	22.5–60 cm (9–24 in)
Chlorophytum (spider plant)	HHP	Foliage house plant. Makes an attractive centrepiece for summer display in a container. Prefers partial shade.	30–45 cm (12–18 in)
Cineraria (dusty miller)	HHA	*C. maritima* is widely grown for its fern-like silvery-grey leaves. The small yellow flowers are not showy.	15–37.5 cm (6–15 in)
Coreopsis (tickseed)	HA	The annual forms of coreopsis bear marigold-like flowers all summer in yellow, red or brown.	30 cm (12 in)
Dianthus (annual carnation)	HHA	There are a number of dwarf annual carnations that do not need staking. Fragrant flowers throughout summer.	22.5–45 cm (9–18 in)
Dianthus (sweet william)	HB	Flattened heads of densely packed, flowers in spring–summer. Bicolours are popular.	15–60 cm (6–24 in)
Diascia (diascia)	HP	A 1990s introduction – spurred open-faced flowers all summer on lax stems.	30 cm (12 in)
Eschscholzia (California poppy)	HA	Very easy – sprinkle seed over bare ground in autumn or spring for all summer silky-petalled flowers.	15–30 cm (6–12 in)
Fuschia (fuchsia)	HP or HHP	Many bush varieties are available. Trailing varieties useful for hanging baskets. Most have bell-shaped flowers.	30–60 cm (12–24 in)
Gazania (gazania)	HHA	The most eye-catching S. African daisy. Flowers (throughout summer) have a dark-rimmed yellow centre.	22.5–37.5 cm (9–15 in)
Helichrysum (helichrysum)	HHP	*H. petiolatum* is grown for its attractive display of felted leaves. Usual colour is silvery grey.	Length 60 cm (24 in)
Iberis (candytuft)	HA	Domed clusters of fragrant flowers – white, pink, red or mauve – cover foliage throughout summer.	15–37.5 cm (6–15 in)
Impatiens (busy lizzie)	HHA	One of the most popular bedding plants, flowering continually in sun or partial shade throughout summer.	15–45 cm (6–18 in)
Kochia (burning bush)	HHA	Looks like a young conifer – the neat bushy growth is made up of feathery foliage. Autumn colour.	45–90 cm (18–36 in)
Limnanthes (poached-egg plant)	HA	Attractive plant but may be hard to find. White-edged yellow flowers in mid- to late summer.	10 cm (4 in)
Lobelia (lobelia)	HHA	The no.1 edging and trailing plant for containers. Blue is the usual colour, but white and red available.	10–15 cm (4–6 in)
Malcolmia (Virginia stock)	HA	Not really a bedding plant. Just sprinkle seeds and it flowers 1–2 months later.	10 cm (4 in)
Nemophila (nemophila)	HA	Low-growing carpeting plant with blue flowers throughout summer. Best sown where it is to flower.	15–30 cm (6–12 in)
Nicotiana (tobacco plant)	HHA	Grow one of the modern dwarfs rather than an old-fashioned tall one. Flowers all summer.	30–60 cm (12–24 in)
Nigella (love-in-a mist)	HA	Very easy to germinate – just sow seed in autumn or spring where it is to grow. Flowers all summer.	30–60 cm (12–24 in)
Pelagonium (geranium)	HHP	Bedding geraniums are the most important of the bold bedding plants. Flowers all summer.	15–45 cm (6–18 in)
Petunia (petunia)	HHA	Showy funnel-shapes. Blooms throughout summer. Multifloras are free flowering – *P.* 'Surfinia' is a trailer.	15–45 cm (6–18 in)
Primula (primrose)	HP	The most popular type for spring bedding is polyanthus (*P. variabilis*). Yellow-eyed flowers in spring.	22.5–30 cm (9–12 in)
Scaevola (scaevola)	HHP	Lax stems. Flowers (spring–summer) are distinctive – there are petals on one side only.	30 cm long (12 in)
Tagetes (Afro-French marigold)	HHA	Flowers (throughout summer) are larger than French ones; plants smaller than African marigolds.	30–45 cm (12–18 in)
Tagetes (tagetes)	HHA	Dwarf half-hardy marigolds. Popular as edging plants. Flowers throughout summer.	15–22.5 cm (6–9 in)
Tropaeolum (nasturtium)	HA	Grow for edging, ground cover or climber. Flowers all summer. Sow seeds rather than transplanting.	15–45 cm (6–18 in)
Verbena (verbena)	HHA	Small primrose-like flowers (all summer) crown the stems. Upright and trailing types available.	15–45 cm (6–18 in)
Viola (viola, pansy)	HA or HB	Will grow in partial shade and stay in flower for 4–6 months. Winter-flowering Universal strain is now popular.	15–22.5 cm (6–9 in)

*Type key:** HA: Hardy Annual HHA: Half-hardy Annual HB: Hardy Biennial HP: Hardy Perennial HHP: Half-hardy Perennial

One step at a time

Whether you're starting a garden from scratch or trying to make an existing garden less labour intensive, an important design principle for the low maintenance garden is to try not to tackle too much at a time. It is much easier to build, revamp or plant one area at a time, only moving on to the next feature when the first is well under control. Planned and planted for easy management, once it is completed it should require minimal time and attention, leaving you free to devote the time you can spare to developing the next area – and a little relaxation.

Choosing the plants

The low maintenance garden takes local climatic conditions into careful consideration. If predominantly hot and dry, the garden should be planted on the xeriscape design principles outlined in chapter 10; if you live in an area of high rainfall, then obviously you will choose plant materials suited to damp conditions.

Low maintenance gardens have a predominance of plants native to the area because they are ideally suited to the amount of rainfall, seasonal temperature extremes and local soils. It is tempting but unwise to attempt to grow more than a few exotic plants for which you must create an artificial environment. Even the most hard bitten of gardeners amongst us admit they rarely do well in proportion to the amount of time and labour lavished upon them! If you live in an exposed or coastal situation, check before you buy that the plants are wind tolerant and have some degree of salt tolerance. A list of plants that cope well with climatic extremes follows later in this chapter.

When planning flower beds, it is rarely wise to choose annuals for the easy care garden. Their life span is limited, they look very tatty when they fade and must then be completely removed, leaving a large tract of bare land with huge weed growth potential. There is a wealth of flowering perennials available to give year round colour, bloom and interest and all they require is a light cutting back after their flowering season. They can also be lifted and divided when new plants are required.

To give year round diversity of colour, shape, texture and form, low maintenance plantings should include deciduous and evergreen trees and

Hardy low-maintenance native plants add beauty and interest.

shrubs, including those with red, gold, silver and variegated foliage; natives; perennials; ornamental grasses; bulbs and ground covers. Always ask your nurseryman's advice on whether the plants are hardy and suited to your soil and aspect.

Love is blind

We've all done it. We see a luscious looking plant in the nursery or in a catalogue and must have it. The description on the label makes it quite clear that our site or soil is quite unsuitable for it. But we say, 'What the hell!' and go ahead and plant it, and it becomes another victim on our plant murder list. Or, unable to resist the challenge, we wear ourselves to a frazzle creating the artificial conditions the lime/acid loving plant craves, conditions that are totally absent in our garden. Full of self congratulation we step back and admire the treasure. It survives for a while, but promptly keels over when its roots discover the true nature of the soil to which it has been committed.

Harden your heart and select plants suited to your natural environmental conditions rather than endeavouring to adapt the environment to suit the plant. The expenditure of vast amounts of time, money, effort and disappointment can be avoided by choosing the right plant for the right place.

Native plants are both unique and beautiful but this doesn't mean that we can't have any of the lush exotica for which our hearts yearn. A huge range of both are available; we simply have to choose from them species best suited to our climate and soil type. The golden rule is don't plant another of anything that has twice turned up its toes and died, despite your best efforts engineering the conditions it demands. See reason, and accept that there is a fairly fine line between optimism and foolhardiness!

The creative sustainable gardener knows that no matter how wet, dry, hot cold, sunny or shady an area, there are plants that will adore it there and romp away with little help from human hands. Identify those areas in your garden and plant accordingly. Happy plants are healthy plants. It's always tempting to try out luscious new cultivars, but be strong and stick to tried and tested varieties until your redesigned garden allows you time to pander to the demands of the odd tender exotics of the heart.

Plant hardiness

Plant breeders are inclined to use the magic word 'hardy' on the plant label to lull gardeners into thinking the plant is fail-safe. A plant is only hardy in the soil type and climatic conditions it likes best. For example, a 'hardy' silver-leafed plant will certainly thrive with little help from you if planted on a sun-baked clay bank or in any dry well drained area, but put it in a heavy, poorly

A rosaphile's lament

With all this talk of hardy easy-to-grow plants, I can almost hear rosophiles, hands over hearts, screaming 'What about my roses?' Rest assured, I've had more than a few dark nights of the soul over this one. You can still have roses, but choose the delightful old-fashioned shrub varieties or the *rugosa* species, both of which are hardy and require little pruning and spraying. Of ancient lineage, rugosas are a much underplanted and under-valued species. They're so hardy that in England and Europe they're used as hedges, as barriers on polluted motorways and as coastal plantings. They have rich dark green heavily veined leaves and double or semi-double flowers with tissue-paper-fine petals.

Many cultivars are richly scented and their flower colours include deepest crimson-purple 'Roseraie de l'Hay', Silver-pink 'Frau Dagmar Hastrupp' and 'Conrad F. Meyer', creamy yellow 'Agnes', soft pink 'Belle Poitevine', dark crimson 'Carmen', and two beautiful whites with creamy stamens, 'Schneezwerg' and 'Nyveldt's White'.

Another white, a personal favourite, 'Blanc Double de Courbet', is often referred to as the 'muslin rose' because its richly fragrant petals are as fine as tissue paper. The blooms are traditionally used in England and Ireland to make bridal coronets and bouquets. There are many other delightful *rugosa* cultivars. Most are

Rugosa 'Frau Dagmar Hastrupp'.

recurrent, and all have large ornamental hips of burnished orange or rosy red that are intriguingly winged and spurred. With beauties like these at your disposal, you can phase out labour-intensive modern varieties and hybrid teas. There is little place for them in the low maintenance garden if their care leaves you no time to enjoy them.

Easy-care bulbs

Name	Site and soil	Notes/planting depth*
Allium (flowering onion)	Sunny site, well-drained soil	In early or midsummer clusters of flowers appear on leafless stalks. These blooms may be wide- or narrow-petalled. Height 22.5 cm (9 in), planting depth 10–15 cm (4–6 in).
Anemone (windflower)	Sun or light shade, well-drained soil	The daisy-flowered anemone is easiest to grow. First to flower is *A. blanda* (spring). *A. apennina* a little later. Height 15 cm (6 in), planting depth 5 cm (2 in).
Brimeura (Spanish hyacinth)	Sun or light shade, well-drained soil	Uncommon but worth trying. Flower stalks bear 10–15 blue or white bells in early summer. Height 15 cm (6 in), planting depth 10 cm (4 in).
Bulbocodium (spring saffron)	Sunny site, well-drained soil	Young flowers goblet-shaped like a crocus, but open wide as they mature. Height 10 cm (4 in), planting depth 7.5 cm (3 in). Lavender flowers early spring.
Camassia (quamash)	Sun or light shade, moist soil	A tall plant with stiff floral spikes of starry blooms in late spring. Height 60–90 cm (24–36 in), planting depth 10 cm (4 in). White, lavender or blue.
Chionodoxa (glory of the snow)	Sun or light shade, well-drained soil	Loose and dainty sprays bear about 10 blooms on each stalk. Usually white-centred blue. Good for naturalising. Height 15–25 cm (6–10 in), planting depth 7.5 cm (3 in).
Colchicum (autumn crocus)	Sun or light shade, humus-rich soil	Wineglass-shaped flowers appear in autumn before the leaves. Plant in mid-summer. Height 15–22.5 cm (6–9 in), planting depth 7.5 cm (3 in).
Convallaria (lily of the valley)	Partial shade, humus-rich soil	Dainty fragrant bells hang from arching stems. Can spread rapidly – good ground cover under trees. Height 20–30 cm (8–12 in), planting depth 2.5 cm (1 in).
Crocus (crocus)	Sun or light shade, well-drained soil	The spring-flowering species are very popular – goblet-shaped flowers in a wide range of colours. Autumn ones also available. Height 7.5–12.5 cm (3–5 in), planting depth 7.5 cm (3 in).
Cyclamen (cyclamen)	Partial shade, humus-rich soil	Winter-, spring-, summer- and autumn-flowering varieties. Hardy types have 2.5 cm (1 in) flowers. Good ground cover. Height 10–15 cm (4–6 in), planting depth 2.5 cm (1 in).
Eranthis (winter aconite)	Sun or light shade, well-drained soil	A glossy yellow carpet of flowers appears in late winter–early spring. Each bloom has a frilly green collar. Height 7.5–12.5 cm (3–5 in), planting depth 5 cm (2 in).
Erythronium (dog's-tooth violet)	Partial shade, humus-rich soil	*E. dens-canis* bears flowers in late spring with bent-back petals on top of wiry stems. Leaves have brown blotches. Height 15 cm (6 in), planting depth 7.5 cm (3 in).
Fritillaria (fritillary)	Light shade, well-drained soil	*F. meleagris* is excellent for the rockery or naturalising in grass. Pendulous blooms (spring) with a checkerboard pattern. Height 30 cm (12 in), planting depth 5 cm (2 in).
Galanthus (snowdrop)	Light shade, moist soil	White hanging bells appear in late winter/early spring. Dry bulbs transplant badly – divide in late spring. Height 15 cm (6 in), planting depth 10 cm (4 in).
Gladiolus (gladiolus)	Sunny site, well-drained soil	Pick one from the hardy species group – *G. byzantinus* bears small red flowers in early summer. Height 60 cm (24 in), planting depth 10 cm (4 in).
Ipheion (spring starflower)	Sun or light shade, well-drained soil	Varieties of *I. uniflorum* bear 2.5 cm (1 in) wide star-shaped blue or white flowers in late spring. Good for rockery or woodland. Height 15 cm (6 in), planting depth 5 cm (2 in).
Iris (iris)	Sunny site, well-drained soil	Several types available – the popular early spring ones are *I. danfordiae* (yellow) *and I. reticula* (blue). Height 15 cm (6 in), planting depth 7.5 cm (3 in).
Leucojum (snowflake)	Sun or light shade, humus-rich soil	There are spring-, summer- and autumn-flowering varieties. Looks like a tall snowdrop but petals are different. Height 15–69 cm (6–27 in), planting depth 7.5 cm (3 in).
Lilium (lily)	Sun or light shade, well-drained soil	Pick one of the Mid-Century hybrids that is compact and sturdy such as *L.* 'Enchantment' – height 90 cm (36 in), planting depth 15 cm (6 in), flowers early summer.
Muscari (grape hyacinth)	Sunny site, well-drained soil	Tiny bell- or flask-shaped flowers are massed on top of leafless fleshy stem in early spring. Height 10–30 cm (4–12 in), planting depth 7.5 cm (3 in).
Narcissus (narcissus, daffodil)	Sun or light shade, well-drained soil	The single white and yellow varieties are the most common. For something different choose doubles, pinks or split coronas. Height 7.5–60 cm (3–24 in), planting depth twice bulb height.
Ornithogalum (star of Bethlehem)	Sun or light shade, well-drained soil	*O. umbellatum* produces white starry flowers that face upwards and close at night. Grow in rockery or grassland. Height 30 cm (12 in), planting depth 5 cm (2 in).
Oxalis (wood sorrel)	Sunny site, well-drained soil	Choose a hardy non-invasive species such as *O. adenophylla*, white/pink flowers mid-summer. Height 7.5 cm (3 in), planting depth 7.5 cm (3 in).
Puschkinia (striped squill)	Sun or light shade, well-drained soil	Easy and attractive, but less popular than its bluebell relatives. Pale blue open bells with a dark stripe in spring. Height 15 cm (6 in), planting depth 5 cm (2 in).
Schizostylis (Kaffir lily)	Sun or light shade, humus-rich soil	Gladiolus-like spikes and crocus-like pink or red flowers autumn–early winter. Height 60 cm (24 in), planting depth 5 cm (2 in).
Scilla (bluebell, squill)	Sun or light shade, well-drained soil	Most common are spikes of hanging blue bells in spring, but there are also white and pink ones and varieties with round heads. Height 7.5–45 cm (3–18 in), planting depth 5–10 cm (2–4 in).
Sisyrinchium (sisyrinchium)	Sunny site, humus-rich soil	*S. striatum* has whorls of creamy flowers on upright stems in early summer. Usually bought as a growing plant. Height 45 cm (18 in), planting depth 2.5 cm (1 in).
Tulipa (tulip)	Sunny site, well-drained soil	Choose one of the botanical (sp) tulips such as *T. kaufmanniana*, *T. fosteriana* or *T. greigii*. Flowers spring. Height 10–50 cm (4–20 in), planting depth 10 cm (4 in).

*Planting depth – the distance between the top of the bulb and the soil or compost surface.

drained soil and hardy it is not. Similarly, a member of the damp-loving hosta family will gasp piteously in a dry sunbaked coastal or Mediterranean-type garden, and eventually fail altogether.

Selecting hardy plants is easier than ever before. We have at our disposal a wealth of compact, disease-resistant plants and dwarf versions of lanky old favourites. The latter reduce time and energy spent on staking and tying up, and are also perfect for small space gardens and container specimens. With careful selection, every plant in your garden can look attractive as well as serving some practical purpose such as providing shade, fruit, flowers, fragrance, shelter or privacy – and pleasure.

'Instant' gardens

Whether you're designing a low maintenance garden from scratch or revamping one that is labour intensive, remember there are hundreds of products designed to save time in our frenetic world. Some are designed to save minutes, others hours, but when it comes to trees and shrubs, it's possible for busy gardeners to cheat and save years!

Modern nursery techniques have made it possible to buy large bare-rooted specimens with which, in return for a little extra care with planting, we can create an instant garden in hours. They're invaluable in situations where a garden must be started from scratch, and where weather-damaged mature specimens must be replaced. If you are prepared to pay a little more for larger plants, shelter, shade, privacy and foundation plantings can be enjoyed instantly. This way, someone else has taken care of the labour intensive propagation and vulnerable early life of the plant.

An 'instant' tree or shrub will have severely trimmed roots, and good site preparation and staking is vital. Dig a hole large enough to allow a good root run, and plant the specimen in a mix of soil and compost containing water retention crystals and slow release fertiliser granules. Good staking prevents the 'root rock' that occurs when plants are continuously blown back and forth by the wind; this movement will snap small new roots before they can properly anchor the tree into position. Secure the plant trunk between two strong stakes driven in at the edge (not through!) the root ball.

Carefree maintenance
The value of mulch
Mulch is probably the most important single aspect of a low maintenance garden. Mulch inhibits weed growth, conserves moisture, keeps the soil cool in summer and warm in winter, encourages myriads of beneficial soil organisms and earthworms, improves soil structure and drainage, and is aesthetically pleasing. Mulch tree and shrub areas with weed mat covered with bark

\	\	\
Easy-care rock garden plants		
Name	**Site and soil***	**Notes and hardiness****
Acaena (New Zealand burr)	Sun or light shade, ordinary soil	HP. Spreading carpeter for cracks in paving. A. 'Blue Haze' forms silvery sheets – height 5 cm (2 in), spread 60 cm (24 in).
Achillea (alpine yarrow)	Sunny site, sandy soil	HP. Choose A. tomentosa – height 15 cm (6 in), spread 30 cm (12 in), heads of tiny yellow flowers throughout summer.
Aethionema (aethionema)	Sunny site, non-acid soil	HP. Popular one is A. 'Warley Rose' with spring–summer rounded pink flower clusters. Height 15 cm (6 in), spread 30 cm (12 in).
Allium (flowering onion)	Sunny site, ordinary soil	B. Choose a non-invasive one – e.g. A. beesianum. Height 30 cm (12 in), planting depth 10 cm (4 in), blue flowers in mid-summer.
Androsace (rock jasmine)	Sun or light shade, gritty soil	HP. A. carnea is an evergreen cushion-forming type – height 10 cm (4 in), spread 10 cm (4 in), tiny pink flowers in late spring.
Anenome (wildflower)	Sun or light shade, humus-rich soil	B. A. blanda and A. apennina are recommended. Another rocky one is A. nemorosa – 20 cm (8 in) high flowers in spring.
Antennaria (cat's ear)	Sunny site, ordinary soil	HP. Good for cracks in paving – can be walked on. Height 10 cm (4 in), spread 45 cm (18 in), small flower heads in late spring.
Aquilegia (alpine columbine)	Sun or light shade, moist soil	HP. Grow a dwarf species such as A. flabellata – white/violet flowers in early summer. Height 15 cm (6 in), spread 15 cm (6 in).
Arabis (rock cress)	Sun or light shade, ordinary soil	HP. A. Ferdinand-colurgii 'Variegata' is not invasive – height 10 cm (4 in), spread 30 cm (12 in), white flowers in spring.
Armeria (thrift)	Sunny site, ordinary soil	HP. Hummocks of grass-like leaves. Globular flower heads in early summer. Height 20 cm (8 in), spread 30 cm (12 in).
Artemisia (artemisia)	Sunny site, ordinary soil	HP. Grown for its leaves. A. schmidtiana 'Nana' forms mounds of silvery fern-like foliage. Height 15 cm (6 in), spread 30 cm (12 in).
Asperula (alpine woodruff)	Sunny site, sandy soil	HP. Choose a smooth-leaved one such as A. gussonii – height 10 cm (4 in), spread 30 cm (12 in), pink flowers in late spring–summer.
Aster (mountain aster)	Sunny site, ordinary soil	HP. A. alpinus has large white, blue or pink daisy-like flowers in late spring. Height 15 cm (6 in), spread 45 cm (18 in).
Astilbe (rockery astilbe)	Light shade, moist soil	HP. The popular one is A. chinensis pumila – height 22.5 cm (9 in), spread 30 cm (12 in), mauve flowers in late summer.
Campanula (bellflower)	Sunny site, non-acid soil	HP. C. carpatica is popular – height 22.5 cm (9 in), spread 30 cm (12 in), cup-shaped flowers (white or blue) all summer.
Chamaecyparis (false cypress)	Sunny site, acid soil	DC. Choose one of the dwarf varieties of C obtusa, such as 'Nana'(round, dark green) or C. pisifera 'Boulevard' (silvery-blue).
Cotoneaster (cotoneaster)	Sun or light shade, ordinary soil	DS. There are several ground-hugging cotoneasters useful for clothing rocks and bare patches. Red berries in autumn.
Crocus (crocus)	Sun or light shade, ordinary soil	B. All can be grown in rockery. Favourite ones are the winter flowering varieties, e.g., C. 'Cloth of Gold'.
Cyclamen (cyclamen)	Partial shade, humus-rich soil	B. All the hardy ones can be grown in rockery. C. hederifolium (flowers autumn) is the easiest.
Cytisus (broom)	Sunny site, sandy soil	DS. Pea-like flowers in spring. Choose a true dwarf such as C. decubens 15 cm (6 in) or C. ardoinii 20 cm (8 in).
Dianthus (rockery pink)	Sunny site, ordinary soil	HP. Grey or green foliage. Examples are D. alpinus – 10 cm (4 in) high and D. deltoides – 20 cm (8 in) high. Flowers all summer.
Dicentra (bleeding heart)	Partial shade, ordinary soil	HP. Arching stems, pendant flowers. Grow a dwarf such as D. cucullaria – yellow-tipped white flowers in spring, height 15 cm (6 in).

chips, and flower and vegetable beds with generous quantities of nutritious organic compost. Mulching saves both water and long tedious hours of hand pulling weeds. Refer back to chapter 3 for the details of organic mulches.

Leisurely meals

The basic tenet of the sustainable gardener's faith is that nothing beats a soil enriched and conditioned with organic materials and mulches. But there are a wealth of labour saving commercially prepared slow release fertilisers in granular, liquid and soluble powder form to supply plants with booster nutrients. These organic fertilisers are detailed in chapter 3 (and information about those used in container planting is given in chapter 7). When in doubt, cheat!

Most iris cultivars make hardy neglect-proof plants.

Name	Site and soil*	Notes and hardiness**
Draba (whitlow grass)	Sunny site, ordinary soil	HP. Mounds of tiny leaves. The easiest is *D. aizoides* – height 7.5 cm (3 in), spread 15 cm (6 in), yellow flowers in spring.
Dryas (mountain avens)	Sunny site, ordinary soil	HP. Excellent ground cover. Popular one is *D. octopetala* – height 10 cm (4 in), spread 60 cm (24 in), white flowers in early summer.
Erica (heather)	Sunny site, ordinary soil	DS. For winter to spring flowers grow one of the varieties of *E. carnea* – height 22.5 cm (9 in), spread 60 cm (24 in).
Erigeron (fleabane)	Sunny site, ordinary soil	HP. Choose a non-invasive species such as *E. aureus* – height 15 cm (6 in), spread 60 cm (24 in), golden flowers in mid-summer.
Erinus (summer starwort)	Sun or light shade, sandy soil	HP. Small starry flowers. Height 7.5 cm (3 in), spread 10 cm (4 in), flowers late spring and all summer .
Erodium (storksbill)	Sunny site, ordinary soil	HP. *E. chrysanthum* forms 22.5 x 22.5 cm (9 in x 9 in) mounds of ferny leaves. Cup-shaped yellow flowers appear in late spring.
Frankenia (sea heath)	Sunny site, sandy soil	DS. Prostrate plant with tiny leaves. Looks like heather. Height 7.5 cm (3 in), spread 30 cm (12 in). Flowers mid-summer.
Geranium (crane's bill)	Sunny site, ordinary soil	HP. Flowers in summer. Choose a rockery one such as *G. cinereum* – height 15 cm (6 in), spread 30 cm (12 in).
Hebe (veronica)	Sun or light shade, ordinary soil	DS. Choose a dwarf such as *H. pinguifolia* 'Pagei' – grey-green 22.5 cm (9 in) mounds with white flowers in spring-summer.
Hypericum (St. John's wort)	Sunny site, ordinary soil	DS. The most popular dwarf is *H. olympicum* – height 15 cm (6 in), spread 30 cm (12 in), yellow flowers in mid-summer.
Iris (rockery iris)	Sunny site, well-drained soil	B/HP. Choose bulb irises *I. dandfordiae* and *I. reticulata*. Non-bulb dwarfs include *I. pumila* – 10 cm (4 in), and *I. lacustris* – 7.5 cm (3 in).
Juniperus (juniper)	Sunny site, acid soil	DC. Ground covers are available. *J. sabina* 'Tamariscifolia' is an example – height 30 cm (12 in), spread 240 cm (95 in).
Narcissus (dwarf narcissus)	Sun or light shade, ordinary soil	B. Miniature and dwarf hybrids are available for early spring flowers. A typical example is *N.* 'Jack Snipe' – 20 cm (8 in).
Phlox (dwarf phlox)	Sunny site, moist soil	HP. Many varieties available. Height 10-15 cm (4-6 in), spread 45 cm (18 in), flowers in late spring.
Primula (rockery primrose)	Sunny site, ordinary soil	HP. Large choice of varieties. *P. wanda* is popular – height 7.5 cm (3 in), spread 15 cm (6 in), flowers in spring.
Sedum (stonecrop)	Sunny site, ordinary soil	HP. Many varieties. Usual form (e.g, *S. pathulifolium*) has low-growing stems, fleshy leaves and star-like flowers in early summer.
Sempervivum (houseleek)	Sunny site, ordinary soil	HP. Ball-like rosettes of green or coloured fleshy leaves. Thick flower stems appear in mid-summer. A good choice for dry spots.
Thymus (thyme)	Sunny site, sandy soil	HP. *T. serpyllum* is the basic species – height 5 cm (2 in), spread 60 cm (24 in), flowers in mid-summer.
Tulipa (tulip)	Sunny site, ordinary soil	B. Grow dwarf spp tulips rather than garden hybrids. Examples are *T. greigii*, *T. kaufmanniana* and *T.* 'Fusilier'.
Veronica (rockery speedwell)	Sunny site, ordinary soil	HP. *V. prostrata* is the most popular one – height 10 cm (4 in), spread 45 cm (18 in), flowers in late spring and summer.
Viola (violet)	Sun or light shade, ordinary soil	HP. Numerous types for spring–summer flowers are available. Height 5-22.5 cm (2-9 in), spread 15 cm (6 in).

*Site and soil – The prime requirement of rock garden plants is good drainage. Other basic requirements for top-quality plants are listed here.

**Hardiness key – HP: Hardy Perennial   B: Bulb   DS: Dwarf Shrub   DC: Dwarf Conifer

Blue-flowered
Ajuga and
Coleonoma
'Sunset Gold'.

Slippery pavers

On to more mundane problems....You've dutifully replaced your swathes of velvet greensward with brickwork and pavers, but they become slippery and slimy with algae growth during damper, colder months. There are a number of chemical cleaners and washes that claim to remove algae growth and moss, but they are just what they say – chemicals. Many contain bleach, caustic agents or chlorine. They'll run off pathways into the roots of bedding plants, and if used in high foot traffic areas, harmful residue will cling to childrens bare feet and pets' paws. They are also expensive and time consuming to apply.

Ground-cover plants

Name	Type*	Notes
Ajuga	HP/E	Blue flowers. Height 10 cm (4 in), spacing 45 cm (1½ ft). Variegated spp.
Alchemilla	HP/D	Lime-green flowers. Height 45 cm (1½ ft), spacing 45 cm (1½ ft).
Ballota	HP/E	Grey woolly leaves. Height 30 cm (1 ft), spacing 45 cm (1½ ft).
Bergenia	HP/E	Bold fleshy foliage, pink spires. Height 45 cm (1½ ft), spacing 45 cm (1½ ft).
Calluna	S/E	Heather for acid soil. Height 15-45 cm (6-18 in), spacing 30 cm (1 ft).
Cotoneaster	S/E	Prostrate shrub, colourful berries, spreading growth habit.
Epimedium	HP/SE	Shade tolerant, bronze in autumn. Height 22.5 cm (9 in), spacing 30 cm (1 ft).
Euonymus	S/E	Ground cover shrubs, prostrate habit. Height 22.5 cm (9 in), spacing 30 cm (1 ft).
Euphorbia	HP/D	Taller. Height 60 cm (2 ft), spacing 45 cm (1½ ft).
Geranium	HP/D	Sprawling. Height 45 cm (1½ ft), spacing 45 cm (1½ ft).
Hebe	S/E	Small compact ground cover. Height 45-90 cm (1½-3 ft), spacing 45 cm (1½ ft).
Hedera	S/E	Ground cover or spreading climber. White, yellow or gold leaf varieties.
Heuchera	HP/E	Tiny white, red, pink bell flowers. Height 60 cm (2 ft), spacing 45 cm (1½ ft).
Hosta	HP/D	Taller ground cover, many leaf colours. Height 60 cm (2 ft), spacing 60 cm (2 ft).
Hypericum	S/SE	Low growing ground cover shrub. Height 60 cm (2 ft).
Iberis	S/E	*I. sempervirens* bears white flowers. Height 30 cm (1 ft), spacing 30 cm (1 ft).
Juniperus	C/E	Dwarf/spreading ground cover shrub. Many species.
Lamium	HP/SE	White-marked leaves for shade. Height 10 cm (4 in), spacing 30 cm (1 ft).
Lysimachia	HP/D	Creeping jenny for damp soil. Height 5 cm (2 in), spacing 30 cm (1 ft).
Nepeta	HP/D	Blue flowers, spreading form. Height 60 cm (2 ft), spacing 45 cm (1½ ft).
Pachysandra	S/E	Good under trees. Height 10 cm (4 in), spacing 30 cm (1 ft).
Polygonum	HP/E	*P. affine* is invasive. Height 30 cm (1 ft), spacing 60 cm (2 ft).
Pulmonaria	HP/D	White-spotted leaves. Height 30 cm (1 ft), spacing 30 cm (1 ft).
Rosa	S/D	Many ground cover spp – recommend flower carpet vars. Height 75 cm (2½ ft).
Sedum	HP/E	Fleshy-leaved ground cover, spreading habit. Many spp.
Stachys	HP/E	Silver-felted leaves, mauve flower. Height 45 cm (1½ ft), spacing 45 cm (1½ ft).
Tiarella	HP/E	Tiny white flowers. Height 30 cm (1 ft), spacing 30 cm (1 ft).
Vinca	S/E	Trailing ground cover. Blue/white flowers. Can be invasive. Height 15 cm (6 in).

*Type key: HP: Hardy Perennial S: Shrub C: Conifer E: Evergreen SE: Semi-evergreen D: Deciduous

The answer is to invest the money in a water blaster, which will also be useful for all sorts of external domestic cleaning jobs. There are a wide range of highly efficient water blasters available that make cleaning all types of surfaces quick and easy. The type you choose will be dictated by the size of area you have to keep clean.

Preventing frost damage

Many countries such as USA and Great Britain suffer long hot summers and prolonged sub-zero winters. Judge the frost potential of your garden by observation. Even in a small area, frost damage can vary enormously. Imagine frost as a body of cold air flowing like water. It settles in hollows and open spaces but is easily blocked by fences, hedges and hardy plants. There are only three options with frost:

- Protect the garden from it;
- Buy only frost hardy plants;
- Ensure slow thawing for tender specimens.

If you live in an area suffering severe winters, you'll be aware when choosing plants that they must be frost hardy. But most of us like to include some tender treasures and are prepared to devote a modicum of time and labour to their protection. Garden centres stock a range of reasonably priced frost protection cloths of various weights, together with pegs to hold them down safely. Old sacking or hessian is an alternative for covering tender shrubs or perennials that have died down. It's not suitable for small developing plants as it tends to exclude light and become heavy when wet.

Other protective materials for semi-dormant or dormant plants include mulches of pea straw, fine bark, bracken or heaps of shrub prunings piled over their crowns. Plastic cloches, sheets of polythene and glass are also advocated for frost cover but in my experience, while they do offer some protection they are not as efficient as cloth. Layers of newspaper or cardboard also provide good insulation, but need to be held down with mulch to prevent them blowing about or disintegrating in the rain.

The best way to avoid frost damage is to listen to the weather forecast and to believe it!

Frost causes the water in plant cells to freeze and swell; when they thaw the swollen cells burst causing plant death. The worst damage occurs

A rowan tree underplanted with *Nandina domestica*, purple berberis and *Coleonoma* 'Sunset Gold'.

when plants thaw rapidly. If possible give plants a gentle but thorough watering before the sun strikes them. This way, the cells gradually relax instead of bursting. Even totally frozen plants can be rescued in this way. Increase the thawing time with 'blankets' of shade cloth or old newspapers.

Frost and wind tolerant plants

Following are details of temperature drops and wind conditions and lists of the trees and shrubs that can cope with this. Most of these larger plants are suitable as foundation and shelter plantings to create a wind filtering framework for the garden and will grow in the USA, Australia, New Zealand and most parts of the UK. Specific perennials and smaller plants are not listed because, provided they are given conditioned soils, most varieties will grow within a sheltering framework once it is established. (A comprehensive list of other hardy low maintenance plants is given in the quick reference planting guides throughout this chapter.)

Trees

Temperature drop to -15°C (4°F). Wind tolerant plants, suitable for coastal planting.

Acer negundo (box elder maple), 17m/55ft. Fast growing deciduous tree. Autumn colour.

Buddleia davidii (butterfly bush), 5m/16ft. Semi-deciduous, lilac, white flower spires.

Casuarina cunninghamiana, 12m/39ft. Fast growing evergreen. Fine needle-like foliage.

Cupressus macrocarpa 'Aurea'. Fast growing conifer to 12m/39ft. Excellent shelter belt.

Cupressocyparis leylandii, 25m/82ft. Fast growing evergreen conifer. Excellent shelter.

Cordyline australis (cabbage tree), 9m/29ft. Evergreen NZ native, swordlike foliage.

Fraxinus excelsior (European ash), 25m/82ft. Deciduous specimen tree. Autumn colour.

Platinus oreinetalis (plane), 25m/82ft. Handsome deciduous tree. Autumn colour.

Pinus radiata, 30m/98ft. Fast growing evergreen, provides excellent wind/shelter belt.

Populus alba (white poplar), 20m/65ft. Fast growing. Deciduous. Good autumn colour.

Salix matsudana 'Tortuosa', 15m/49ft. Fast growing. Deciduous. Attractive branch form.

Tamarix chinensis. Deciduous shrub to 5m/16ft. Soft fine foliage, pink-red flower clusters.

Temperature drops to -15°C (4°F). Plants tolerant to moderate winds, unsuited to coastal planting.

Cedrus atlantica 'Glauca', 20m/65ft. Evergreen. Handsome needle-like silver blue foliage.

Cedrus deodara, 30m/98ft. Evergreen. Handsome grey-green foliage. Slow growing.

Chamaecyparis lawsoniana 'Silver Queen', 8m/26ft. Evergreen. Good shelter and hedging.

Chamaecyparis pisifera 'Boulevard', 30m/98ft. Attractive evergreen grey-blue foliage.

Dacrycarpus dacridiodes (white pine), 36m/118ft. Evergreen. Prefers moist soils.

Eucalyptus leucoxylon, 12m/39ft. Fast growing, pink flowered gum. Evergreen.

Larix decidua (European larch), 30m/98ft. Deciduous. Autumn colour.

Liquidamber styraciflua, 30m/98ft. Deciduous. Maple-like leaves, autumn colour.

Malus floribunda (crab apple). Deciduous. Flowers followed by fruit.

Metasequoia glytostroboides (redwood), 17m/55ft. Deciduous. Autumn colour.

Populus nigra (black/Lombardy poplar), 25m/82ft. Deciduous. Fast growing.

Prunus avium (sweet cherry), 15m/49ft. Deciduous.

Prunus serrulata 'Kanzan', 8m/26ft. Deciduous. Scented flowers.

Salix alba var vitellina (golden willow), 25m/82ft. Deciduous. Pendulous branches.

Temperature drops to -15°C (4°F). Plants not wind tolerant.

Acer palmatum (Japanese maple), many spp/heights/colours. Palmate foliage.

Acer platanoides (Norway maple), 18m/59ft. Deciduous. Autumn colour.

Dacrydium cupressinum (red pine), 30m/98ft. Evergreen. Weeping needle-like foliage.

Fagus sylvatica (European beech), 20m/65ft. Deciduous. Autumn colour.

Gleditsia tricanthos (honey locust), 30m/98ft. Deciduous. Golden form available.

Sorbus aucuparia (rowan), 15m/49ft. Deciduous. Autumn colour, bright red berries.

Taxodium distichum (swamp cypress), 30m/98ft. Deciduous. Red-bronze in autumn.

Shrubs

Temperature drops to -3°C (26°F). Wind tolerant plants, suitable for coastal planting.

Araucaria heterophylla (Norfolk pine), 30m/98ft. Evergreen. Symmetrical habit.

Arbutus unedo (strawberry tree), 9m/29ft. Evergreen. White flowers, red fruit.

Banksia serrata, 9m/29ft. Evergreen with decorative cream-yellow flowers.

Camellia japonica, 7m/23ft. Evergreen. Red, pink flowers. Good hedging.

Coprosma robusta, 5m/16ft. Evergreen. Brownish-green leaves. Excellent shelter.

Garrya eliptica (catkin bush), 5m/16ft. Evergreen. Grey green catkins.

Griselinia littoralis, 5m/16ft. NZ native. Evergreen. Excellent shelter plant.

Hoheria populnea (lacebark), 7m/23ft. Evergreen. White flowered NZ native. Requires moisture.

Ilex aquifolium (holly), 12m/39ft. Evergreen. Variegated form available. Red berries.

Ilex cornuta (Chinese holly), 4m/13ft. Evergreen. Green/variegated leaves. Red berries.

Leptospermum scoparium (tea tree), 5m/16ft. Flowering NZ native. Evergreen.

Myoporum insulare (Australian ngaio), 4m/13ft. Evergreen. White flowers, purple berries.

Myoporum laetum (NZ ngaio), 14m/46ft. Evergreen. White flowers, red-purple fruit.

Phebalium squameum (satinwood), 3–10m/10–30ft. Evergreen. Erect linear habit – hedging.

Phoenix canariensis (date palm), 12m/39ft. Evergreen.

Pittosporum tenuifolium (lemonwood), 10m/30ft. Evergreen. Excellent shelter tree.

Racosperma longifolium (Sydney golden wattle), 5m/16ft. Evergreen. Golden flowers.

Racosperma melanoxylon (Tasmanian blackwood), 30m/98ft. Evergreen.

Sophora microphylla longicarinata (NZ kowhai), 12m/39ft. Semi-deciduous. Golden flowers.

Temperature drops to -3°C (26°F). Plants tolerant to moderate wind. Unsuited to coastal planting.

Casuarina glauca (swamp oak), 18m/59ft. Evergreen. Hardy. Excellent shelter.

Magnolia campbelli, 20m/65ft. Deciduous. Fragrant lilac-pink flowers.

Magnolia grandiflora, 10m/30ft. Evergreen. Handsome glossy foliage, cream flowers.

Prunus campanulata (Taiwan cherry), 8m/26ft. Deciduous. Magenta blossom.

Quercus palustris (pin oak), 18m/59ft. Deciduous. Autumn colour.

Temperature drops to -15°C (4°F). Wind tolerant plants suitable for coastal planting.

Ceanothosus papillosus 'Roweanus' (Californian lilac), 3m/10ft. Evergreen. Blue flowers.

Cotinus coggygira (smoke bush), 5m/16ft. Deciduous. Purple foliage, smoke-like blooms.

Cotoneaster horizontalis. Spreading habit. Deciduous. White flowers. Orange berries.

Cotoneaster lacteus, 4m/13ft. Evergreen. White flowers, red berries. Excellent hedging.

Viburnum japonicum, 3m/10ft. Evergreen. Fragrant white flowers, red berries.

Hebe cupressiodes (whipcord hebe), 2m/6½ft. Slow growing evergreen. Fine foliage.

Temperature drops to -15°C (4°F). Plants tolerant to moderate winds. Unsuitable for coastal planting.

Berberis darwinii, 4m/13ft. Evergreen. Orange-yellow flowers. Blue berries.

Chamomeles speciosa (Japonica), 2.5m/8ft. Deciduous. Hardy. Red flowers.

Hamamelis mollis (witch hazel), 4m/13ft. Fragrant orange-yellow winter flowers.

Pieris japonica, 1–5m/3–16ft. Evergreen. Handsome foliage. Sprays white-pink flowers.

Potentilla fruticosa, 1m/3ft. Deciduous. Yellow flowers.

Rhododendron luteum (azalea), 1.5m/5ft. Deciduous. Red or yellow flowers.

Thuja occidentalis 'Rheingold'. Conifer. Semi-prostrate evergreen. Bronze foliage.

Viburnum davidii, 1.2m/4ft. Evergreen. White flowers, blue berries.

Viburnum opulus 'Sterile' (snowball tree), 4m/13ft. Deciduous. Decorative round flower heads.

Viburnum x burkwoodii, 2.5m/8ft. Semi-evergreen. Pink-white flowers. Autumn colour.

Weigelia florida (apple blossom), 2m/6½ft. Deciduous. Variegated available. Pink blossom.

Temperature drops to -3°C (26°F). Plants suitable for coastal planting.

Abelia x grandiflora, 2m/6½ft. Evergreen. handsome hedge, shelter plant. Pink flowers.

Massed flowers on hardy New Zealand tea tree.

Easy-care hardy perennials

Name	Site and soil	Notes
Acanthus (bear's breeches)	Sun or light shade, well-drained soil	*A. spinosus* is the usual one – height 1.2 cm (4 ft), spacing 75 cm (2.5 ft). Flowers (white/purple) in summer.
Achillea (yarrow)	Sunny site, well-drained soil	Yellow flat-topped flower-heads in summer. Look for a dwarf 60 cm (2 ft) variety – e.g. 'Moonshine'.
Ajuga (bugle)	Sun or light shade, ordinary soil	Creeping ground cover – height 10 cm (4 in), spacing 1½ ft (45 cm). Choose a coloured leaf variety.
Alchemilla (lady's mantle)	Sun or light shade, well-drained soil	*A. mollis* is an old favourite – height 45 cm (1½ ft), spacing 45 cm (1½ ft). Flowers (small, greenish-yellow) in summer.
Anemone (anemone)	Sun or light shade, well-drained soil	Saucer-shaped blooms in spring-summer. Leaves are deeply lobed. Height 90 cm (3 ft), spacing 45 cm (1½ ft).
Artemisia (wormwood)	Sun or light shade, well-drained soil	*A. ludoviciana* is grown for its silvery feathery foliage – height 90 cm (3 ft), spacing 60 cm (2 ft).
Aruncus (goat's beard)	Light shade, ordinary soil	Dark green foliage and branching plumes of white flowers in early summer. Height 1.5 m (5 ft), spacing 1.2 m (4 ft).
Astilbe (astilbe)	Light shade, moist soil	Feathery plumes of tiny flowers in summer. Many varieties available. Height 75 cm (2.5 ft), spacing 45 cm (1½ ft).
Astrantia (masterwort)	Light shade, well-drained soil	*A. major* produces pink-tinged white flower-heads throughout summer. Height 60 cm (2 ft), spacing 45 cm (1½ ft).
Bergenia (bergenia)	Sun or light shade, well-drained soil	Ground cover with large fleshy leaves. Hyacinth-like flower spikes in spring. Height 45 cm (1½ ft), spacing 45 cm (1½ ft).
Coreopsis (tickseed)	Sunny site, well-drained soil	*C. grandiflora* is the usual one – yellow daisy-like flowers throughout summer. Height 45 cm (1½ ft), spacing 45 cm (1½ ft).
Cortaderia (pampas grass)	Sun or light shade, well-drained soil	Grow *C. selloana* as a focal point – 45 cm (1½ ft) silvery plumes on 1.2–3 m (4–10 ft) stalks in early autumn.
Crambe (crambe)	Sun or light shade, well-drained soil	A bold bushy plant with large leaves and sprays of tiny white flowers in early summer. Height 1.8 m (6 ft).
Dicentra (bleeding heart)	Light shade, well-drained soil	*D. spectabilis* is the popular one – arching stems with white/pink flowers in late spring. Height 75 cm (2.5 ft), spacing 45 cm (1½ ft).
Doronicum (leopard's bane)	Sun or light shade, well-drained soil	*D. orientale* is an early flowering dwarf – yellow daisy-like flowers in spring. Height 30 cm (1 ft), spacing 30 cm (1 ft).
Epimedium (bishop's hat)	Partial shade, ordinary soil	Ground cover for shade – turns bronze in autumn. Spring flowers are insignificant. Height 22.5 cm (9 in), spacing 30 cm (1 ft).
Erigeron (fleabane)	Sun or light shade, well-drained soil	Looks like a small Michaelmas daisy. Flowers in early summer. Height 45 cm (1½ ft), spacing 30 cm (1 ft).
Eryngium (sea holly)	Sunny site, well-drained soil	Thimble-shaped blue flowers above thistle-like leaves throughout summer. Height 60 cm (2 ft), spacing 45 cm (1½ ft).
Euphorbia (spurge)	Sun or light shade, well-drained soil	Masses of flower heads in spring-summer – colour usually yellow but there is an orange one. Height 60 cm (2 ft), spacing 45 cm (1½ ft).
Geranium (crane's-bill)	Sun or light shade, well-drained soil	Excellent ground cover. Flowers (white, pink, red or blue) in spring–mid-summer. Height 45 cm (1½ ft), spacing 45 cm (1½ ft).
Helleborus (hellebore)	Partial shade, moist soil	Two types – Christmas rose (winter-spring) and Lenten rose(spring). Height 30 cm (1 ft), spacing 45 cm (1½ ft).
Hemerocallis (day lily)	Sun or light shade, ordinary soil	Large lily-like trumpets (pale yellow to deep red) in early summer. Height 90 cm (3 ft), spacing 60 cm (2 ft).
Heuchera (coral flower)	Sun or light shade, well-drained soil	Tiny bell-shaped blooms (white, pink or red) on top of slender stems in early summer. Height 60 cm (2 ft), spacing 45 cm (1½ ft).
Hosta (plantain lily)	Partial shade, ordinary soil	Excellent ground cover grown for its attractive foliage and spikes of flowers in mid summer. Height 60 cm (2 ft), spacing 60 cm (2 ft).
Iris (iris)	Sunny site, well-drained soil	Some of the bearded irises (with hairs in petals) are easy-care plants. Example is *I. pallida* – height 75 cm (2½ ft), spacing 60 cm (2 ft).
Liriope (lily-turf)	Sunny site, well-drained soil	*L. muscari* has spikes of violet flowers in spring and summer and aromatic leaves. Height 60 cm (2 ft), spacing 45 cm (1½ ft).
Nepeta (catmint)	Sunny site, ordinary soil	Popular edging plant. Small lavender flowers in spring and summer and aromatic leaves. Height 60 cm (2 ft), spacing 45 cm (1½ ft).
Oenothera (evening primrose)	Sunny site, well-drained soil	Grow a hardy one like *O.* 'Fireworks' – yellow poppy-like flowers in summer. Height 45 cm (1½ ft), spacing 45 cm (1½ ft).
Polygonum (knotweed)	Sun or light shade, ordinary soil	Evergreen ground cover. Choose a *P. affine* variety – height 30 cm (1 ft), spacing 60cm (2 ft), pink flowers all summer.
Primula (primula)	Partial shade, humus-rich soil	Many are easy-care plants. An example is *P. denticulata* – flowers in spring, height 30 cm (1 ft), spacing 30 cm (1 ft).
Pulmonaria (lungwort)	Partial shade, moist soil	Leaves are generally silver-spotted and evergreen. Height 30 cm (1 ft), spacing 30 cm (1 ft), flowers in spring.
Rudbeckia (coneflower)	Sun or light shade, ordinary soil	Dark-centred blooms all summer. Popular one is *R. fulgida* 'Goldstrum' – height 60 cm (2 ft), spacing 60 cm (2 ft).
Salvia (salvia)	Sun or light shade, well-drained soil	Blue flowers all summer. Usual species is *S. superba* – height 90 cm (3 ft), spacing 45 cm (1½ ft).
Saxifraga (saxifrage)	Sun or light shade, humus-rich soil	The most popular one is London pride, with starry flowers in spring and early summer. Height 30 cm (1 ft), spacing 45 cm (1½ ft).
Sedum (stonecrop)	Sunny site, well-drained soil	*S. spectabile* is an old favourite with 10 cm (4 in) wide flower-heads late summer to autumn – height 45 cm (1½ ft), spacing 30 cm (1 ft).
Solidago (golden rod)	Sunny site, well-drained soil	Grow a dwarf such as *S.* 'Golden Thumb' – yellow flower heads in late summer. Height 45 cm (1½ ft), spacing 45 cm (1½ ft).
Stachys (lamb's ears)	Sun or light shade, well-drained soil	*S. ianata* is a good ground cover – woolly leaves and mauve flowers in mid-summer. Height 45 cm (1½ ft), spacing 45 cm (1½ ft).
Tiarella (foam flower)	Sun or light shade, ordinary soil	Good ground cover with evergreen leaves and tiny white flowers in early summer. Height 30 cm (1 ft), spacing 30 cm (1 ft).
Tolmiea (piggyback plant)	Sun or light shade, ordinary soil	A house plant that can be used as ground cover. Tiny flowers in early summer. Height 22.5 cm (9 in), spacing 45 cm (1½ ft).
Tradescantia (spiderwort)	Sun or light shade, ordinary soil	Hardy varieties have sword-like leaves and silky flowers throughout summer. Height 45 cm (1½ ft), spacing 45 cm (1½ ft).
Veronica (speedwell)	Sun or light shade, well-drained soil	Wide range of heights. *V. spicata* has spikes of small flowers in early summer – height 45 cm (1½ ft), spacing 30 cm (1 ft)

Artemisia arborescens, 1–2m/3–6ft. Evergreen. Aromatic silver foliage.

Bachyglottis compacta, 1m/3ft. Dark green foliage, silver reverse, yellow daisies.

Corokia cotoneaster, 1.75m/5½ft. Evergreen. NZ native. Small yellow flowers.

Euonymus japonicus, 4m/13ft. Glossy leaves, star-shaped green flowers, pink fruits.

Grevillea rosmarinfolia, 2m/6½ft. Evergreen. Red, yellow or pink flowers.

Hebe hulkeana (NZ lilac), 1m/3ft. Evergreen. Decorative lilac-pink flowers.

Hebe speciosa, 2m/6½ft. Evergreen. Very hardy. Lavender-purple flowers.

Hebe townsonii (hebe), 2.5m/8ft. Evergreen. Very hardy. White flowers.

Leucadendron 'Safari Sunset', 2.5m/8ft. Evergreen. Colourful red-gold bract flowers.

Leucospermum reflexum, 2–4m/6½–13ft. Evergreen. Orange-red pin cushion flowers.

Myrtus communis, 3m/10ft. Evergreen. Fragrant white flowers. Good hedge/shelter.

Nandina domestica 'Pygmaea' (heavenly bamboo), dwarf to 80cm. Evergreen. Colourful foliage.

Olearia albida, 2.5m/8ft. Evergreen. NZ native. Light green foliage, white daisies.

Olearia traversii, 6m/20ft. Evergreen. Tough leaves, white reverse, greenish-white flowers.

Phormium spp (flax), NZ native. Wide range colours, heights. Evergreen. Very hardy.

Photinia 'Red Robin', 4m/13ft. Evergreen. New growth glossy coral-red. Excellent hedge.

Prostanthera incisa (Australian mint bush), 1m/3ft. Evergreen. Green/variegated, lilac blooms.

Telopea speciosissima (waratah), 3m/10ft. Evergreen. Showy crimson-red flowers.

Drought tolerant plants
Refer back to lists given in chapter 10.

High performance, low maintenance plants
The lists of easy-care plants in this chapter offer the low maintenance gardener a huge diversity of flowers, foliage, form, colour and texture. Imagine a golden robinia tree (*Pseudocacia* 'Frisia'), underplanted with the mahogany-purple shrub *Cotinus*

Hebe speciosa, hardy evergreen with long-lasting flower sprays.

Sweetly scented *Nicotiana*, an easycare perennial.

'Royal Purple', and beneath that, the light, graceful and blue grass, *Helictotrichon sempervirens*; for flower power add daylilies with exotic blooms which belie their hardy nature. The permutations are endless – the choice is yours – and you *will* have time to sit in the shade!

Easy-care trees, shrubs and climbers

Name	Type	Notes	Height after 10 years
Aucuba (aucuba)	S/E	Variegated varieties of *A. japonica* are popular. Can be planted where little else will grow.	2.1 m (7 ft)
Berberis (barberry)	S/D or E	Popular spiny shrub – many varieties are available. Yellow or orange flowers in spring.	30 cm–2.4 m (1–8 ft)
Betula (birch)	T/D	Graceful specimen tree. A dwarf variety of *B. pendula* (silver birch) is the one to grow.	3.6 m (12 ft)
Chaenomeles (japonica)	S/D	An old favourite grown for its spring flowers (white, pink or red) and autumn fruits.	1.5 m (5 ft)
Choisya (Mexican orange)	S/E	Attractive rounded bush with glossy foliage. Flat heads of white flowers in spring.	1.8 m (6 ft)
Cotinus (smoke bush)	S/D	Feathery flower-heads in mid-summer; leaves turn golden in autumn. Sold as *Rhus cotinus*.	3 m (10 ft)
Cotoneaster (cotoneaster)	S/D or E	Lots of showy berries and good foliage colours in autumn. Varieties in all shapes and sizes	15 cm–4.5 m (½–15 ft)
Crataegus (hawthorn)	T/D	Specimen tree or hedging plant. White, pink or red flowers in late spring; red or orange berries in autumn.	7.6 m (25 ft)
Daphne (daphne)	S/D or E	The deciduous *D. mezereum* is the popular variety – purple-red flowers in February.	90 cm (3 ft)
Elaeagnus (oleaster)	S/D or E	The evergreen *E. pungens* 'Maculata' with yellow-splashed leaves is the popular variety.	2.1 m (7 ft)
Erica (heather)	S/E	Many varieties from ground cover to framework shrubs. Most, but not all, need acid soil.	15 cm–3 m (½–10 ft)
Escallonia (escallonia)	S/E	Choose one of the hybrids. e.g., *E.* 'Apple Blossom'. Flowers are white, pink or red.	1.8 m (6 ft)
Euonymus (euonymus)	S/D or E	The popular ones are the variegated evergreens, e.g., *E. radicans* 'Silver Queen'. Excellent ground covers.	30–60 cms (1–2 ft)
Garrya (silk tassel bush)	S/E	Rounded bush with oval leaves – long and tender catkins drape down in January and February.	3 m (10 ft)
Gaultheria (checkerberry)	S/E	The best known is *G. procumbens* – a shiny-leaved ground cover with white flowers.	15 cm (½ ft)
Genista (broom)	S/D	The one to grow is *G. lydia* – a spreading low bush, with golden flowers in May/June.	60 cm (2 ft)
Hamamelis (witch hazel)	S/D	Fragrant spidery flowers appear in winter before the leaves. Good autumn foliage colour.	2.4 m (8 ft)
Hebe (shrubby veronica)	S/E	Many types available, but some are tender. Choose a small variety such as *H.* 'Autumn Glory'.	45–90 cm (1½–3ft)
Hedera (ivy)	C/E	Widely used as a climber or ground cover. Many leaf variegations available – white, yellow or golden.	3–4.5 m (10–15 ft)
Hydrangea (hydrangea)	S or C D	Many lacecap or mophead varieties are available. *H. petiolaris* is a self-clinging climber	1.5 m (5 ft)
Hypericum (St. John's wort)	S/semi E	A low-growing bush that will grow almost anywhere. Yellow flowers all summer and autumn.	60 cm (2 ft)
Ilex (holly)	S/E	Many forms – smooth leaves, yellow berries, etc. Buy a self-fertile one to ensure berry production.	1.5–4.5 m (5–15 ft)
Jasminum (winter jasmine)	S/D	The popular variety is *J. nudiflorum* – yellow flowers on lax leafless stems from November to February.	3 m (10 ft)
Lavandula (lavender)	S/E	Clumps of greyish-green leaves. White, pink or lavender flowers. Flowers from November to February.	3 m (10 ft)
Lonicera (honeysuckle)	S or C D or E	A vast genus with a shrubby group and an even larger climbing group. Growth of climbers rather untidy.	90 cm–6 m (3–20 ft)
Mahonia (mahonia)	S/E	Small ones widely used for growing under tree. Large ones (e.g., *M. japonica*) used as specimen plants.	60 cm–2.4 m (2–8 ft)
Osmanthus (osmanthus)	S/E	*O. delavayi* is the one to choose – white fragrant blooms on arching stems in April.	1.5 m (5 ft)
Parthenocissus (Virginia creeper)	C/D	Tall spreading vines used for wall cover. Leaves of *P. tricuspidata* turn bright red in autumn.	9.1 m (30 ft)
Phormium (phormium)	T/E	*P. cookianum* 'Tricolor' with green/white/red leaves has an exotic palm-like appearance.	1.2 m (4 ft)
Pieris (pieris)	S/E	An excellent choice for acid soil. Young leaves are bright red and spring floral sprays are white.	1.2 m (4 ft)
Potentilla (shrubby cinquefoil)	S/D	Many varieties. An easy shrub that blooms from May to September.	60 cm–1.2 m (2–4 ft)
Prunus (prunus)	S/D or E	Evergreens include Portugal and cherry laurel. *P. triloba* (pink flowers) is a popular deciduous one.	1.2–4.8 m (4–16 ft)
Prunus (ornamental cherry)	T/D	Very popular flowering tree. Blooms between January and June depending on variety. Flowers single or double.	90 cm–7.6 m (3–25 ft)
Pyracantha (firethorn)	S/E	Widely planted wall shrub grown for its massive display of red or orange berries in autumn.	1.8–3.6 m (6–12 ft)
Rhododendron (azalea)	S/D or E	A low-growing evergreen or Japanese azalea is a must for the mixed border if you have an acid soil.	30 cm–4.5 m (1–15 ft)
Ribes (flowering currant)	S/D	*R. sangineum* is seen everywhere. Pink or red flowers on pendant heads in spring. Quick growing.	1.8 m (6 ft)
Robinia (robinia)	T/D	*R. pseudoacacia* 'Frisia' is eye-catching, spreading layers of golden yellow leaves all season long.	7.6 m (25 ft)
Salix (willow)	S or T D	Ordinary varieties are far too large for most gardens – choose a dwarf like *S. Kilmarnock*.	1.5–3 m (5–10 ft)
Skimmia (skimmia)	S/E	Neat and compact. White flowers in spring. Male and female plants needed for berry formation.	90 cm (3 ft)
Sorbus (mountain ash)	T/D	Colourful graceful tree with white flowers, yellow or red berries and golden autumn leaves.	4.5–7.6 m (15–25 ft)
Spiraea (spiraea)	S/D	Spring-flowering varieties have white flowers; summer ones are deep pink or red.	60 cm–1.8 m (2–6 ft)
Viburnum (viburnum)	D or E	A vast genus of plants with winter- and spring-flowering as well as autumn-berrying types.	1.5–3 m (5–10 ft)
Vinca (periwinkle)	S/E	A trailing ground cover to carpet banks or bare ground with white or blue flowers all summer long.	15 cm (½ ft)

Type key: S: Shrub T: Tree C: Climber D: Deciduous E: Evergreen

Easy-care hedging plants

Name	Style*/Type**	Notes
Acer (maple)	F/D	The field maple (*A. campestre*) hedge is much less common than beech, but it flourishes in all soil types and the plants quickly grow together. Trim in late autumn.
Berberis (barberry)	I/D or E	Several evergreens such as *B. stenophylla*, *B. darwinii* and *B. julianae* make splendid informal hedges with yellow flowers in spring. *B. thunbergii* is deciduous. Trim Berberis after flowering.
Berberis (barberry)	D/D	*B. thergii atropurpurea* 'Nana' produces a compact formal hedge about 45 cm (1½ ft) high. The foliage is reddish. Trim after leaf fall.
Carpinus (hornbeam)	F/D	A quick growing hedge which quickly reaches 2.4 m (8 ft) if left untrimmed. Usually keeps its dead leaves like beech. Reliable in heavy soil. Trim in late summer.
Escallonia (escallonia)	I/E	The evergreen *E. macrantha* is popular in coastal areas as it tolerates salt-laden air. Red flowers appear in early summer. Trim when the flowers fade.
Fagus (beech)	F/D	*F. sylvatica* has green- and purple-leaved varieties – all can be trimmed to produce a tall formal hedge. Brown leaves persist over winter. Trim mid-summer. Tackle any hard pruning in early spring .
Ilex (holly)	F/E	*I. aquifolium* forms a dense barrier that is colourful when berries are present or a variegated variety has been used. Trim in late summer.
Lavandula (lavender)	D/E	A popular low growing hedge with purple flowers, aromatic grey foliage. Cut off stalks once flowers fade. Trim to shape in late spring.
Prunus (laurel)	F/E	Portugal laurel (*P. lusitanica*) and cherry laurel (*P. laurocerasus*) make fine tall hedges with dense shiny leaves, but plenty of room is required. Trim in early spring.
Prunus (sloe)	I/D	The sloe or blackthorn (*P. spinosa*) has long been used for hedging fields. White flowers appear in spring. Cut back unwanted growth in winter.
Pyracantha (firethorn)	I/E	The popular *P. coccinea* can be used for hedging but *P. rogersiana* is usually recommended. Cut back in summer to expose berries.
Ribes (flowering currant)	I/D	This plant is usually grown as a shrub, but it can be grown at 30 cm (1 ft) intervals to produce an attractive hedge. Trim when the flowers fade.
Rosa (rose)	I/D	Some shrub roses make good hedges, but only informal ones as they cannot stand regular trimming. Remove unwanted growth in spring.
Taxus (yew)	F/E	This old favourite need not be dull – there are bright golden varieties. No trouble, but it is slow to establish. Trim in late summer.
Thuja (thuja)	F/E	Western red cedar (*T. plicata*) is the conifer to grow if you want cypress-like foliage. Unlike the popular Leyland Express it needs only one trim (early spring) each year.

*Style key:
F: Formal hedge – a line of hedging plants rimmed to form a smooth surface. Foliage types are generally treated this way.
I: Informal hedge – a line of hedging plants that not trimmed.
D: Dwarf hedge – a line of low-growing hedging plants pruned to 90 cm (3 ft) or less. The hedge may be formal or informal.
**Type key: D: Deciduous E: Evergreeen

Easy-care conifers

Name	General notes	Species and variety	Type*	Height after 10 years	Species notes
Abies (fir)	Most are giants; choose with care.	*A. balsamea* 'Hudsonia'	D	30 cm (1ft)	Good for rock gardens
		A. koreana	M	1.8 m (6 ft)	Dark green foliage
Chamaecyparis (false cypress)	Popular. Range from rockery dwarfs to stately giants.	*C: lawsoniana* 'Allumii'	M	1.8 m (6 ft)	Conical, blue-grey foliage
		C.i 'Columnaris'	M	2.4 m (8 ft)	Narrow, conical. Good specimen tree
		C.i. 'Elwoodii'	D	1.5 m (5 ft)	Popular, grey-green foliage
		C.i. 'Elwood's Gold'	D	1.2 m (4 ft)	Branchlet tips golden-yellow
		C.i. 'Minima Aurea'	D	30 cm (1 ft)	Compact pyramid, bright yellow
		C.i. 'Minima Glauca'	D	30 cm (1 ft)	Round shrub, sea green foliage
		C. obtusa 'Nana Gracilis'	D	60 cm (2 ft)	Dark green rounded sprays
		C. pisifera 'Boulevard'	D	90 cm (3 ft)	Silvery-blue feathery sprays
Juniperus (juniper)	Dwarfs and spreading types popular.	*J. chinensis*	D	1.5 m (5 ft)	Blue-green foliage
		J. communis 'Compressa'	D	30 cm (1 ft)	Columnar, grey-green foliage
		J. c. 'Depressa Aurea'	D	30 cm (1 ft)	Spreading, golden foliage
		J. horizontalis 'Glauca'	P	30 cm (1 ft)	Spreading, blue carpet
		J. media 'Pfitzerana'	D	1.2 m (4 ft)	Very popular, wide spreading
		J. squamata 'Meyeri'	D	1.2 m (4 ft)	Erect, blue-grey foliage
		J. virginiana 'Skyrocket'	M	1.8 m (6 ft)	Narrow column, blue-grey foliage
Pinus (pine)	Usually too tall, but dwarf varieties available.	*P. mugo* 'Gnom'	D	60 cm (2 ft)	Globular shaped rockery pine
		P. nigra	T	3 m (10 ft)	Dark green foliage
		P. strobus 'Nana'	D	60cm (2 ft)	Spreading, silvery foliage
Taxus (yew)	Suitable for shade. Generally slow growing.	*T. baccata*	M	1.8 m (6 ft)	Dark green tree or hedge
		T. b. 'Fastigiata'	M	1.8 m (6 ft)	Conical. Irish yew
		T. b. 'Fastigiata Aurea'	M	1.8 m (6 ft)	Yellow-edged dark-green foliage
		T. b. 'Semperaurea'	D	60 cm (2 ft)	Spreading, golden foliage
Thuja (arbor-vitae)	Similar to false cyprus. Good range of colours.	*T. occidentalis* 'Rheingold'	D	90 cm (3 ft)	Conical, bronze foliage
		T. orientalis 'Aurea Nana'	D	60 cm (2 ft)	Globular, golden foliage
		T. plicata	T	4.8 m (16 ft)	Pyramid-shaped specimen tree
Tsuga (hemlock)	Most types are too tall.	*T. cadadensis* 'Pendula'	D	60 cm (2 ft)	Spreading, weeping branches

*Ultimate height key: P – Prostrate: under 45 cm (1½ ft) D – Dwarf: 30 cm–4.5 m (1–15 ft) M – Medium: 4.5–15 m (15–50 ft) T – Tall: over 15 m (50 ft)

CHAPTER TWELVE
TREES – THE LUNGS OF THE WORLD

The glory of the forest was best seen in the morning and evening. At daybreak, all of the valleys and hollows were shrouded in mist. As the sun began to glint on faraway hills, tuis began chorusing from the ancient trees, and the pigeons would tumble in a flash of green and white. Muted birdsong greeted another day, but with the full rising of the sun and the lifting of the mist, a deep silence prevailed over all again. In the evening with the sun going down behind the far ranges, there would often be a blaze of light and colour in the sky. The forest lay underneath, dark and foreboding, and your mind's eye conjured up the vision of the Patupaiarehe, the ancient dwellers of Maori mythology, gliding softly upon the forest tracks. Then darkness came, the moon rose, the forest glistened in different shades of darkness, and the white mists slipped in, and settled again in the valleys and hollows. The only sound was the haunting call of the morepork calling to a mate way down in the valley.

Des Ogle, New Zealand Forest Ranger, 1941–1982.

Grass has been poetically dubbed the hair of the earth, while trees are sometimes referred to as its lifeblood, its lungs, and sheltering arms.

From the earliest human habitation, trees have provided shelter, sustained the world's people and animals, and have been the backbone of life as we know it. They control pollution, conserve water, stabilise and protect the earth, they are our life breath, the air cleaners, the rain makers and they are amongst nature's most precious and magnificent creations. Almost every aspect of our modern life is influenced in some way by trees. We depend upon them for shade, shelter and privacy; their wood builds our homes, our furniture and tools, our boats and bridges.

Above: Chinese Gardens, Sydney, framed by skyscrapers. Mature trees control pollution and provide a sheltering oasis in the heart of the city.
Opposite: The forest, nature's most magnificent and most abused creation.

163

The forest is Nature's most beautiful and most abused creation.

Their fruits feed and sustain us; their dead tissue has been transformed over millions of years to the fossil fuels of gas, coal and oil on which our industrialised modern world depends. They give us the blessing of fire and warmth, and make it possible for us to travel the world by sea, air and land.

Trees supply us indirectly with almost everything we need in life, yet for generations we have slaughtered them and cut them down without replacing them, without thought for the future, which seemed so far off. That future is not just dangerously close. With the new millennium it has arrived.

The reality is that green canopies of many of the world's forests hide a legacy of centuries of grazing and felling. The floor of the forest has been stripped of new growth. This presents a frightening problem for future generations – geriatric trees with no offspring, no regenerative powers.

Entire nations have been denuded of their native forests, and the resulting atmospheric pollution by the carbon monoxide that they would have converted into life-giving oxygen is a grave threat to life on earth. Scientists have established that the destruction of forests is bringing changes in the world climate that could ultimately bring to an end man's reign on earth.

We must replant now, and continuously, to try to halt and heal the damage done to all animal life, to our climate and to the world's entire ecology. Our weapons of survival against the greed of governments, the apathy of politicians, the short-sightedness of land developers and farmers lie in restoring forests and replanting trees in every situation, large and small – in cities, on lifestyle blocks, on farms and horticultural land, on eroded hillsides once clothed with native forest. If we try to plant native trees we replace our country's lost green mantle. There is room in even the smallest garden for at least one tree.

We, the families of the new millennium, must plant those trees in any space we can, the trees without which our civilisation could never have begun – and without which it certainly has no future.

Where shall we begin?

As always, we must begin in our own backyard! An average garden has room for five medium-sized trees at most. If we choose wisely, not only will these provide precious shade, shelter and privacy, but they will also bless us with flowers and fruit – part of the diet of every living creature. The tree's flowers attract legions of fertilising insects, and when their petals have fallen they leave behind berries, nuts and seeds, which contain the life of a new generation of trees. The birds that eat the fruit are directly responsible for the regeneration of forests because they excrete the seeds, which then grow into new trees. But the birds and bees will only come into our gardens if we plant the flowering trees that provide them with pollen and nectar.

When we plant a tree we give a priceless gift to future generations. We start a plant on a journey that may take hundreds of years. Biblical text reads: 'He that planteth a tree is the servant of God. He provideth a kindness for many generations, And faces that he hath not seen shall bless him.'

In researching this chapter, I came across the

following story from a book published in the early 1950s called 'The Man Who Planted Trees' by Jean Giorno. It tells of a tramper who discovers a shepherd living in a remote area of the French Alps, many days walk from the nearest village. An ancient weathered oak tree grew near the shepherd's hut, and every day when he took his flock up onto the bare and degraded hillsides, he planted 100 acorns. From some 1,000,000 planted before the tramper arrived, 10,000 seedlings had survived both sheep and the elements. The shepherd continued his work throughout his lifetime and over about 20 years, the land became revegetated; he extended his range of species by begging seeds of beeches and birches.

The infant forest retained water and old streams came back, bringing with them regeneration of the forest floor, and the germination of the dormant seeds of willows, rushes and grasses. The shepherd had planted trees for the next generation and the next, and still lived long enough to sit with his animals in their shade. Eventually his life's work was recognised and the forest was placed under a conservation order. The story does not say whether this happened in his lifetime, but for us in our modern world it is a parable of the power of one.

A tree for all reasons

Even the tiniest plot can give life with the planting of one small tree. (See chapter 7 for trees suitable for inclusion in small plots.) Since most of us have small to medium sized gardens the trees we have room for must be as versatile and as multi-purpose as possible. Those listed below do not include the treasured traditional fruiting orchard trees such as apples, pears, peaches, plums, citrus, and subtropical fruit trees, since these have already been discussed in chapter 8.

In addition to shape, form and colour, which give visual appeal in landscape design, many trees offer amenity values such as stock fodder and shelter, flower displays, firewood, timber and bee and bird food. The list below is by no means exhaustive but offers a selection of recommended multi-purpose species that are tolerant of diverse soils and climatic conditions. (See also lists of hardy trees and shrubs in chapters 7 and 11.) The following trees are all of medium to large size at maturity and ideal for planting in larger and rural

The smallest garden has room for at least one tree – this one is the deciduous *Acer* 'Aurea'.

gardens, on lifestyle blocks, around dams, in wetlands, on farms and in animal paddocks.

Food and protection for animals

Life-style block owners and rural gardeners know that animals exposed to the elements do not thrive because they burn up body heat and energy trying to keep warm or cool according to the season. Newborn animals often perish through lack of shelter in inclement weather. Plantings of the correct trees offer them both protection, food and good health. The following trees offer stock both shelter and food. (The parts of the trees given in the list are those edible by animals.)

Acacia spp (wattle) – all parts
Fagus/Northofagus (beech) – nuts
Chamaecytisis palmensis (tree lucerne) – pods
Gleditsia triacanthos (honey locust) – pods
Morus alba (mulberry) – fruit
Populus spp (poplar) – foliage
Quercus (oak) – acorns
Salix spp (willows) – foliage

Abundant gifts

The following trees comprise the groups cypress, acacia, eucalyptus, poplar, pine, willow, deciduous hardwood (oak, elm, ash, robinia, walnut). In addition to creating handsome specimen trees, these are classified as multi-purpose trees because they provide several of the following attributes: shade, shelter, privacy, erosion control, timber crops, flowers and fruit, autumn colour, hardiness to coastal locations, stock feed and shelter, and tolerance of diverse soils and climatic conditions.

Key: D – deciduous. E – evergreen. Fl – flowers. Fr – fruit. Gr – growth rate. S – size. FW – firewood. T – timber. AC – autumn colour. SF – stock fodder. DT – drought tolerant. RS – recommended species.

Climate/hardiness (CH) key:

H – Tender: requires conditions generally free from frost; prefers hot climate, subtropical to tropical.

T – Half-hardy or hardy: Tolerates light to medium frosts; thrives in any temperate to warm climate.

C – Very hardy: Tolerates all frost (30°C/86°F and lower); grows in cold-winter areas.

Acacia (wattles, mimosa, jasmine). E. Fl. Fr. Gr – fast. S – small to medium. FW. T. SF. DT. CH – T/H. Decorative flowering evergreens native to Australia, Africa, Asia, America. Massed fluffy flowers followed by seedpods. RS – *A. dealbata* (silver wattle), *A. mearnsii* (black wattle), *A. melanoxylon* (Australian blackwood).

Agathis australis (kauri). E. Fl. Gr – slow. S – large, tall. T. CH – C/T. Native to Australia, Malay Archipelago, Fiji, New Hebrides, New Caledonia and one magnificent species is native to New Zealand. Forest giant mass slaughtered for centuries for the masts of ships and for its resinous gum. Beautiful and valuable timber. Suitable for medium to large gardens.

Albizia julibrissen (silk tree). D. Fl. Gr – fast. S – medium. DT. CH-C/T/H. Native to Africa, Australia and Asia, but grows in many parts of the world. Beautiful shade tree, fine fern-like foliage and powder puffs of pink/red silken flowers.

Alnus cordata (alder). D. Fl. Fr. Gr – fast. S – med. T. CH – T/C. Native to Europe and temperate countries. Versatile trees, hardy to many soils, tolerant infertile sites. Improve soil conditions by fixing nitrogen and leaf drop builds up soil struc-ture. Valuable timber tree. Pyramid shaped, dark green glossy heart-shaped leaves, catkins and fruit. RS – *A. glutinosa* (black alder), *A. rubra* (red alder).

Araucaria heterophylla (Norfolk pine). E. Gr – fast. S – large, tall. DT. CH – T/H. Dramatic tree with broad based pyramidal silhouette, open tiered horizontal branching with sharply pointed, dark green upstanding leaves. Resistant to salt winds, provided coastal landscaping and shelter.

Banksia integrifolia (banksia). E. FL. Gr – slow. S – medium-large. T. DT. CH – C/T/H. Tree with leathery sharply toothed leaflets, long lasting spikes of gold/red/orange tubular flowers in parallel rows. Nectar-rich flowers attract many insects and birds. Tolerant poor sandy soils and coastal conditions.

Brachychiton (Illawarra flame). D. FL. FR. SF. DT. Gr – slow. S – large. CH – T/H. Spectacular Australian native also growing in California, South Africa, Mediterranean. Massed red flowers. RS – *B. discolour*, red/gold, *B. populneum*, cream flowers lightly speckled brownish-green. Used as stock food in drought areas.

Nectar-rich flowers of *Banksia integrifolia* provide a banquet for birds.

Casuarina glauca (swamp she-oak). E. Gr – fast. S – medium-large. T. DT. CH – T/H. Australian natives – fast growing conifer-like trees, broad pyramidal shape, long sweeping branches, finely textured deep-green needle-like foliage. Timber suitable cabinet making, wood-turning, furniture. Tolerant wet/dry soils, salt and sandy soil, good coastal shelter. RS – *C. stricta, C. cunninghamiana*.

Cassia many spp. (senna or shower tree). D/semiD. FL. FR. Gr – fast. S – large. Native to temperate areas northern and southern hemispheres, N. America and Australasia. Pinnate leaves, long lasting yellow, red, orange, white or pink flowers followed by pea-like pods – source of tannin and medicinal senna.

Chamaecytisus palmensis (tree lucerne). E. FL. Gr – fast, but short lived. S – small–medium. DT. CH – T/H. Nitrogen fixing tree/shrub, drought and salt tolerant. Good short term soil improver, shelter coastal situations.

Coprosma spp. E. Gr – medium-fast. DT. CH – T/H. Large shrubs/small trees, many forms. Glossy foliage, variegated cultivars, tolerant many soils, salt winds, poor coastal soils.

Cordyline australis (cabbage tree). E. Fl. Gr – med–fast. DT. CH – C/T/H. NZ native, bold architectural form, sword-like foliage and scented berry-flowers. Variegated, yellow, purple, red cultivars. Tolerant of wet and dry conditions.

Crataegus (hawthorn). European native, growing many parts of world. D. Fl. FR. AC. Gr – fast. S – med. CH – C/T. Thorny tree often densely planted as hedging. English hawthorn, *C. oxyacantha* bears prolific red, pink, flowers followed by clusters red berries.

Cryptomeria japonica (Japanese cedar). E. Gr – med–fast. S – large. T. DT. CH – C/T. AC. Fast growing cedar, broadly columnar or slender pyramid in shape. Foliage deep reddish-bronze autumn-winter. Excellent large screen/shelter tree, tolerant salt winds, well drained soil. Good timber.

Cupressus (Mexican cypress). E. Gr – fast. S – tall. T. DT. CH – C/T. Timber boat building, furniture and turning. Withstands dry conditions, salt winds, exposed sites. RS – *C. lusitanica, C. macrocarpa* (Monterey cypress).

X Cupressocyparis leylandii (Leyland cypress). E. Gr – fast. S – large and tall. T. DT. CH – C/T.

Sterile cross between *C. macrocarpa* and *Chamaecyparis Nootkatensis*. Valued timber and shelter tree. Hardy to salt winds, dry conditions, poor but well drained soils.

Darycarpus dacrydiodes (kahikatea/white pine). E. FL. FR. Gr – med. S – large. T. CH – C/T. NZ native, silver-green foliage on handsome pyramidal tree. Prolific crops berries edible to birds and humans. Prefers swampy, poorly drained land, but tolerant of most sites.

Erythrina spp. (coral tree). D. FL. FR. Gr – fast. S – large. CH – T/H. Native to temperate areas of Africa, Central America, Australasia, Asia, East Indies, Hawaii. Flamboyant flowers coral-red on bare branches before leaves appear. Widely used for erosion control.

Eucalyptus (gum tree). E. FL. Gr – fast. S – large. T. DT. CH – T/H. Australian native, huge genera now growing almost worldwide. *E. botryoides* (southern mahogany) will withstand salt winds, dry and wet conditions, exposed areas. Useful coastal shelter. *E. saligna* (Sydney blue gum), provides good furniture veneers and building timber. Stringy barks. Valued for durability of their timber. Also recommended for timber – *E. gobida, E. microcorys, E. muelleriana, E. pilularis*. Many eucalypt species flourish in barren deserts and some species in swamps. Now exported as timber and land stabilisation trees worldwide. Eucalypts have aromatic silver-grey foliage, intriguingly patterned and peeling bark, and attractive red, cream, white and golden flowers.

Fraxinus oxycarpa (claret ash). D. AC. T. CH – C/T. Popular for its rich purple-black foliage, is also valued for timber in Europe and America. RS – *Fraxinus excelsior* (European ash).

Ginkgo biloba (Ginko). D. Gr – slow. S – large. CH – T/C. Ancient tree species, golden deeply lobed foliage shaped like that of the maidenhair fern. Tolerant salt winds, most soils.

Grevillea robusta (silky oak). D/semi-D. Fl. Gr – fast. S – large, tall. T. DT. CH – T/H. Australian native now grown in most temperate areas worldwide. Silver backed ferny leaves, vivid orange, comb-like inflorescences in summer.

Gleditsia triancanthos (honey locust). D. Gr – med. to fast. DT. CH – C/T/H. Native to Central America, now growing worldwide. Golden, emerald green or ruby pinnate leaves. Tolerant of most soils, many climatic conditions.

Griselinia littoralis (broadleaf). E. Gr – fast. S – small. DT. CH – C/T/H. Small trees native to New Zealand and Chile. Tolerance of heavy pruning makes them excellent specimen/shelter/hedging trees. Bold glossy foliage, variegated available. Tolerant many soils, salt wind. RS – *G.l.* 'Green Jewel', *G.l.* 'Dairy Cream', *G.l. lucida.*

Juglans nigra (American black walnut). *Juglans regia* (European walnut). D. Fl. FR. Gr – Med. S – large. T. AC. CH – C/T. Handsome tree bearing nuts. Requires shelter, deep moist soils.

Leptospermum scoparium (manuka/tea tree). E. FL. S – small–med. FW. T. DT. Ch – C/T/H. New Zealand native, many fine flowering varieties. Oil used for medicinal purposes. Tolerant diverse soils and climatic conditions, manuka is an excellent primary coloniser. Excellent (hard) firewood and used for outdoor furniture and fencing.

Leptospermum laevigatum (coastal tea tree). Australian native, salt and wind resistant, valuable for windbreaks, stabilising eroded land or coastal dunes. White flowers. RS – *L. petersonii*, lemon-scented tea tree.

Magnolia grandiflora (American evergreen magnolia). E. FL. FR. Gr – slow. S – large. T. CH – C/T/H. Tolerant of wind, climatic extremes, dry soils. Hardy magnolia makes spectacular flowering, shady specimen tree.

Malus (crab-apple). D. Fl. FR. Gr – fast. S – small–med. CH – C/T. Small trees bearing abundant oriental-looking blossom on bare branches before leaves appear, often bearing edible fruit. Native of Asia, Europe, America. Hardy most soils but prefers temperate climates.

Melaleuca (paperbark). E. FL. Gr – fast. S – med–large. CH – T/H. Australian genus now growing in temperate areas worldwide. Decorative peeling bark, colourful 'bottlebrush' flower spikes of white or cream. Hardy in wet and dry soils, coastal conditions.

Melia azedarach (China/India berry or Persian lilac). D. FL. FR. DT. Gr – fast. S – variable. CH – T/H. Grown worldwide in temperate climates. Hardy to many soils, frost tolerant. Sprays of lilac flowers in spring followed by golden-yellow berries. Popular shade tree since delicate foliage filters sunlight rather than totally excluding it.

Nyssa sylvatica (tulepo or black gum). D. DT. Gr – slow. S – med–large. CH – C/T. AC. Native North America, tolerating wet, poorly drained conditions, but drought tolerant in summer. Brilliant autumn colours.

Olea europa (olive). E. Fl. FR. Gr – slow. S – small–med. CH – C/T. Grown primarily for commercial crops, silver-leafed olive makes an attractive ornamental specimen tree and is hardy to poor soils, wind and drought.

Paulownia tormentosa (empress or foxglove tree). D. FL. FR. Gr – fast S – large. T. CH – C/T. Native of China, named for Anna Paulownia, daughter of a Russian tsar. Beautiful tree grown for quick timber crops in many countries. Large racemes of lavender-blue foxglove-like flowers, huge heart-shaped leaves, bronze coloured seed capsules. Deep, moist soils, shelter from strong winds.

Pinus (many spp). E. FR (pine nuts), Gr – med–fast. S – large, tall, but many compact cultivars. CH – C/T. Native to many countries, generally fast-growing, hardy, medium to large tree with blue-green needle-like foliage. Cold hardy, tolerant of dry soils and coastal locations. Many species provide excellent shelter trees and timber. *P. radiata* is an important commercial timber tree.

Pittosporum (mock orange). E. Fl. FR. Gr – fast. S – small–med. CH – T/H. Small trees with attractive green/variegated foliage and scented flowers native to Australia, New Zealand, eastern Africa, Asia, Japan and Hawaii. Tolerant many soils, climatic extremes, coastal positions, undemanding, valuable multi-purpose tree.

Platanus acerifolia (London plane). D. Gr – slow–med. T. AC. S – large. CH – C/T. Pollution-resistant tree growing in cities worldwide. Large handsome light green foliage, shade tolerant, autumn colours, valued for timber.

Populus x *euroamericana* (European poplar), *P. yunnanensis* (Chinese poplar). D. Gr – med. S – tall. SF. AC. T. DT. CH – C/T/H. Poplars widespread throughout world. Tolerant dry soils, wind. Handsome rich green foliage, golden autumn foliage. Valued for erosion control and shelter. Timber light, strong, non-resinous. Provides stock food, abundant pollen for bees and beneficial insects.

Quercus spp (oaks). D. E. Gr – med. S – large. T. AC. CH – C/T. Large family of deciduous and evergreen trees native from temperate to tropical countries. Many species available for garden planting forming handsome specimen trees with brilliant autumn colour. Durable and beautiful timber. RS – *Q. coccinea* (scarlet oak), *Q. palustris* (pin oak), *Q. robor* (English oak), *Q. palustris* (America), *Q. rubra* (America).

Robinia pseudocacia (black locust). D. Gr – fast. S – med. CH – C/T/H. T. DT. Common throughout USA, Europe and Australasia, fast growing highly regarded timber tree. Excellent erosion control tree, tolerant dry conditions, infertile soil. RS – *R.p.* 'Frisia' beautiful golden leafed cultivar favoured by landscapers as both specimen and shade tree.

Salix (willows, many spp). D. Gr – fast. SF. CH – C/T. AC. Native many countries. Smaller growing, shrubby and dwarf willows provide attractive garden trees bearing ornamental catkins in spring. All willows need cool damp soils. Many have weeping foliage, attractive near water. Larger specimens valuable for erosion control, long pliable branches used for plaited fences, screens, plant supports. Willows tolerate very wet, poorly drained conditions. RS – *S. alba* x *matsudana* (Italian willow), bred for fast growth rate and erosion control; S. alba var. 'Vitellina' (golden willow), attractive cultivar with golden foliage and stems; *S. purpurea* (purple osier), shrub willow used for erosion control; *S. matsudana* var. 'tortuosa' ('corkscrew'), contorted branches, fine green foliage, excellent contrast of form with other trees.

Sequoia sempervirens (California redwood). E. Gr – fast. S – large, tall. CH – C/T/H T. Large handsome tree with pyramidal crown atop long slender trunk, fine needle-like foliage. Hard, durable timber.

Sophora spp. (kowhai, Pagoda tree). D. Fl. Fr. T. Gr – fast, S – small–med. Ch – C/T. Native to southern hemisphere, Japan, Chile, Hawaii and USA. Bears nectar-rich golden tubular flowers in spring, delicate fern-like foliage. Attractive to native birds and insects. Grows well along lake and river margins, tolerates most soils and coastal conditions. Timber tough, hard, durable with beautiful colour and grain.

Taxodium distichum (swamp cypress). D. Gr – med. S – large. AC. CH – C/T. One of the few deciduous conifers. Elegant American native, erect, pyramidal form, delicate feathery leaf sprays, open branched habit. Spectacular orange-bronze foliage in autumn. Tolerant poorly drained wet soils.

Flowers of the New Zealand kowhai attract a number of native birds.

Ulmus procera 'van Houtte' (golden elm). D. Gr – slow–med. S – med. T. AC. CH – C/T. Wind tolerant, golden elm is a popular garden tree, yellow foliage throughout summer, gold in autumn. Excellent shade tree tolerating most soil conditions, hard, tough, heavy wood. RS – *U. procera* (English elm), *U. glabra* (Wych elm), *U. hollandica* (Dutch elm – purchase Dutch-elm-disease resistant).

Controlling erosion

Soil conservation and tree planting go hand in hand. Farmers, horticulturists, and the owners of large rural gardens and lifestyle blocks are often faced with the necessity for clearing unprofitable scrub in order to develop the land, or they may have inherited land that is badly eroded through clear felling and failure to replant. When land is cleared, the risk of erosion can be reduced by leaving in place on fragile areas any existing trees, native plants, or forest trees, particularly on steep slopes or in gullies.

How can I reduce the risk of erosion and stabilise the land in my care?

- Clear and replant small manageable areas at a time. When plants are rooted, growing and easily manageable, tackle an adjacent area.
- Establish a grass or ground cover over cultivated, cleared or eroded land as soon as possible.

Once covered with native forests, these hills are now dusty landscapes of tussock and rock.

- Cultivate along the contour, not up and down the slope.
- Choose the appropriate season and method of cultivation for the land. In other words, understand the type of soil and the predominating climatic factors and choose plants suited to those conditions, whether they be coastal, hot and dry, cold and wet, windswept, wetland, heavy poorly drained soil, etc.

How do trees improve land stability?

- They bind the soil together with their roots.
- They protect the land from the direct impact of heavy rainfall, thus preventing topsoil washing away.
- They protect the land from scouring winds, which blow away existing topsoil.
- They remove excess moisture from the ground, helping create healthy oxygenated soil.
- They build up existing topsoil by feeding and enriching it with leaf fall and vegetative debris.

Gully and streambank erosion

A predominant feature of land suffering from erosion is that it has been carved into deep gullies by heavy rainfall, overflowing streams or rivers. In any stabilisation programme these areas should be planted first because they often trigger off other forms of erosion such as land slips. *Salix* spp (willows) are well suited for healing gully erosion because their wide-spreading fibrous roots travel out to tie and bind the land. Gully or stream bank planting should incorporate pairs of trees planted directly opposite each other to confine the water in the channel. The trees' roots also drink up excess water, thus preventing flooding from washing off further topsoil.

Tree spacing will be dictated by the severity of the problem. For severely eroded areas, tree pairs should be 4–5 m (13–16 ft) apart. For potentially erodable areas, tree pairs can be as far apart as 10–20 m (30–60 ft).

Salix purpurea (shrub willow) is useful on smaller streams where animals must have access to water, but remember to protect these trees from the animals until they have become established. Further up the sides and top of the banks *Populus* spp (poplars), and *Alnus* spp (alders) are effective. Plant only on the outside of the bends so as not to force water onto the opposite side of the bank.

Slippery slopes

Listed shortly are suggestions for dealing with slips, slumps and earthflows, depending on the severity of the problem. Often the movement is accelerated by water running through a gully, which can undermine the slopes above. Suitable plantings for less severe problems include poplar, willow or *Erythrina skyesii* at 5–10 m (16–30 ft) spacings, and plantings of *Eucalyptus*, *Pinus radiata*, *Cypressus*, and *Alnus* spp. at 8–10 m (26–30 ft) spacings.

Close planting 4–5 m (13–16 ft) apart with poplar and willow stakes or trees is recommended at the bottom of the slope, moving planting out to 6–10 m (20–30 ft) apart further up. Alternative planting could include *Acacia melanoxylon*, and poplars and willows. Animal grazing will need to be restricted while newly planted grass, ground cover and trees become established, or to give existing vegetation time to recover. As the trees mature thinning will need to be carried out to allow light to penetrate the canopy and encourage the development of understory vegetation.

Underground movement: tunnel gully erosion

Underground movement causes gullies to be carved by water beneath the soil surface. The underground gully eventually collapses, leaving a series of holes in its path. It is difficult to predict where further holes will develop, but the roots of trees planted along suspected tunnel lines will bind the soil together and prevent further tunnelling.

Wind erosion

Wind erosion can affect both coastal and inland areas. For this type of erosion it is important to keep to the following principles:

- On exposed hillsides, earthslips and slumps require planting from the bottom up, as the majority of control is achieved in the bottom third. Plantings should extend onto the solid ground to the sides above and below the movement.
- Do not plant in cracks in the ground, as these will dry out and open up in summer, causing the tree roots to dehydrate.
- To prevent death by waterlogging, do not plant any trees except willows in areas that water is likely to flood.

Shelter from the storm

The aim of a shelterbelt is to filter the wind rather than to cut the wind out altogether. A solid impenetrable windbreak such as a fence or wall will deflect wind completely, causing erosion and turbulence in other areas. The most effective windbreak is created by groupings of different trees and shrubs, some with foliage cover to ground level.

To achieve an efficient vegetative shelter it is important to plant both taller and lower growing species at the same time; otherwise, when foliage gaps in the maturing screen of vegetation become evident, it will be much harder for new plants to

Trees suitable for erosion control
Agathis australis – kauri
Alnus cordata – black alder
Acacia melanoxylon – Australian blackwood
Cupressus lusitanica – Mexican cypress
C. macrocarpa – Monterey cypress
Cupressocyparis x *leylandii* – leyland cypress
Dacridium cupressinum – rimu
Eucalyptus botryoides – southern mahogany
　　E. globoida – white stringy bark
　　E. globoidea, E. microcorys, E. muelleriana
　　E. pilularis, E. saligna
Gleditsia triacanthos – honey locust
Paulownia spp – paulownia
Pinus radiata – radiata pine
Populus spp – poplars
Quercus robor – English oak
Robinia pseudocacia – robinia, black locust
Salix spp – willows
Sequoia sempervirens – Californian redwood
Podocarpus totara – totara

establish themselves in their shade.

Another point to consider is that although solid windbreaks such as fences and walls are useful initially in helping plants establish and in protecting them as they grow, there is the danger that as these plants grow taller than the solid barrier, they will receive the full force of the wind and may snap, suffer wrenched roots or blow over altogether. A shelterbelt will be most efficient at a height of approximately 5 m (16 ft), with taller, most-hardy trees on the outside, and shorter trees or shrubs on the inside. Relatively close planting is essential to provide deflective foliage density, and to allow for the fact that some plants may not survive.

Under wraps

Protection for young trees is particularly essential in coastal areas where wind carries salt and sand. Salt is toxic; it retards bud growth and when allowed to accumulate on the surface of the new leaves it will burn them. This may be counteracted by spraying regularly with water while plants are young.

Constant sand blasting has more serious effects, damaging exposed trunks and stems, espe-

Exotic and richly fragrant flowers of the frangipani.

cially those of young plants, and restricting sap flow and thus plant growth. Protection may be given by erecting shade-cloth shelters around establishing plants, or by enclosing them in drums or plastic shields.

Small but sturdy

There is a wide variety of smaller trees and shrubs that will provide windbreak hedging for both coastal and inland gardens. *Abelia grandiflora* is a small evergreen tree to 3 m (10 ft) with glossy leaves toned bronze-purple in autumn and winter, followed by pink-red flowers. The larger shrubs, such as silver *Artemisia* spp and *Ceanothus* spp, make excellent underplantings to taller trees, and the common olive tree, *Olea europa*, is an adaptable Mediterranean tree useful for screen and windbreak purposes. Sea buckthorn, *Hippohae rhamnoides*, is valued for stabilising sand dunes and develops into a small, attractively gnarled tree with silver foliage. The evergreen *Euonymus japonica*, a fast growing small tree offering variegated foliage forms, is hardy to many soils and climatic conditions. Similarly useful is *Raphiolepsis indica*, which bears sprays of delicate pinkish-white flowers over glossy leathery leaves.

New Zealand hebes, attractive flowering shrubs hardy to both cold and temperate climates, come in many sizes and are becoming sought-after in a number of countries as resistant under-cover shrubs.

Trees with flower power

Once a foundation of sheltering trees has been established, more tender trees treasured for their flowers, fragrance and beauty of foliage may be planted. These might include the maples, *Acer* spp, which come in many sizes, forms and colours, along with a wealth of dwarf species with exquisitely fine foliage; the *Prunus* spp, bearing blossom and fruit; flowering magnolias of sizes to suit every garden; the taller growing rhododendrons, azaleas and camellias; and the deciduous American dogwoods, *Cornus* spp, with great beauty of foliage, form, and colour and bearing unusual bract-like flowers – many with coloured stems of vibrant coral, which shine on winter days.

We do not live for practicality alone! Some of the world's favourite trees are grown purely for their beauty as specimen trees. However, space here allows mention of only an unforgettable few. (For key to codes used below, refer back to the beginning of the list of multipurpose trees given earlier in this chapter.)

Acers (described above)

Aesculus (horse chestnut). D. Fl. Fr. Gr – fast. S – large. AC. CH – C/T. Popular trees in northern hemisphere, planted extensively in parks, streets, larger gardens. Also native to Europe and N. America. Striking finger-shaped leaves of tender green, tall candles of white or pink (*A. carnea*) flowers, followed by large round spiny fruits about size of golf ball, containing large round seeds with glossy brown coats.

Bauhinia (orchid tree). D. Fl. Fr. Gr – fast. S – large. CH – T/H. Native to the Americas, Asia, Africa and Australia. Flowering tree, white, reddish-purple or mauve-pink blossoms with five curving petals, long stamens.

Betula (silver birches, many spp). D. AC. Gr – med–fast. S – variable. CH – C/T. Popular garden trees with delicate airy structure, ornamental bark. Native to northern hemisphere but grown in many temperate climates. Dwarf weeping forms available.

Callistemon (Bottlebrush tree, many spp). E. Fl. Fr. Gr – fast. S – variable. DT, CH – T. Hardy tree, many sizes and varieties, spectacular upright, long-lasting flower spires resembling bottlebrushes. Flower colour – many shades of crimson-scarlet, cream, white, pink, and green and violet in less common species.

Catalpa (Indian bean tree). D. Fl. Fr. Gr – med. S – large. CH – C/T. Lush tree with tropical appearance, yet frost hardy, originating from northern climates (Asia and North America). Huge heart-shaped leaves, green or golden according to variety. Fragrant foxglove-like flowers of white, pink or lemon-tinted purple or yellow. Flowers followed by long pods.

Hibiscus. E. Fl. Gr – fast. S – small–med. CH – T/H. Small trees with flamboyant exotic flowers, growing in warm climates worldwide. Fijian, Hawaiian cultivars treasured for magnificent, often bi -and tri-coloured blossoms.

Hymenosporum (Australian frangipani). E. Fl. Gr – fast. S – med–large. CH – T/H. Australian native now grown in many temperate countries. Handsome glossy foliage, perfumed creamy frangipani-type flowers.

Jacaranda (blue haze tree). D. Fl. Gr – fast. S – large. CH – T/H. Beautiful blue-flowered tree with delicate fern-like foliage.

Plumeria (frangipani, temple flower). D. Fl. Gr – fast. S – small-med. CH – T/H. Treasured worldwide, found in many subtropical and tropical climates. Handsome glossy elongated leaves, richly perfumed cream flowers with golden hearts. *P.* x 'Scott Pratt' is dark pink, and *P. rubra* is red.

Striped and stippled: variegated foliage trees

Liriodendron (tulip tree). D. Fl. Gr – fast. S – large. CH – C/T. Related to magnolias, magnificent tree native to eastern N. America. Leaves are unique – long stemmed, four-lobed, blunt apex. Some varieties have variegated cream, green, gold foliage. Though fast growing, the tulip tree is slow to bloom, but flowers resemble great lime-gold tulips with orange hearts – definitely worth waiting for!

Tristania (water gum). E. Fl. Fr. Gr – fast. S – large. CH – C/T. Native to Australia, New Caledonia and India. Cultivar *T. conferta* has beautiful golden-green foliage and sprays of fragrant creamy-white flowers, followed by round seed pods that remain on tree giving year round interest.

Cornus kousa 'variegata' (dogwood, wedding cake tree). Beautiful large tree, cream and green variegated foliage, open spreading branches arranged in tiers. Many American dogwoods offer

Flamingo-pink spring foliage of the toon tree, *Cedrela sinensis*.

handsome bi-toned foliage and magnificent autumn colour.

Other handsome variegated trees include those from the *Ilex* (holly) genera and Acers (maples).

Planting and staking

Trees are often raised by commercial breeders as mass plantings in paddocks. They're delivered bare rooted to nurseries, where they're 'heeled in' (temporarily 'planted') in beds of mulching materials and compost. A bare-rooted tree will have severely trimmed roots, so good site preparation and staking is vital. Dig a hole large enough to allow a good root run, and plant the tree in a mix of soil and compost containing water retention crystals and slow release fertiliser granules.

Staking all young trees is important because it prevents 'root rock' – which will cause small new roots to snap before they can properly anchor the tree into position. Secure the trunk between two strong stakes driven in at the edge of the root ball.

The tree should be positioned between two stakes that are set far enough apart to allow the growth of a sturdy framework and allow a little trunk movement. The stakes should be positioned on the prevailing windward side of the tree, so that it will be blown away from them rather than

Our remaining forests

In 1998, the Worldwide Fund for Nature stated that 10 per cent (8750) of the 80,000 to 100,000 of the world's known tree species now face extinction. Some 77 species have already disappeared and almost 1000 others are now listed as critically endangered.

Threats to the earth's remaining forests include
- felling for timber and wood fuel
- agriculture
- expansion of human settlements
- uncontrolled forest fires
- invasive exotic species and introduced animal pests
- unsustainable forest management.

There is only one species that can save them.

Trees are the lungs of the world.

against them. The ties should be of material such as cloth, rubber or plastic (strips of old panty hose are ideal), which will not cause damage to the trunk as it moves in the wind.

Sustainable forestry management

We know that increasing world population must inevitably continue to put great pressure upon our remaining forests. It would be unrealistic to imagine otherwise. People must be fed, clothed and housed, and have books and newspapers to read. But if we destroy our remaining forests, we destroy ourselves.

The answer lies in sustainable management, in trying to take only what we need and to put back what we take. It is the only solution we have, and it must be done if we are to survive.

Towards the end of the eighteenth century, with great omniscience the English poet and philosopher William Blake wrote: 'The tree which moves some to tears of joy is to others only a green thing which stands in the way.'

Decisions are too often made by out-of-touch government officials who sit in urban offices. They have never trodden a forest floor, or gazed up at its cathedral roof of sunlit dappled green, listening to its peace or to the greatest orchestra on earth, the songs of native birds, and answering the whispering of its myriad tiny creatures. They have never acknowledged that the survival of the forests means the survival of humanity.

When the saws, bulldozers and helicopters scream destruction, they crush not only the forests but also all that dwell within. For every creature we make extinct, 40 others which were dependant upon it in the ecological chain perish also. Can your garden, your family, replace one fallen tree, two, three? These small numbers multiplied across the globe can reach out green hands to become forests again.

Trees make up the rapidly diminishing forests that once sheltered the earth, that rise from the world's driest places and draw most of the rain. They are the levees whose roots hold the earth when the elements erode and destroy; and the green filters that embrace poisonous carbon dioxide and in return give oxygen. They are the lungs of the world.

CHAPTER THIRTEEN
GARDEN STYLES FOR SPECIFIC ENVIRONMENTS

The flora, fauna and landscape of a nation contribute to the identification of a national soul.

Gordon Ford, *The Natural Australian Garden*

The traditional garden has been regarded for centuries as an enclosure in which to create exotic and somewhat anachronistic designs far removed from the natural landscape beyond its boundaries. An example of this is our gardening endeavours to grow luscious exotics entirely unsuited to our climates, or our struggles to maintain gardens with lush lawns and labour intensive herbaceous borders in desert denizens of heat and drought! We know in our hearts that such gardens are sustained only by endless cultivation, water-

ing, pruning and spraying, and in general as gardeners we are at odds rather than in harmony with nature.

The key to a sustainable, low maintenance garden is in choosing a design and planting materials suited to one's specific environmental, geographical and climatic conditions. Provided that they are given enriched and conditioned soil, the plants employed then become self-sustaining.

English essayist and gardener Alexander Pope wrote of garden landscaping: 'Consult the genius of the place and then exploit it.' Echoing the character of the immediate environment helps create a garden that looks both natural and in harmony

Above: A lush subtropical garden designed for the steamy heat of Queensland, Australia.

with its context. It reflects its own climate, soil type, flora, fauna and cultural traditions. The wise gardener learns as much as possible about the climate, altitude, soil types, prevailing winds and what sort of plants colonise the area if it is left uncultivated. If we design and plant with these principles in mind, we celebrate the distinct and diverse glories of our individual countries and do not continue to destroy their unique regional identity. A new type of garden emerges, one that is truly of its place and time, and this garden is, of course, subject to sustainable management.

Checklist: identifying your conditions

Identify your climatic and geographical conditions, giving consideration to the following factors:

- hot, dry, low rainfall
- seasonal extremes – long hot summers and freezing winters
- high rainfall, humidity and damp soils – sub-tropical or tropical conditions
- coastal or exposed area conditions with salt-laden high winds
- temperate climate with balanced amounts of sunshine and rainfall
- specific soil type

Choose which category your garden environment falls into, then take the following actions:

- Go for walks in the area and study which plants grow best there.
- Observe which native plants are thriving – they will always be the natural colonisers of your specific soil type, geographical location and climatic conditions; that is, they will thrive where little else will grow and where exotics will certainly fail.
- When you are sure of the specific characteristics of your gardening environment, withdraw from the library books detailing plants suited to these conditions. Most books of this type give maps and charts of nation-wide geographic and climatic zones along with relevant plant lists. Seed packets usually give similar zone maps indicating in which zones specific plants will thrive. (See also plant lists at the end of chapter 11).
- Seek advice from your local nursery expert on selecting plants suited to your environment
- Read plant labels carefully and believe them!

(For example, if you garden on a wind whipped coastal hillside, stay away from the roses!)
- Remember that plants labelled 'hardy' or 'easily grown' will still only do well if given the environmental conditions they like best.

Having identified the constraints and virtues of your specific environment and determined which plants will grow well there, you are now equipped to:

- design a garden which is in harmony with your natural landscape,
- choose plant materials suited to that garden,
- manage the garden according to the low maintenance and sustainable principles and techniques outlined in this book, and
- sit back and enjoy a stunning garden giving you maximum all seasons performance!

Culturally cosmopolitan

Having understood the need and accepted the underlying philosophies of choosing the right garden for the right environment, we look at translating and reconciling these concepts into a style. Although we go forward sharing the common bond of sustainable management and natural landscaping, our interpretation of style will always remain eclectic and highly individual. It is an expression of self and identity, which is exactly as it should be. So let us consider styles across the globe.

England, America, Australia and New Zealand, although worlds apart in terms of geographical location, time and distance, all share close common bonds in gardening. With the exception of Great Britain, where summers are more temperate, in various regions of our countries we all share the climatic extremes of freezing winters and long hot summers, and all have areas that are subtropical to tropical. This means that in addition to indigenous species, we can each grow almost the same huge diversity of exotic plants because plant breeders and international seed catalogues make them available to us all.

Many cold hardy native plants from New Zealand and Australia are treasured by garden landscapers worldwide. Plants such as native ornamental grasses, phormiums (flaxes) and cabbage trees (*Cordyline australis*) are keenly sought after for their bold sculptural effects; and gardeners

'English Garden' rose produced by British breeder David Austin.

in Australasia can't get enough of British breeder David Austin's English roses! The American heirloom seed company W.P. Burpees will mail seeds of antique USA plant species worldwide. Plants transcend all barriers of time, place and nationality, and by sharing them we assume a little of each other's identity, even as we seek to establish one that is uniquely our own. This is especially true when we share each other's native plants. If gardens in these four countries alone share for example, an English rose, a New Zealand flax, an Australian eucalyptus and a selection of American heirloom vegetables, we gardeners are helping to perpetuate genetic plant diversity across the globe.

The native and integrated garden

The native garden features trees, shrubs, ornamental grasses, bulbs, ferns, and a huge diversity of other plants indigenous to its country. The plants grow in self-sustaining colonies because they are growing in the climatic and geographical locations they like best. This type of garden is beautifully integrated with the natural landscape because the plants placed in the garden situation reflect those present in the environment. The eye travels easily between the two and the overall ambience is one of harmony with the natural world.

The native garden is becoming referred to as the 'integrated garden' – a definition perhaps of the most sustainable kind of garden. The plant material is chosen to echo and enhance, but never

to compete with views of sea, sky, sand, bush, beach, mountain, lake, river, and tree. The colours that predominate are those of the natural landscape, silver-grey river hues, sky and sea blues, sand-golds, warm red terracotta and rich dark greens. Warmth and contrast of colour are often provided by flowering plants of bruised plum and vibrant garnet reds.

The integrated garden draws existing natural features into its overall design, features such as a range of distant hills or a lake framed by a stand of trees. Low plantings can draw the eye over magnificent vistas of borrowed landscape beyond the confines of the garden itself. The 'borrowed' feature may be as simple as a stunning tree in a neighbour's garden!

For many years, while other garden styles such as the cottage garden predominated, native plants in many countries were dismissed as 'dull and boring' or 'having no flowers', but nothing could be further from the truth. They offer just as much colour, excitement, fascinating floral form, diversity of foliage, texture and shape as any imported exotics, and many provide year round interest.

Selection of the species

Because native plants have evolved over millions of years to suit the geographical location and climatic extremes of their individual countries, they are hardy to their natural environment and therefore remain healthy and are generally easily grown. Drought resistant plants have evolved in dry continents such as Australia and in parts of America, while in cool damp climates with high rainfall such as the UK and Europe, many species of flowers, trees and shrubs evolved to become deciduous to protect themselves against long freezing winters.

As though to compensate for their absence in the winter months, these deciduous plants are known for the beauty of their spring foliage, their summer flowers and the drama of their autumn colours. The traditional cottage garden with its brief season of flowering glory is ideally suited to the short summers of the northern hemisphere.

Some countries such as America and New Zealand have a wide range of climatic conditions ranging from the subtropical, temperate and mild, with desert plains and tussock grasslands, through boiling mud pools and geysers, to snow-swept alps and subzero winters. In New Zealand alone, the immense diversity of native plants that range from vast tracts of green velvety bush feathered with giant tree ferns and ancient towering kauri trees to tiny native orchids and alpines is awe inspiring.

America also has this topographical and climatic variation. Giant redwood forests merge into sun and windswept prairie and tussock plains and desert reaches where cacti and succulents predominate; cloud-tickling glacial mountains sail above her face and giant canyons rest in her bowels; there are temperate areas where carpets of wild

flowers or alpines come each to their season, and tropical regions where coconuts and banana palms flourish.

The vast continent of Australia has aromatic drought resistant eucalyptus forests, a great giant desert heart where lonely oaks and ancient bottle-shaped baobab trees crouch to protect the earth, and dried up river beds and creeks of scoured pebbles punctuated by sentinel gums with trunks bleached skeleton white by the ever present sun and wind. There are lush, humid subtropical rain forests and fertile river valleys embroidered with wild flowers where major cities cling to ocean coastlines. Our countries are shaped by millions of years of chaotic upheavals within the earth and sculpting by the elements, and we all share something of this rich and enormous natural diversity.

As every gardener knows, no matter how hot, cold, wet or dry an area is, there are plants that will adore it there! We have just begun to realise that many of those plants are natives – evolved to perfectly suit our own lands. Planted in our gardens in harmonious combinations of foliage and flower form of contrasting colour, shape and texture, they're superb. They are our identity.

We are equally fortunate in that this cosmopolitan plant culture enables us to share a diversity of garden styles. England gave many countries the traditional, internationally beloved cottage garden. It is a style which will never really lose its appeal, but as nations like Australia and New Zealand move away from the northern hemisphere garden scene and seek their own southern hemisphere identity, subtropical plants, natives and exotics of hot colours are being integrated to create gardens of a unique South Pacific flavour. The truth is that as far as identity goes we can establish our own but still enjoy the best of all worlds.

Container culture

Container gardening plays a vital role in the sustainable garden of the future as space for homes and gardens grow smaller, but it is not a new concept. The plantaholic Queen Hatshepsut of ancient Egypt lived in a very arid area and she had acres of choice specimens in pots. Huge areas of the Hanging Gardens of Babylon and the gardens of ancient Persia were actually planted in no soil situations, but it has to be said that armies of serfs were available for tending them.

Container gardening – currently enjoying an unprecedented revival – has revolutionised the types of plants that can be grown in northern hemisphere countries suffering severe winters. Frost tender subtropical exotics and fruits, many available in dwarf forms, if planted in containers and moved into sheltered positions during winter, can be grown in the coldest climates, given there is sufficient sunshine and warmth during the summer months. A friend in London has a selection of Australasian citrus, Californian peaches, and exotic Hawaiian and Fijian hibiscus bushes in an inner-city walled garden.

Pub fronts in England are famous for their containers, hanging baskets and window boxes; these now contain New Zealand flaxes and phormiums as contrast of foliage and form to the froth of flowers. Traffic islands, public parks and gardens in European countries now feature these and other southern hemisphere plants such as hebes and grevilleas together with cold-hardy American palms and grasses. The world is the gardener's oyster as far as plants are concerned.

Garden styles

Having identified the constraints and virtues of your specific environment and the types of plants suited to it, you may still need advice on choosing a particular style – on getting it together. In addition to environmental considerations, human energy and time, the use of mechanical power and water are also vital equations. Whether you are planning a new garden or revamping an old one to be more environmentally friendly, these factors

are directly influenced by the chosen design of garden. A breakdown follows on the predominant styles that are taking us into the twenty-first century and their suitability for both sustainable and low-maintenance management.

Bold design concepts, simplicity of form, shape and design together with the employment of drought tolerant architectural and native plants is the keynote of the garden of the twenty-first century. Its versatility allows it to be created in both hot and cold climates, in spaces large or small. Designed to maximise every inch of space, it is uncluttered, unfussy and has great visual impact, sometimes offering a fun-filled wild and whacky ambience created with garden furniture and containers painted in electric colours.

There is a move away from the traditional 'garlands and cherubs' stone statuary to modern sculptures in warm terracotta colours, and animals and figures are more related to those of today than of yesteryear. This style of garden reflects the clear-cut angular lines of the architecture of the modern homes they surround.

The design of the millennium garden is planned to integrate both house and garden as a harmonious whole, each enhancing the other. The minimalist style is particularly suited to homes in

Keynote of the new millenium garden: bold design concepts using the simple architectural forms of drought tolerant exotics and natives.

urban areas where, because garden space is at a premium, each element is chosen and placed with care for maximum visual impact. Hardscaping materials, wood, gravel, pebbles, rocks and stone are dominant, and plant interest is provided by a small number of bold architectural plants, such as agaves, aloes, succulents, native plants, palms or, in colder climes, with hardy trees, shrubs and plants that display dramatic leaf shape, form, texture and colour.

Futuristic, sophisticated and minimalist
The garden of the future has a minimal lawn area and favours instead a water feature designed with bold uncluttered lines. The water feature is very important to all styles of garden but it is an enormously therapeutic element in inner-city or urban living. Entertaining areas are paved and feature a barbecue and often, if space allows, a small swimming pool.

Gardens of the future will also feature an efficient night lighting system because they are very much an extension of indoor living and entertaining space.

Angled timber, steel water sculpture, hardy plants and hardscaping materials characterise the garden of the twenty-first century.

Pebbles replace lawns, and plants offering strong, simple forms provide the design elements.

Maintenance is minimal in the millennium garden because it is sustainable in a surprising number of ways. It relies mainly on structural features for visual impact and maximises space; it is drought resistant or has low water requirements, since the plants chosen are hardy, often natives of the region and therefore suited to predominating climatic factors such as rainfall and heat.

The plants are unlikely to require the use of chemical sprays since plantings are minimal and hardy, and hardscaping materials preclude weeds and therefore the use of herbicides. The design is economical in terms of human time and energy and does not involve mechanical power other than electricity for night lighting. With living space constantly diminishing, this garden for the future is very much a garden for living and playing in.

Architectural gardens

These are usually gardens closely resembling the futuristic natural garden in style where the hardscaping is generally more dominant than the plants. Stone, statuary, water, brick, pavers, gravel and planted containers chosen for their decorative values take centre stage. Plants are chosen for their bold sculptural structure rather than for their flowers and are therefore hardy to extreme climatic conditions. Paved entertaining and play areas replace lawns and a water feature is generally an important part of the overall design.

Maintenance is generally low. Many of the plants in the all-seasons architectural garden are hardy evergreens with slow growth habit thus requiring little spraying or pruning. Since hardscaping materials predominate there is no mowing and little weeding.

The informal natural garden

This is a more basic semi-formal garden dominated by a pleasing integration of native plants and easy-care shrubs and trees. Flowers are limited to attractive hardy perennials, but colour, shape, texture and form is provided by foliage rather than by floral plantings. Hard landscaping replaces lawns with bricked or paved patios, play and entertaining areas. Beds and borders have a good mix of deciduous and evergreen shrubs underplanted with hardy perennials, bulbs, ornamental grasses and ground covers.

This style of garden offers ease of maintenance and year round interest. It requires some annual pruning of trees and shrubs, cutting back and dividing spent perennials, and occasional renewing of mulch materials and weeding on beds.

The cottage garden

This universally popular, ancient and traditional style of garden design originated in England and Europe many centuries ago. The style has endured because where they found similar temperate conditions in their adopted countries, early European settlers recreated the gardens of their northern hemisphere homes across the face of the globe. The design is informal with many types of plants, including edibles, all tumbled together in a bee-embroidered profusion. Plants are allowed to self sow freely and new additions are included wherever there is room. The emphasis is on flowers rather than form and foliage; richly scented heritage roses and old fashioned perennials dominate beds and borders, and lawns are usually minimal.

The unrestrained and billowing abundance of the cottage garden is relaxed, full of scent and colour. It has a gentle and romantic ambience. The style is beloved and has possibly also endured through a sense of nostalgia for yesteryear. Deciduous, natural woodlands with ferns and streams are also predominant features of northern hemisphere gardens.

The vegetable garden is an important feature of the cottage garden. Flowering companion plants and edibles are planted together potager style to create an edible garden that is both aesthetically pleasing and productive.

Now I must shatter this romantic vision! I can tell you absolutely definitely that, despite popular conception, the cottage garden is a high maintenance garden.

Although the overall design of our gardens at Valley Homestead are basically a harmonious integration of native New Zealand plants together with exotics, the gardens immediately surrounding the old colonial homestead are purely cottage garden in style. Each enhances the other perfectly, which is possibly why this European design has endured for centuries around the old villa and bungalow homesteads of New Zealand, Australia and parts of America. However, that air of soft billowing abundance and 'naturalness' is knife-edge stuff – it is constantly just a hairline from being a wild impenetrable mess. Cottage garden beds and borders must be strictly controlled to prevent a jungle effect; they involve constant deadheading and cutting back to keep the plants in flower, and require constant watering.

Overall, despite exacting a higher degree of care from its designer, the diversity of plant material in the cottage garden offers home and sustenance to a wide variety of beneficial predatory insects, birds, bees, butterflies, hedgehogs, frogs and other creatures.

The formal garden

Gardens and other landscapes fall into two main classes – the formal and geometrical, and the informal, asymmetrical and natural. In the formal garden there is no attempt to disguise the fact that the design has been imposed upon the landscape by people. Such gardens are characterised by straight lines, regular curves and symmetrical balance. In the formal garden, whatever is put on one side of the main axis is repeated on the other. Repetition, rather than diversity of planting, and emphasis on strong form are the predominant features.

The strong classical appeal of formal gardens is enjoyed worldwide and the style is often chosen where harsh climatic factors prevail. The plant materials selected are usually hardy, evergreen and often containerised, thus requiring minimal maintenance except for occasional trimming and pruning. Formal garden design features artificially

Hardy architectural plants, paved walking areas, planted containers and painted timber frames create a striking combination in this Australian garden.

shaped shrubs, trees and hedges. Other design elements include strictly defined parterres of plantings behind hedges of yew and box or set within walls and courtyards. In the larger formal garden there may be grand herbaceous borders, walkways lined with pleached trees (trees with shoots or branches interlaced), sophisticated water features, classic statuary and sculpture.

Knot gardens in which symmetry and pattern are paramount predominate and these are usually confined behind clipped dwarf hedges, but grand techniques can be recreated on a smaller scale! Classical garden design is versatile and equally well suited to the small modern garden. The clean uncluttered lines of the formal style will enhance a small area that would look chaotic and claustrophobic if crammed with informal cottage garden plantings.

Symmetrical groupings of flowers and ground covers, punctuated by an even number of standard or topiaried shrubs in elegant containers, might

Topiary

Traditional containerised topiary specimens are invaluable for lending elegance and symmetry to almost any style of garden but they are traditional to the formal garden, enhancing its basically geometrical structure. However, since they offer maximum elegance in return for minimum maintenance and generally suffer from few pests and diseases they are becoming a popular design element in sustainable modern gardens, and the ancient art of topiary will play an important role in landscape architecture of the future. For these reasons a DIY guide follows.

Smaller shrubs and ornamentals have been containerised and trained as topiary specimens and standards since ancient Roman and Egyptian civilisations. To the novice gardener, the art of pruning to shape topiary specimens appears to be a somewhat technical and on occasions dangerous horticultural skill to master! Those elegant standards are also desperately expensive when purchased from the nursery, which is always a compelling reason to try one's own hand.

It is reassuring to remember in the learning stages that very few plants will die as the result of incorrect pruning – at worst your specimen may not produce any flowers or fruit for a season or two, but it will certainly survive!

It's as well, however, to be aware that not all shrubs and trees make successful subjects for topiary. Some cannot tolerate severe cutting, eventually losing their vigour. Some grow much too quickly so that they become labour intensive, while others produce foliage that is too open to allow any impression of shape. The following species suffer from none of these drawbacks. They are generally slow growing and densely leafed, and will respond to trimming by producing new shoots each year.

English box (*Buxus sempervirens*) and yew (*Taxus* sp) are the traditional shrubs for topiary, but they are slow to mature, and the latter can grow very large. *Lonicera nitida* will shape as well as box and in half the time. Holly (*Ilex* spp) trees with glossy (and somewhat prickly) leaves are ideal for clipping into simple shapes. Many of the larger thuja conifers (*Thuja* spp) train into stout hedges and will also prune well to simple geometric shapes.

More complicated shapes do take more skill since they involve plants trained over wire frames, and one must, as the saying goes, possess one's soul in patience while the plants grow. For the modern gardener a steady hand and just a little patience are all that is required in learning how to develop plant sculptures. It can take many years to develop an impressive geometric head on a tall stem. But if you are in a hurry, you can cheat!

Choose a suitable tree or shrub (preferably two, for symmetry) from the nursery with a strong, straight central trunk and a full, well-developed head. Remove all the lower branches to the height you desire, and then trim the head lightly to a chosen shape and a couple of passable topiary standards may be had in a few hours instead of years. For the beginner topiarist it is wise to stick to simple geometric shapes such as balls, cubes, columns and triangles. You can experiment with advanced shapes on frames when you have gained experience.

It may be wise to provide a strong stake for taller standards, because the density of their heads can make them a little top heavy and susceptible to strong winds. Use soft ties so that the trunk does not suffer injury. Any new shoots that appear on the trunk should be promptly removed, and new growth on the head should be pinched back regularly to encourage even more shoots, which will provides the density of foliage you require to train into a desired shape. Other traditional shrubs that make attractive standards or topiary specimens include roses, conifers, camellias, bay trees (*Laurus nobilis*), upright rosemary (*Rosmarinus officinalis*), lavender varieties (especially *Lavendula dentata*, which has strong upright growth and is quick growing), citrus, orange blossom (*Philadelphus coronaria*) and hydrangeas.

Many more small trees and shrubs clip well into these forms and in addition to providing vertical accents and focal points they are highly ornamental, take little space and lend grace and dignity to any style of garden. Above all they are well suited to life in containers, so may be enjoyed in gardens of all sizes and geographic locations.

Townhouse topiary.

occupy no more than the sides of a modern drive-way, a tiny front or back garden, or an inner-city courtyard. There is no need to own a country estate if a traditional classical garden is your desire!

The amount of maintenance required for a formal garden varies according to size. It will obviously be high if the garden is large and there are miles of hedges to clip, sweeps of lawn to mow, and herbaceous borders to maintain. In the small formal garden where flower plantings are usually minimal, maintenance will be low and should mainly involve occasional clipping of topiary specimens and dwarf hedges.

The semi-formal garden

This universally popular style surrounds millions of suburban homes in temperate zones. Although lacking the linear confines, symmetry and restraint of the formal garden, everything in the semi-formal garden is neat and ordered. The design is dominated by manicured lawns, which are edged or intersected with flowerbeds and borders cut in geometric shapes. There are often island beds planted with annuals and perennials and several rose beds. The back garden features a flat open-bedded allotment style vegetable garden, and there are plantings of single trees and shrubs in individual positions.

The semi-formal garden is a high maintenance garden. It requires time and patience and some

degree of commitment. Lawns must be mowed regularly and their edges hand trimmed. Bedding plants must be replaced, and roses deadheaded, sprayed and pruned. Other flowers must be cut back and deadheaded, and flowerbeds and vegetable gardens kept hoed, watered and weed and disease free.

The large garden

Generally situated in more rural areas, the large garden usually features classic design elements such as sweeping lawns, tall hedges, topiary, plantings of mature trees and shrubs, wide herbaceous and perennial borders, rose walks and gardens, extensive water gardens and ornamental structures such as gazebos, pergolas, rose arbours and arches. This style of garden almost always includes an extensive vegetable garden laid out in the potager or open bed design, and an orchard.

Maintenance of the large garden is high. It requires considerable human energy, time and mechanical power – such as ride-on lawn mowers, electric or petrol driven strimmers, weed eaters, hedge clippers and chainsaws. Herbaceous borders are labour intensive and the garden requires a high degree of weeding, pruning and disease and pest prevention. Water requirements are also high.

The coastal garden

For many, the spell of the sea is so hypnotic they choose to make their homes beside it, and having

The gravel pathways of this drought tolerant Mediterranean garden are lined with flowers and herbs that give off sweet or spicy smells.

succumbed to its magnetism, the first requisite after setting up home is to establish a garden. The lesson is rapidly learned that idyllic coastal sites suffer 'sea-changes' too, and strong salt-laden winds and spray can batter precious plants. The old adage of choosing the right plant for the right place is never more essential than here.

In designing the seaside garden it is important to study the vegetation that is already thriving in the area. Exposed coastal locations contain a wealth of self-sustaining plants that have evolved over centuries in harsh conditions and are consequently ideally suited to dry sandy areas. By planting species indigenous to coastal locations we add to the character and identity of the neighbourhood, and are spared a good deal of heartache and expense from failed and unsustainable plantings! Another bonus is that such plants provide habitats and sustenance for birds, butterflies and insects native to the coast.

Providing shelter from the wind is an essential element in the design and success of the coastal garden. Windbreaks are formed by the use of screens, shade-cloth, fences or trellis frames, by plantings of trees and shrubs of varying heights, or by a combination of both.

Many seaside gardens enjoy stunning ocean vistas, and an important consideration in designing the sheltering framework is to allow gaps or 'windows' – the object is to shut out the wind but not the view. A workable design incorporates vegetative windbreaks that filter, absorb and deflect the wind's energy; plantings of drought tolerant and tenderer plants can then be established within.

A coastal garden demands a medium amount of maintenance. Soils in coastal areas are thin and sandy, and require regular additions of nutritious organic matter to improve structure and moisture retention. The choice of drought tolerant hardy plants is essential; sandy soils are porous and if tender specimens are employed, they will dehydrate rapidly unless given copious amounts of water. While becoming established, most young plants, even of hardy variety, will require some wind protection, combined with regular hosing of salt from their foliage. Trees and shrubs need firm staking.

Constant wind and good air circulation generally minimises disease and pest infestation in coastal gardens, encouraging self-sustaining plant colonies.

The Mediterranean drought tolerant garden

The sustainable gardener learns many great truths in the course of creating and maintaining a garden, and the greatest of these is that despite the harshness of poor dry soils in windblown, mountainous and rocky terrain, there are a wealth of plants that will thrive there. Areas where hot dry conditions predominate also cover a good deal of the earth's surface. This need not be a case for despair but for rejoicing, because the number of plants that worship the sun far exceeds those that like to paddle or freeze!

First, refer back to chapter 10 for details of drought resistant plants. The Mediterranean garden features gravel hillsides, sweet and spicy perfumed herbs, lavenders, artemisias and other grey-foliaged plants, and groves of olives.

The climatic factors affecting the Mediterranean garden are low annual rainfall and long, hot, dry summers. The gardener's style is firmly under the constraints of climate and soil, so plant materials are (on the whole) restricted to those that thrive naturally in these conditions, thus requiring little maintenance.

The water garden

Regardless of the rigours of climate and geographical location, water is an indispensable feature in gardens of every shape, size, design and style. A garden under sustainable management requires more than healthy chemical-free crops and flowers. It must also provide the gardener with spiritual food. Water offers a variety of moods and sounds. A small still pool offers reflective tranquillity, the rushing of a cascade or the tumbling of a waterfall give a sense of movement and excitement. The peaceful trickle of water amongst rocks, the murmur of a slow moving stream, or the swish of the gracefully arching plumes of a fountain all create an aura of peace and well-being in a garden haven. The smallest expanse of water can give reflections of the sky in its infinite variety, the tracery of overhanging trees and mirror images of flowers, people and buildings. The pattern of its surface changes constantly with the turning of the seasons and the moods of the elements.

In addition to providing the means to grow fascinating aquatic plants, water attracts wildlife in many forms and provides it with a valuable habitat. Darting fish bring animation and movement; birds, along with butterflies, dragonflies

and other insects, skim the margins to drink; and toads and frogs hold noisy courtship rituals before populating the water with tadpoles.

In style and design, a water feature may constitute a grand lake across which swans sail in the traditional manner; an inner-city high-tech aquatic showpiece of concrete, steel or floral fountains; a pool of classical design set in topiary gardens; an oriental garden planted with whispering bamboo and pools of exotic fish; a small still pond in a relaxed cottage or woodland setting; an ornamental wall-hanging recirculating water into a basin; or simply a miniature waterlily floating on the surface of an attractive container on a tiny patio or verandah. While the water features we will design for the new millennium will certainly not be as grandiose as those from earlier centuries, they are as important to both modern landscaping architecture and gardener enjoyment as they were in the drought-stricken gardens of ancient Persia and Egypt.

The subtropical garden

Subtropical to tropical conditions predominate in many parts of the United States, New Zealand and Australia. Modern Australasian gardeners are seeking their own national identity and an adaptation of their gardens to suit climate, environment and lifestyle. They perceive themselves not as satellite countries of the United Kingdom, but as Pacific Rim countries.

Garden design, with increased bias towards native and subtropical plantings and movement away from the pastel parterres of the northern hemisphere, clearly reflects this impetus. Their aim is to create a Pacific paradise, integrating southern hemisphere natives with a range of tropical delights from the Pacific Rim – the region that includes coastal New Zealand, Australia, California and Mexico, the Pacific islands and the Indonesian Archipelago.

Australasian gardeners are said to be 'blessed among gardeners'. They have the best of both worlds – gardens in which the hardy and subtropical grow side by side. The southern hemisphere garden offers lush foliage, flamboyant colour, opulent flowers, plants of bold structure, and

Bold foliage plants, a sculptured bowl and bamboo pipes give this water garden sculptural appeal.

shadowed canopies of tree ferns and palms. Overhead, rampant vines and climbers let fall flashy blossoms of crimson, pink, and gold as they scramble towards the sunlight. Integrated with natives, such plants also inspire the creation of secret pools where canna lilies, orchids, hibiscus and *Vireya* (subtropical rhododendrons), along with bougainvilleas and other flamboyant subtropical climbers, create mirror images in the water. Plants in the Pacific Rim garden do not whisper – they make bold statements!

Although brilliant flower colour sets an exotic mood, this happy combination of subtropicals, natives and old English favourites will fold into a sheltering framework of natives such as hebes, phormiums (New Zealand flaxes), cordylines (Cabbage trees), coprosmas, pittosporums, native tussock grasses, palms, flowering acacias, eucalypts, grevilleas and tree ferns. Your natives need not be common or garden varieties either, but can include spectacular hybrid varieties that are keenly sought after by landscapers and horticulturists worldwide.

Pacific pride

The Pacific Rim garden is extremely versatile because it may be created in large and small places, in containers in less temperate areas, around decking, verandahs and patios. The garden is well suited to townhouses or courtyard areas where shelter provided by walls, hedges or other buildings creates a microclimate favourable to subtropical species. It is suited to hot arid locations where drought defying phormiums, gums, and cordylines might combine with fleshy succulents, spectacular agaves, aloes and the spiked silhouettes of cacti of many forms to create all the drama of a desert landscape.

At its other extreme, the garden may have all the atmosphere of a tropical rain forest where the burning sand and sun-baked pebbles are replaced by a woodland floor damp with mosses beneath a canopy of clematis, palms and tree ferns. In warm, moist locations the luxuriance of its green depths has all the beauty of a South Seas jungle.

Although New Zealand and Australia are also subject to seasonal cycles such as those experienced by the UK and the USA, the southern hemisphere garden is a dynamic year round garden because growth and bloom in all but the

coldest areas are sustained by the more temperate conditions of these seasons. When the subtropical and cottage garden flowers have fallen there is a solid foundation of hardy natives with evergreen foliage maintaining colour, form and texture.

Australia and New Zealand enjoy the best of imported specimen trees, but native species such as the towering kauri (*Agathis australis*), the golden blossomed kowhai (*Sophora tetraptera*), tree ferns (*Cyathea dealbata*), cabbage palms (*Livistona australis*), nikau palms (*Rhopalostylus sapida*), and towering bone-bleached Eucalypt gums firmly proclaim their countries' national gardening identity.

New Zealand and Australia are cosmopolitan societies experiencing increased migration of Asian peoples. This encourages further the present diversity in garden design, bringing a combination of Asian-Pacific styles that offer scope for visual excitement and dramatic garden architecture. This skilful integration of natives with exotic imported plant materials creates gardens that integrate harmoniously with their unique South Pacific landscape – gardens that take Australasia and the Pacific islands into the new millennium with the unmistakable identity of the southern hemisphere.

Although the Pacific Rim garden has a unique identity, it employs a diverse range of plant material that engenders differing degrees of maintenance. In its natural state and environment the subtropical garden is largely self-sustaining, but when recreated within the confines of a garden, its luxuriant exuberance may need some degree of cutting back and control.

Trends on the world scene

The move to a new kind of gardening based on sustainable principles has burgeoned in recent years in Australia, New Zealand, England and America. Along with increasing awareness of the value of indigenous plants there is a desire to work in sympathy with the landscape and a move away from imposing alien styles and design upon it. Leading new-age landscape designers include John Brookes of England and London-based New Zealander Anthony Paul. Piet Oudolf and Ton der Linden are leading practitioners of Dutch and European garden design. Oudolf weaves rich tapestry mosaics reflecting the wild landscape in terms of form and structure; der Linden brings the eye of the artist to his airy compositions, abundant with grasses, where the effect of light is maximised. They overlay their designs with natives and non-native material planted in nature's way – in bold swathes that are in harmony with the scale of the landscape.

Brookes and Paul emphasise that basic design must be stronger than ever in natural gardens to avoid a chaotic look. Both include innovative designs for small, city gardens, which at first glance might appear to be unsuitable for a natural approach. While advocating the use of native plants generally, they prefer a mix of introduced and wild plants for greater scope and diversity. Brookes has recently brought out a book *The New Garden: How to Design, Build and Plant Your Garden with Nature in Mind.*

Aimed squarely at a worldwide audience he discusses the basic design elements of natural gardening, and takes the reader round the globe to look at gardens on the coast, in desert conditions, in shady woodlands, in wet and dry areas, in grasslands, in temperate, Mediterranean, and tropical regions, and at those in urban areas.

The 'New American' garden

The term 'New American' garden has become synonymous with the work of two American landscape architects Wolfgang Oehme and James van Sweden. They have pioneered the move away from the confines of formality towards a naturalistic, free-spirited style revelling in the rich plant diversity and strong architectural elements of late twentieth-century America. Their designs show a heightened awareness of native plants and grasses. Used in a naturalistic way these plants are an integral part of their designs, imbuing the garden with life and movement as they react to sun and wind, while providing structure and year round interest.

Water features are also important, and both designers have written extensively on these elements in *Gardening with Nature* and *Gardening with Water*. Their book *Bold Romantic Gardens: The New World Landscapes of Oehme and van Sweden with Susan Rademacher*, published in 1990, began the move towards gardening naturally and struck a chord with landscape architects and gardeners throughout the world.

Low maintenance is another key element in

The skilful integration of natives and exotics creates a bold and colourful South Pacific garden landscape.

the new millennium garden. America in particular has no tradition of demanding, time-consuming garden maintenance, with the obvious exception of large open plan lawns. These are now becoming much reduced in area, and flower interest is provided by hardy perennials, and bulbs rather than short-lived annuals. Wildflowers are welcomed as natural colonisers and growth and change according to the season breathes life and interest into the garden.

It may seem ironic that a new American style should come about through the work of a German and an American of Dutch descent, but the seeds of discontent with the labour intensive traditional European garden had already been sown years before by Danish-born landscape architect, Jens Jensen. Part of the Prairie School, a movement inspired by the great American plains of the Midwest, Jensen promoted the use of native plants in low maintenance gardens wherever possible.

After the long time constraint of open plan lawns dotted with a few shrubs, such a free, wild pioneering image struck a nostalgic chord among American gardeners, and began a strong movement away from endless streets of uniform grassed gardens with no screening other than a few foundation plantings around the house.

Southern style

With the explosion of suburbia after the Second World War, Thomas Church, who designed California-style gardens, took on Jensen's work. Realising even then that a changing world and lifestyles meant less time and money for the upkeep of expensive labour intensive gardens, Church wrote a book called *Gardens are for People*. The emphasis was on low-maintenance, functional gardens. He created practical easy-care outdoor living areas, with swimming pools, verandahs, barbecues and native planting combinations designed for the ease and convenience of their owners.

Church's physical designs for living have been an integral part of Australian and New Zealand gardens for many years. Southern hemisphere gardeners too, tutored by landscape architects such as Jacob De Ruiter, Isobel Gabitas and plant expert Graeme Platt, have eagerly embraced the move towards low maintenance natural gardens involving large numbers of indigenous plants. Their philosophy is to capture something of the magic of the natural landscape; to tie the garden more closely to the landscape by drawing on the incredible richness and diversity of everything from lush subtropical forests to vast tussock lands, from wild uninhabited coastlines to bush clad mountains. They use associations of native plants in the wild to create blueprints for the garden, translating the big picture into small garden settings that echo the natural palettes and unique character of the landscape.

Shared philosophies

Thus, the evolving modern garden comes from the shared philosophies and work of international landscape architects from around the world. No matter how grand, humble, large or small our individual backyards we are offered a wealth of inspiration. Also encouraging is that horticulturists, farmers and landscape artists are consulting with environmental specialists, recognising that of necessity, gardening in the new millennium must have a strong conservational bias. Based on ecological principles, sustainable management and natural plant associations, their shared philoso-

phies are moving towards working with nature for the health and well-being of people and of the earth. Each of us, as global gardeners seeking to create our own garden identity in the twenty-first century, has much to offer each other.

A case of identity

Having studied together the garden styles that predominate as we move into the twenty-first century, the most important thing of all is that your garden, regardless of design, must be what you want it to be; it must offer the facilities you and your family require. Your only constraints and influences should be those of gardening in environmental harmony with your geographical location, climate and available space. Taking these factors into consideration, your garden must still be essentially a reflection of your own personality and tastes – your identity.

It should be uninfluenced by fads and fashions, but contain at least some of the low maintenance features and native plantings of the New Age natural garden, and be managed in a sustainable manner.

Your garden is a reflection of the lifestyle you've chosen for your family – it is the vehicle that allows you to make it a reality. It is your place of refuge from the stress and pace of modern living; the place where you can grow healthy chemical-free food for your children; the place where, in creating a garden in harmony with your natural landscape and environment, you can exercise your creative talents to the full.

It will be your piece of paradise born of your personal gardening philosophies, because what you create there will be as unique as the new millennium.

EPILOGUE

Man, nature, horticulture and environmental conservation – a symphony for four players, a quartet united in a harmony of mutual trust and respect, an arpeggio of inextricably interwoven notes without which the music of our earth cannot endure.

Gardening is said to bridge the gap between nature and man. The balance of nature we disturb at our gravest peril; it is an exquisite spider's-web equilibrium upon which all life is sustained. This book is essentially about sustainable horticulture, but it rings loud and clear the clarion call of environmental conservation, for both are halves of an indivisible whole.

One of the main tenets I have offered you in this book is that people-power wins. It can move mountains; it can create forests; and it can overturn governmental policies. There is an old Maori saying: He-aha te mea nui o te ao? He Tangata! He Tangata! He Tangata! (What is the most important thing in the world? People! People! People!)

Throughout the twentieth century we have lived without thought for a future that seemed so far off. That future is not just dangerously close. With the new millennium it has arrived. The earth is now entrusted to the people of the twenty-first century.

We are those people. We can save our planet; live beyond three score years and ten; organise organisms other than ourselves to work the soil; stop wasting and degrading the earth's resources; grow healthy chemical-free food and throw some pretty impressive dinner parties to celebrate! We can do all this by burning less fossil fuels, and by planting trees, using the minimum water and running vehicles as little as possible; we can do it by reducing domestic materials that involve disposal by land use, fire and machinery, by monitoring and controlling the actions of scientists and biotechnological companies and by insisting on the identification and labelling of genetically modified foods. By doing all this we can help create an environment of poison-free crops, people, birds and animals.

The wonder of it is that we can all start from this very moment – in our own backyards. All our journeys will be different, but the destination is the same: care of the earth, care of the people, the recognition of the intrinsic value of every living thing and its vital place in the ecological chain. In instituting sustainable systems of horticulture and agriculture, we work with and for nature and not against it. We take out only what we need, and we put back what we take out.

May we have the courage to take the next step on our journey, to unite as a global family, and to do what it takes to bring these changes about.

Bibliography

Allardice, Pamela, *Companion Planting*, Angus & Robertson/HarperCollins, Australia, 1996

Anthony, Diana, *New Zealand Potager: The Ornamental Vegetable Garden*, David Bateman, NZ, 1998

Arthur, Hodges, LeHunt, *The Water Efficient Garden*, Random House, Australia, 1993

Ashworth, Suzanne, *Seed to Seed*, Seed Savers Inc. USA

Bird, Richard, *Companion Planting*, Headline Book Publishing, UK, 1990

Buczacki, Stefan, *Best Garden Doctor*, Hamlyn, UK, 1997

Buczacki, Stefan, *Garden Warfare*, Souvenir Press, UK, 1998

Capek, Karel, *The Gardener's Year*, 1929, Reprinted by University of Wisconsin 1984

Carson, Rachel, *Silent Spring*, Hamish Hamilton, UK, 1963

Church, Thomas D., *Gardens are for People*, University of California Press, 1995

Fanton, Michel and Jude, *The Seed Savers' Handbook*, Seed Savers' Network, Australia, 1994

Ford, Gordon and Gwen, *The Natural Australian Garden*, Bloomings Books, Australia, 1999

French, Jackie, *The Organic Garden Problem Solver*, Angus Robertson, Australia, 1994

Hadlington, P.W. and J.A. Johnston, *Australian Trees*, NSW University Press, 1979

Hamilton, Geoff, *The Ornamental Kitchen Garden*, BBC Books, UK, 1995

Hessayon, D.G., *Easy Care Gardening Expert*, Transworld, UK, 1996

Jeavons, John, *How to grow more vegetables than you ever thought possible on less land than you can imagine: a primer on the life-giving biodynamic French intensive method of organic horticulture* (5th edn), Ten Speed Press, California, 1999

Jekyll, Gertrude, *Wood and Garden*, UK, Macmillan Publishers, 1874

Macoboy, S., *Trees for Flower and Fragrance*, Lansdowne Press, Sydney, 1982

Mitchell, Alan, *Trees of Britain and Northern Europe*, Dragon's World Publishing, UK, 1985

Mortimer, J. and B., *Trees for the NZ Countryside*, Silverfish, NZ, 1984

Phillips, Roger and Martyn Rix, *Vegetables*, Random House, UK, 1997

Van der Ryn, Sim, *The Toilet Papers: Recycling Waste and Conserving Water*, Chelsea Green Publishing Company, California, 1995

Van Sweden, James and Wolfgang Oehme, *Bold Romantic Gradens*, Watson-Cuphill Pubns., 1998

Van Sweden, James, et al, *Gardening with Nature*, Random House, UK, 1997

Van Sweden, James, et al, *Gardening with Water*, Random House, UK, 1995

Watts, Meriel, *The Poisoning of New Zealand*, Auckland Institute of Technology Press, 1994

Woodrow, Linda, *The Permaculture Home Garden*, Penguin Books, Australia, 1996

Woodward, Penny, *Pest Repellent Plants*, Hyland House Publishing, Australia, 1997

Acknowledgements

The author and publisher gratefully acknowledge the following for permission to reproduce copyright material in this book. The author has attempted to contact all copyright holders and regrets any omissions, and welcomes approach from any copyright holder she has been unable to contact.

Carson, Rachel, *Silent Spring*, Hamish Hamilton, UK, 1963

Ford, Gordon and Gwen, *The Natural Australian Garden*, Bloomings Books, Australia, 1999

Ogle, Des, *Beyond the Twenty Foot Stump*, Northland Historical Society, N.Z. 1998

Van der Ryn, Sim, *The Toilet Papers: Recycling Waste and Conserving Water*, Charles Green Publishing Company, California, 1995

Vellve, Renee, *Saving the Seed: Genetic Diversity and European Agriculture*, Genetic Resources Action International, 1992

Photographic Acknowledgements

Grateful thanks to Gil Hanly for photographs: front cover, bottom left; back cover; pp. 8, 44, 58, 78, 88, 118, 142, 162 and 182.

Also thanks to Dr Nicholas Martin and Peter Workman of Crop & Food Research, Auckland, NZ, for photographic material of biological control agents.

I would also like to thank the gardeners in UK, USA, Australia and New Zealand who have allowed me to include photographs of their wonderful gardens in this book, and for their great and much appreciated hospitality.

Index

Quick reference tables